Value Theory in Philosophy and Social Science

Value Theory in Philosophy and Social Science

Edited by

ERVIN LASZLO
and
JAMES B. WILBUR

State University of New York
College of Arts and Science at Geneseo

GORDON AND BREACH SCIENCE PUBLISHERS

New York   London   Paris

Copyright © 1973 by

Gordon and Breach, Science Publishers, Inc.
One Park Avenue
New York, N.Y. 10016

Editorial Office for the United Kingdom

Gordon and Breach, Science Publishers Ltd.
42 William IV Street
London W.C.2.

Editorial office for France

Gordon & Breach
7 - 9 rue Emile Dubois
Paris 14^{e}

PREFACE

The annual Conferences on Value Inquiry bring together philosophers, scientists and humanists to discuss the many facets of the problem of value in the experience of the individual and in contemporary society. The keynote is sounded best perhaps in the opening quotation of the first speaker at the First Conference. "Americans currently face a period in which few institutions, beliefs, or values can any longer be taken for granted. All are under strain; all are challenged. Basic transformations of man and society are now underway, and many vital choices of values must be made" (p.1, below). Americans, and indeed all peoples of the world, are confronted with the necessity of making vital choices of value; traditional values crumble under the impact of rapid technological and societal change and new ones are not available ready-made. In the face of this challenge philosophers, scientists and humanists must assume their traditional roles and responsibilities and apply themselves to the urgent task of discussing the nature of human values, the dynamics of value change, the available options and choices and the procedures for justifying and verifying assessments of value.

One of the criteria in choosing papers for the Conferences is the ability to stimulate such discussion and clarification among the participants. And it is in the hope and belief that they will serve the wider audience in the same way that the annual publication of the *Proceedings* is undertaken within this same series.

The papers in the present volume, originally presented at the First and Second Conferences on Value Inquiry (The University of Akron, 1967, 1968), show deep concern with the problems and responsibilities mentioned above. Part I, devoted to the First Conference, centers on the problem of value in philosophy. The papers by Kurt Baier, "The Concept of Value," and Nicholas Rescher, "The Study of Value Change", are the fruit of a joint project at the University of Pittsburgh. They present penetrating analyses of the nature and varieties of value, and of the modes and expectations of value change. They are followed by Arnold Berleant who, in "The Experience and Judgment of Values" throws light upon the distinction between *valuation*, the having of an experience, and *evaluation*, the making of a judgment upon that experience.

In "Formal Axiology and the Measurement of Values," Robert S. Hartmann presents not only a summary of the main points of his much read theory of value but concentrates on the more particular question of how values can be measured. The papers of Robert Herzstein and J. Prescott Johnson are historical in nature, the former, entitled "The Phenomenology of Freedom in the German Philosophical Tradition: Kantian Origins," traces the influence of the Kantian ideal of "freedom" upon selected themes in German intellectual history and the latter, entitled "The Fact-Value Question in Early Modern Value Theory" discusses the development of this dichotomy in the works of the Post-Kantian German thinkers Lotze, Windelband, Rickert, Brentano, Ehrenfels and Meinong.

The last paper, by Ruth Macklin, "Actions, Consequences and Ethical Theory" takes issue with a consequentialist theory of ethics by pointing out the difficulties in marking out the line between the description of an action, and the consequences which follow upon that action.

The papers of the Second Conference, contained in Part II, establish the broadly interdisciplinary concern also characteristic of subsequent Conferences. This Conference called upon philosophers and social scientists to discuss the problem of value as encountered in social theory. In the first study, "Phenomenology as a General Theory of Social Action", Robert Friedricks considers the relevance of phenomenology in the work of such American social theorists as Peter Berger, Thomas Luckman and Edward Tiryakian. In the second and third articles, John Petras and Larry and Janice Reynolds consider the value dimension of the social theories of Charles Horton Cooley and Claude Levi-Strauss, respectively. Joseph Margolis maintains in his paper "The Use and Syntax of Value Judgments" that it is a mistake to suppose that there is any single adequate model of uniform usage for value judgments either in general, or within the separate domains; i.e. moral, aesthetic, legal, prudential, or technical. Then, in his article "Values, Value Definitions and Symbolic Interaction", Glenn Vernon considers the problem of value within the framework of symbolic interaction theory, of which he is a major spokesman.

The last two papers concern themselves with the value problems of Marxist philosophy. John Somerville, in "The Value Problem and Marxist Social Theory" distinguishes between the theoretical and practical aspects of what he calls the Fallacies of Misplaced Value Function, holding that Marxist value theory can best be understood as the attempt to avoid these fallacies. In "Classical Marxism and the Totalitarian Ethic," A. James Gregor explores the relationship between "classical Marxist ethics" and the ethics of the social order created by contemporary Communism.

The editors would like to thank Martinus Nijhoff of The Hague, Holland, for permission to reprint materials which originally comprised Vol. I, No. 1 (Spring, 1967) and Vol. II, No. 1 (Spring, 1968) of *The Journal of Value Inquiry*. They also wish to express their appreciation to Freda Hark and Susan Perkins for their valuable help in preparing and typing the manuscript.

Ervin Laszlo
James B. Wilbur

TABLE OF CONTENTS

PART I

Value Theory in Philosophy

THE CONCEPT OF VALUE

Kurt Baier

Leaving aside actual revolutions, no time in history has seen more extensive, more fundamental, and more rapid social changes than the present. It is probably safe to say that "Americans currently face a period in which few institutions, beliefs, or values can any longer be taken for granted. All are under strain; all are challenged. Basic transformations of man and society are now underway, and many vital choices of values must be made." (Robin M. Williams, *American Society: A Sociological Interpretation*. Alfred A. Knopf. 1951). It is also generally recognized that in the determination of people's behavior their values play an important role and that the direction in which values change importantly affects the welfare of individuals and of societies. However, empirical investigators do not have available to them a conceptual apparatus suitable even for specifying the values, value systems, or value orientations of particular individuals or societies, at any given time, or changes in these values taking place over a period of time, let alone any theories predicting and explaining such changes, and least of all any understanding of how to assess the desirability or undesirability of any anticipated changes in such values which would enable those in charge of our destiny to take appropriate steps at least to avert disaster if not to lead us to the Great Society. This is a gloomy characterization of the state of the art, but not an uncommon one.

In any case, there would seem to be room for a philosophically oriented overview of the entire conceptual area such as I shall present in this paper. My hope is that the following elucidation of the point and the empirical content of the various types of claim we make with the word 'value', will dispose of many of the theoretical difficulties in the way of an empirical investigation not only of the values which people in fact subscribe to but also of the question of their soundness or unsoundness. These advantages, I hope, will be thought sufficient to warrant the effort necessary to clarify fully the dimensions of the concept which I have had to leave vague.

It will be asked why I have gone to such trouble to lay bare what we ordinarily mean by the word 'value', instead of introducing a new and precise terminology not burdened with the old ambiguities and confusions. The answer is that it would be premature at this stage.

No doubt, eventually the increase in our knowledge of people's values may make it advantageous or even necessary to introduce technical terms departing significantly from the concepts here discussed. However, such new terms have to be introduced and explained by means of the ordinary

1

ones generally used. In the last resort political, social, and moral decisions are made in terms belonging to the everyday conceptual framework, for the troubles to be diagnosed and cured arise in everyday life. To give a medical analogy: hay fever sufferers may perhaps eventually describe their symptoms in terms of fluctuations in the amount of histamine in the blood-stream, but this new and more precise way of speaking will be adequate only if it is a way of describing and explaining the old concerns, i.e., irritations in the eyes and nose, excessive sneezing, headaches and discomfort, and so forth. While this is so (and why should it ever change?) it will be essential to have an unconfused everyday vocabulary capable of drawing the major distinctions required for detailed specifications of values. When we have that, it will be easier to introduce a more precise terminology for describing a person's values and the changes they have undergone over a period of time.

Of the three fields, economics, philosophy, and sociology, in which the idea of value has been most assiduously examined and used, the analytic work of the economists has made the greatest progress and is the most useful for our purposes. This is so despite the fact that the employment of the idea of value in two different areas, for two different purposes, in two different types of theory, has led to a good deal of misunderstanding and confusion (though perhaps mainly among non-economists), and in one area has encountered seemingly insuperable difficulties. These two areas are value theory and welfare economics. In the former, the more successful area, 'value' or 'exchange value' means market price, i.e. the ratio at which commodities come to be exchanged in a market. In this area, value theory is the theory explaining and predicting the changes of these exchange values or ratios of exchange. Exchange values are public, inter-personal phenomena; the resultants of many individuals' estimates of the intrinsic worthwhileness to them of possessing these commodities, of their usefulness, of their cheapness, of their affordability to them, and so on. Despite frequently expressed views to the contrary, exchange value is not a magnitude which does or ought to reflect some other magnitude such as the real value, just price, use value, utility, or what-have-you of that commodity.

In welfare economics, by contrast, an individual's values are the application of his preferences to the alternative possible patterns of his society's resource allocation; social values, the "aggregations" of these individual evaluations into an aggregated ordering of alternative resource allocations open to the society. There are many difficulties in this way of looking upon the relation between individual and social values, and there appears to be no agreement about how normative welfare economics is to proceed.

In view of the serious obstacles in the way of "aggregating" individual welfare functions into social welfare functions, or of even determining individual welfare functions on the basis either of actual preferential choices or verbally expressed preferences, I want to suggest for further development a modification of the concepts used in welfare economics. I follow the economists in distinguishing between questions concerning the good or well-being of the individual and questions concerning the good or well-being of the group of which he is a member. However, instead of the comparatively narrow question of welfare, individual or social, I raise the wider question of what I call *the quality of life;* and instead of conceiving of this crucial property as constructed out of the individuals' *preferences*, I think of it as constructed out of hierarchically ordered answers to different types of question, including those concerning inclinations, preferences, and tastes, but also his needs and interests. Answers to the question of what is in his interest are more important, (make a stronger claim on his resources) than answers to questions of inclination or preference or taste. More about this below.

My key idea is that of something, whether an occurence or an action or state of affairs, *making a favorable difference to a person's life.* To make this more precise, it is important to distinguish two aspects of a person's life which may be so affected: the quality of his life at any given time, and the extent of his ability to raise or maintain that quality.

Consider the quality of some material or substance, such as steel, cloth, tobacco or wine. Imagine this material passing, at a steady flow, some given point of quality control where its quality is periodically inspected, in order to ensure that it continues to be of the required level or standard. If the material falls below the required quality, it is rejected; if it reaches the required level or comes above it, then it passes. By the quality of the material we mean the extent to which it meets the appropriate or legitimate requirements we make of materials of this sort. It is better or higher quality material the more fully it meets the appropriate requirements. Its quality or excellence lies in its ability or capacity to satisfy the appropriate requirements, and the measure of that quality is the extent or magnitude of that ability.

The quality of someone's life is something analogous to the quality of some material: a measure of the excellence of that life in terms of its ability or capacity to satisfy the appropriate or legitimate demands made on it. As in the case of materials, we can try to isolate those factors which favorably affect its quality, those which make no difference to it, and those which unfavorably affect it. In this case, too, we shall naturally be concerned to promote those factors which make for an improvement of its quality and to eliminate or modify those factors which make for a lowering of its quality.

We can distinguish four different classes of demands on a life. (1) The demands a person himself makes on his life: what he wants from or out of life, what he hopes life will hold for him, what he wants life to contain, if he is to call it a worthwhile, satisfying, or good life. (2) the demands others may legitimately make on him, if they are to call it a decent, decorous, law-abiding, or morally adequate life. (3) The requirements one legitimately makes before one calls it a valuable or admirable life; e.g. those that define the heroic, the saintly, the great artist's, the great scientist's life, and so on. These are the contributing, valuable lives. Their high quality lies in the benefit they confer on others. The difference between the morally adequate life and the valuable life is that the former satisfies the demands others may legitimately make on a life, whereas the latter satisfies requirements outside what may be legitimately demanded. The former contains the minimal contributions *anyone* can be expected to make, quite irrespective of any special talents or gifts he may have. The latter acknowledge the performance of the specially gifted individual. (4) The last class of demands are those which a critic may make of the requirements spelled out in the first three sets, those actually in operation in a given society. A critic may find what a given person demands of life excessive, unreasonable in terms of what is possible and so on, or he may criticize it as too unambitious, too modest, too easily satisfied. And analogous criticisms could be offered of the other sets of criteria.

A person reaching maturity in a given society will normally have formed certain demands on his life; what he wants from or out of life. Of course, these demands may change as he grows older and learns to criticize and modify them in the light of what is possible, with the resources at his disposal, and of what is truly rewarding, and what he would regret spending his resources on. Part of his education along these lines will include the rejection of some of the things others would like him to do, and the inclusion of others he had previously ignored or rejected.

Now, we can say that anything which, at a given time, brings his life closer to the satisfaction of the demands which he, at that point reasonably makes on it, favorably affects the quality of his life. Getting a coveted job, finding a long-lost relative, moving into one's dream house, winning an election, discovering a cure for an illness, are such developments which favorably affect the quality of one's life because they constitute the satisfaction of some legitimate demand one makes on life, they are something one wants out of life. In being this, their occurrence confers a benefit on one.

Thus, we mean by *the quality* of a given life the measure of its capacity to satisfy the demands which the person himself could reasonably (vetted by a qualified critic) make on his own life. By contrast, we shall speak of *the worth* of a given life when we consider its excellence on the basis of the other two sets of requirements or criteria which one can apply to a given life. These are relevant when we examine the moral worth and the admirability of a given life, but they are not relevant when we consider whether something confers a benefit on a person, i.e. favorably affects that life's quality, i.e. that life's capacity to satisfy the demands the person himself can reasonably make on it. There can be no doubt about the importance of this point of view or perspective, from which an individual can look upon events in nature (the weather, the crops, and the litters), upon the doings of people around him (the benefactions, aids, assistances) and upon social institutions (schools, churches, police, garbage collection) as potential or actual factors making for the improvement of the quality of his life. The other two points of view, from which he and others can look at his life as itself a potential or actual factor making for the improvement of the quality of life of others are equally important in the appraisal of that life. But since the requirements or demands appropriate to these points of view are capable of conflicting with the demands appropriate to the first, they should be considered separately and must in any case not be included in the account of what confers a *benefit* on someone. For the satisfaction of the requirements appropriate to the latter two points of view may and frequently does compel an individual to employ his resources in ways which lower the quality of his life, or at any rate in ways which differ substantially from those in which he would have employed them had he looked at events with a view simply to improving the quality of his life.

I have so far spoken of events, doings, and institutions as making a direct favorable impact on the quality of someone's life. However, developments may confer a benefit on someone less directly, namely, by improving his ability or power to make, himself, a direct favorable impact on the quality of his life. There are two ways in which developments may do this, either by increasing the individual's own powers or capacities so that *in the same environmental condition* he is better able to maintain or improve the quality of his life, or by so changing his environment that *with the same powers* he is better *able* to do so. Increasing a man's health, strength, skills, knowledge, or wealth falls in the former category; improving the natural or social climate and amenities of life in the latter category. I suggest that we speak of *the climate of life* in a given society where we refer to the degree of orderliness, predictability, security, and trustworthiness of individuals and institutions in that society. The climate of life is the better, the more reliably one can expect the social and personal guarantees of life, liberty, property and contractual undertakings to be respected. We naturally speak of *the quality of life* (as opposed to the quality of a particular life) in relation to the natural and cultural *amenities* provided in a given society. I have in mind the variety and quality of goods and services (including cultural ones, of course) which a society makes available to its members. Clearly, the quality of an individual's life is very largely determined by *the quality of life made available in that society:* the resources one can acquire and the goods and services on which one can spend them. Hence a benefit is conferred on a person, even when there is no direct improvement in the quality of *his* life, by anything that increases his powers to improve the quality of his life in given conditions or by anything that improves the conditions (the climate and quality of life) and so makes it easier for him to improve, by his own efforts and as he sees fit, the quality of his own life.

By a short extension of this line of thought we come also to include in what confers benefits, the possession of such *defenses* as would, or of such powers as could be used to, prevent something which would lower the quality of one's life.

B

Lastly, we must include factors independent of the person's own tastes and demands on life, namely, the satisfaction of those conditions whose satisfaction is a necessary condition of the continuation of his life. Anything bringing about the satisfaction of such a condition, confers a benefit on that person irrespective of whether he knows or believes that it is such a condition or, knowing that it is, wants it satisfied. Of course, it does so only while the continuation of his life *holds* something for him, that is, offers something he wants out of life, or while he thinks there is a chance that it holds something for him in the future. To a person living through the last phases of an incurable disease, life may hold nothing and the medical ministrations designed to prolong that life may not then confer a benefit on him.

These different ways of expending one's resources for the attainment of certain ends whose attainment favorably affects one's life clearly confer *benefits* of different importance. Some of them affect the quality of a person's life only indirectly, yet in a more crucial way than others affecting it more directly and more substantially. For in some cases, the attainment of an end caters to a person's needs, in others to his interest, in yet others merely to his tastes. These different ways of favorably affecting one's life clearly are of unequal *importance* or *weight*. The satisfaction of one's *needs* has a better claim on one's resources than that of one's tastes, preferences, or inclinations, or even than that of one's interest. Some ends are quite objectively *more urgent* than, and therefore have *priority* over others. The attainment of those ends which are the neutralization of, avoidance of, or protection against certain imminent dangers or threats to the individual's very life would seem to have priority over all other claims on one's energy, attention, and wits, as long as the continuation of life promises to be a life of a certain quality, namely one, sufficiently high for the individual to prefer its prolongation to its termination. Clearly while one finds life worthwhile, the satisfaction of the conditions of its prolongation has first priority. Again, policies designed to protect or promote one's *best interest* would seem to be superior to policies designed to prevent minor discomforts, pains, and unwelcomenesses, or to ensure thrills, enjoyments or satisfactions. Nor does it seem impossibly hard to distinguish quite often what end it would be in one's best interest to attain, and what would merely give us satisfaction or enjoyment. Up to a point, (to be fixed in the light of threatening dangers of attack, illness, poverty), ends designed to ensure the security of the agent, have superiority over ends promising comparatively shortlived pleasures even if intense, particularly if they are causally connected with subsequent suffering. Of course, at times, the argument for one end or another may be inconclusive, the considerations being too finely balanced.

Where principles of priority of the kind just outlined point to a specific end and (by way of the course of action necessary to attain the end) to a particular way of attaining it, there we can speak of *norms*, of things the agent *ought* to do, ways in which the agent ought to expend his resources.

I must mention one particular type of norm which is of very great importance in our lives. I mean those norms which we often call *obligations* or *duties*. Where people are linked together in an organization, their power is greatly increased. They can more effectively improve the quality of their own lives and those of others, but they can also lower the quality of the lives of others, or reap benefits greater than those reaped by others making equal or greater efforts in the organization. It is plausible to hold all three of the following: (i) that the climate of life in a particular group is determined by whether or not most of its members follow those norms which direct people not to aim at ends whose attainment would detrimentally affect the lives of others even if at the same time it would favorably affect their own; (ii) that maintaining the climate of life at a high level is a condition of an adequate quality of life for everyone; and lastly (iii) that many people must often be tempted to violate such norms as these. It will therefore be most important to ensure that people generally do follow these kinds of norms. By contrast, there will be other kinds of which this is not true. Thus, there are norms in regard to which no one but the individual himself will care whether he follows them or not (e.g. whether he says his prayers or does his exercises), and there will be norms in regard to which it is safe to assume that an individual will normally follow them if he knows them (e.g. that one ought not to touch a hot stove or drive a car when one is drowsy). With regard to these it will not be important for the community to see that all members follow them; though perhaps the community *should* spread the knowledge of the second kind, and encourage individuals to follow them.

It is thus possible to explain the rationality of policies and norms entirely in terms of the quality of individuals' lives and ways of improving it. Even obligations are explicable in this way by the addition of the three plausible assumptions we just noted. With these preliminaries out of the way we can now make clearer the two main uses of the word 'value', its use in what I shall call "value assessments", and in "value imputations".

Value assessments are assertions to the effect that something did, will or would favorably affect the life of someone. A value assessment may be a particular claim such as "The flash-light (compass, ointment, master key, pistol) you gave me (him, us) was (will be, would be, would have been) of great (little, no) value to me (him, us)"; or it may be a more complex remark such as, "social defense reactions in jackdaws have a high survival value", or "fasting and prayer have incomparable moral value", or "the literary value of the book is nil, but its documentary value is considerable".

By contrast, *value imputations* are assertions to the effect that someone has, holds, or subscribes to some value, V, (e.g. achievement, work, altruism, comfort, equality, thrift, friendship), or that something, V, is one of his values. When we say this of an individual or a whole society, we impute to that individual or to that society a favorable attitude towards the realiza-

tion of a certain state of affairs, one vaguely indicated by the value name,
'V', an attitude he has because he expects (more or less explicitly) that the
realization of that state of affairs confers some benefits on someone, not
necessarily the value holder himself.

Clearly, these two types of value-assertions, value-imputations, and
value-assessments, make different and mutually independent claims. When
Jones says that for him his friendship with Mr. K has great political value,
he *assesses* the value for him of that friendship as being great, but he does
not thereby *impute* to himself the value, friendship, political success or
any other value.

Again, the word 'value' *means* different things in these two kinds of
assertion. Roughly speaking, assessed values are measures of the *capacities*
of various kinds of entities including persons, to confer benefits, and imputed values are measures of *tendencies* of persons to promote certain ends,
for certain reasons.

I have space for only one of the many important philosophical difficulties which have been raised about value, but it is probably the one most
widely and deeply felt. It is the seemingly radical difference between questions of fact and questions of value, and the consequent impossibility of
using, in answering questions of value, the tried and successful methods
for answering questions of fact. The three main accounts of this apparent
impossibility point to certain supposed fundamental differences between
statements of fact and judgments of value. One type of theory claims to
find differences in subject-matter (ordinary, natural facts versus mysterious,
nonnatural values); another finds fundamental differences in point or interest of the two types of claim (statements, reports, assertions, conveying
information versus ejaculations, expressions, evocations, exhortations,
prescriptions, imperations); a third finds fundamental differences in available methods of support for such claims (statements of fact capable of being
established by other statements of fact which constitute conclusive evidence
or reasons, versus value judgments not capable of being conclusively established by statements of fact).

The foregoing analysis of value assessments and value imputations has
already cast some doubt on the reality of this problem. We can now examine
this a little more closely. We must put aside some types of value claim
namely, those which would not be considered properly *evaluative* and so not
value judgments in the sense which gives rise to our problems. For instance,
value imputations would not be considered value judgments, but straight
forward statements of fact. I cannot here attempt to uncover the criteria on
the basis of which some remarks containing the word 'value' are thus identified as evaluative or as value judgments proper where as others are regarded as mere statements of fact. It is however, fairly clear that, whatever
these criteria are, those claims which I have called value assessments and
ose concerning the soundness or otherwise of imputed values would be

classified as value judgments proper. If I am right in this, then such value judgments do not seem to be sufficiently different from statements of fact to give rise to the supposed problems. To make this clearer, let us first distinguish between *unqualified* value assessments, such as 'Your advice was of inestimable value to me' or 'Membership of a fraternity is no longer of any value to anyone today', and *qualified* value assessments, such as 'His book has no *literary value* at all' or 'Stating a person's goal has some *explanatory value*' or 'Regular exercises in self-denial have very great *moral value*'. It is a characteristic feature of unqualified value assessments that either they explicitly refer to the person *for* whom something *has* value, or *to* whom it is *of* value, or else they must be understood as referring to someone or anyone. By contrast, qualified value assessment need not contain or imply such a reference to a particular person or to anyone and everyone. The advice was of value if and only if it was of value to someone, but the book has or does not have literary value, period.

Among unqualified value assessments (the only ones I have space to examine), we must distinguish particular from general ones. 'Your advice was of inestimable value to me' is particular. It says that under the conditions (whatever they were) prevailing on a given occasion, a certain piece of advice made a favorable difference to the speaker's quality of life, and it assesses that difference as being of a certain magnitude, called here inestimable. By contrast, 'In cases where marital tensions arise through financial problems, advice from marriage counsellors is usually of little value' is a general unqualified value assessment. General value assessments assert the existence of a connection between the acquiring of benefits of certain magnitudes by people of certain sorts, when standing in relations of certain sorts, under conditions of certain sorts, to things of certain sorts. The two main differences between general and particular claims can then be characterized as follows. The general ones do not refer to particular occasions and so of course do not say anything about the benefits derived on those occasions. Particular ones do refer to particular occasions and do say something about the benefits derived, from what and by whom. However, unlike general ones, they do not spell out the conditions which must be satisfied if such benefits are to be derived – they do at most imply that such conditions, whatever they may be, must have been satisfied, since the benefits *were* derived.

The only significant way in which such particular or general claims differ from other particular and general claims is that they contain the idea of conferring a benefit on someone or of making a favorable difference to someone's life, or of favorably affecting the quality of someone's life. Does this idea render such claims incapable of empirical investigation? We have already seen that on the face of it there does not seem to be any difficulty in principle about investigating the various factors which favorably or unfavorably affect the quality of a persons's life, any more than there is in

investigating the factors which affect the quality of some material or product. If we can establish quality control of a product, we should be able to
establish quality control of a life, in the sense, that we should at least be
able to *tell whether* the quality of a person's life was the same as or better
or worse than it was at an earlier time, and also to find out what were the
factors which contributed to its being so.

However, it may now be objected that there is something incurably
"subjective" about the concept of the quality of an individual's life; and
that unlike the concept of the quality of a product, the question of how the
quality of a person's life has been affected could be empirically investigated.

The answer to this objection must be given in two parts. The first part
of the answer admits that there are aspects of the concept which are in an
important sense subjective, but insists that there are other aspects which
are not. For as we have seen, questions of *survival, health* and *security* can
be answered in ways which are objective in the required senses: it is possible
to find out empirically and objectively what will prolong or cut short a
particular person's life, what will protect him against dangers and what will
increase his ability to cope with emergencies. Furthermore, it should be
possible to formulate such general claims in ways which apply to all human
beings. As far as survival, health, and security are concerned, conferring a
benefit on someone, or favorably affecting his life, or favorably affecting the
quality of his life (and the opposite) is therefore a change in a person's life
which can be empirically and objectively established, just like other changes
about which we raise no problems. And as we have seen, these benefits are
among the most important which can be conferred on a person.

The second part of the answer to the objection under discussion admits
that there are aspects of the quality of a person's life which are in some
sense non-objective, but shows that this admission is quite harmless, as
far as the possibility of quality control is concerned. It is of course perfectly
true that people differ in their tastes and that settlements in matters of
taste are not objective. For although one can dispute about them, one cannot show another person wrong in matters of taste. Nevertheless, for the
purpose of establishing quality control, it is perfectly sufficient to know
what a person's tastes in fact are. For there really is an aspect of the quality
of his life which is determined by his actual tastes. What makes a person's
life worthwhile, rich, enjoyable, and so forth really is to a considerable
extent determined by the extent to which what life brings caters to his actual
tastes, irrespective of whether they are the same as those of other people.
To the extent to which our economy attempts to be responsive to actual
and varied consumers' tastes and to pump enough resources into their
pockets to enable them to cater to their own individual tastes in the market,
the economy really tries to make a contribution to this aspect of the quality
of everyone's life.

But it is surely not impossible to ascertain empirically and objectively what a person's tastes are, i.e. what sorts of things he likes, i.e. tends to enjoy, and what things he dislikes, and tends to find unpleasant, repugnant, painful and so forth, even though it may sometimes be difficult to tell whether a person failed to enjoy something because his tastes had changed or because some of the conditions for enjoying something for which he has a taste were absent. This uncertainty will need to diminish to the extent to which we increase our knowledge of the conditions under which a person of a given sort with tastes of a given sort enjoys what he has a taste for.

But if I am right in this, then the subjectivity of some aspects of the quality of a person's life is not an insuperable obstacle to finding out whether or not a given thought has favorably affected these subjective aspects of the quality of that person's life, because we can determine whether or not this change is something catering to his tastes. And if it is, then it favorably affects that aspect of the quality of his life.

University of Pittsburgh

THE STUDY OF VALUE CHANGE

Nicholas Rescher

INTRODUCTION

My discussion will fall into three major parts. First I shall deal with two clearly *conceptual* issues, namely how values manifest themselves, and what are some of the principal modes of value change. Next I shall consider the *methodological* issue of how the espousal and the changes in espousal of values can be studied, particularly in a future-oriented, prospective context. Finally I shall present in outline some *empirical* findings regarding probable patterns of change in American values over the next generation (say to 2,000 A.D.).

HOW DO VALUES MANIFEST THEMSELVES?

When we impute to someone (N = Smith, Jones, the Aztecs), subscription to a certain value (X = love of country, devotion to duty, the worship of Mammon), what is it that we say about him and what sorts of grounds can we have for claiming it?

It is clear that value-subscription can manifest itself in two easily distinguishable overt modes: Firstly on the side of *talk* (or thought). In claiming that N subscribes to the value we give grounds for expecting a certain characteristic type of *verbal* action, namely that he would "appeal to this value" (1) in the support or justification of his own (or other people's) actions, and (2) in urging upon others the adoption of actions, courses of action, and policies for acting. Moreover, in addition to such overt verbal behavior we would of course expect him to take the value into proper account in the "inner discourse" *(in foro interno)* of deliberation and decision-making. In imputing a value to someone we underwrite the expectation that its espousal will manifest itself, in appropriate ways, in the justification and recommendation of actions. The prime indicators of value-subscription are those items which reflect the *rationalization* (defense, recommendation, critique) of aspects of a "way of life."

But secondly, on the other hand, we also expect the value to manifest itself on the side of *overt action*. We would draw back from saying that patriotism (financial security, the advancement of learning) is one of N's values unless he behaves *in action* – and not just at the verbal level – so as to implement the holding of this v   by "acting in accordance with it" himself, by endeavoring to promote its adoption by others, etc. In saying that prudence, for example, is one of N's values we *underwrite the presumption* – and to say this is not, of course, to *guarantee the fact* – that N behaves prudently (is a prudent person), and the like for other values (patriotism, intelligence, etc). (The converse, of course, is by no means true: To say that N is prudent no more implies that prudence is one of his values than saying he is impatient implies that impatience is a value of his.)

A value is thus a Janus-headed disposition-cluster – we expect it to orient itself in two directions: both that of discourse and that of overt action. There is of course, the problem of the hypocrite and the dissimulator, the man who merely talks the value, but does not implement it in action. *Per contra*, there is the man who acts in accordance with a typical pattern of value-subscription (for reasons of conformity, by happenstance, etc.), but who does not subscribe to the value at the verbal level, and may even explicitly reject subscription to it. In either event we would have to refrain from a value imputation of any *unqualified* kind. In imputing a value to someone we underwrite the expectation that its espousal will manifest itself in practice as well as in thought.

Subscription to a value is thus a two-sided affair, and value imputations have a double aspect: both verbal and behavioral. When we impute the subscription of N to the value X, we underwrite the grounds for expecting from N a reasonable degree of conformity with the characteristic mani-festation-patterns of X-subscription both in discourse and in action.

We impute a value to N to characterize his vision of "the good life" or at any rate *his vision of how life ought appropriately to be lived* – be this in his judgment "for the good" or not, in some more fundamental sense of the term. "His vision" indicates that we have to do with how *he looks* at the matter: "how life is to be led" indicates that we have to do with *conduct* (action). His way of looking at the matter would be expected to manifest itself – at any rate in ordinary circumstances – by his *dispositions to talk* (to approve, disapprove, recommend, encourage, etc.). His view of how life is to be led would be expected to manifest itself – again, under ordinary circumstances – by *his dispositions to act*, by the things he does and the ways in which he chooses to expend his resources of time, energy, etc.

On the basis of these considerations, we may see readily what are the principle tools by which the value-pattern of a society can be determined.

On the side of behavior, the primary tool will be *budget analysis*, i.e., a scrutiny of patterns of resource-investment, including not only *material* resources, but also time (time budgets), and expenditures of energy, effort, inconvenience, etc.

On the side of talk, the primary tool will be *content analysis*, above all a scrutiny of the pronunciamentos of such publicly recognized spokesmen for values: newspaper editorialists, graduation-exercise speakers, religio-moral sermonizers, and political orators. These data can be extended and supplemented by the content analysis of that methodologically important artifact, the questionnaire. We shall have occasion to return to this prospect below.

MODES OF VALUE CHANGE: A PRELIMINARY TYPOLOGY

We must begin with an explication of what a "value change" is, and explain the different sorts of things that are at issue here. First, one piece of technical terminology:

Value-subscription: A person who subscribes to (i.e., has, accepts, holds, is dedicated to, gives his adherence to, etc.) a certain value will be characterized as a *subscriber* to this value. This idea can obviously be applied to a group of persons as well. *"Dietary propriety,"* for example, is a value for orthodox Catholics (Jews, Muslims – all, to be sure, in different ways), but not at all for Protestants.

We may now consider five very importantly different modes of value change:

1. *Value acquisition and abandonment:* When a person begins to subscribe to a value to which he did not previously give adherence we shall say that he has *acquired* this value. In the reverse case, when he gives up adherence to a value to which he previously subscribed, we shall say that he has *abandoned* this value. Value acquisition and abandonment is the most radical sort of value "change" on the part of an individual value-subscriber with respect to a given value; it is not a matter of more or less and of degree, but rather turns on the yes-no issue of a given value's entering or exiting from a person's set of accepted values. This is the sort of thing one thinks of in connection with a religious or ideological conversion.

2. *Value-redistribution:* A given value is more or less widely distributed throughout a group according as a larger or smaller proportion of members of the group subscribe to it. We may speak of a *value-redistribution* when there is a change in the extent or in the pattern of its distribution in the society. A very common way in which a value becomes a "value of a society" that is, becomes successively more and more generally diffused (i.e., more and more extensively distributed) throughout this society in that most or virtually all of its members subscribe to it – is to start out as the value of some dedicated minority who successfully manage to promote its increasingly widespread acceptance. This has been the history of many of our national values (e.g., *"tolerance"*).

3. *Value-rescaling:* The set of values to which a person (or group) subscribes can generally be compared on a value-scale of higher and lower, and to some extent can even be arranged in a strict hierarchy. This does not turn on the yes-no issue of whether a subscriber does or does not adhere to certain values, but on the extent of his commitment to them. The height of a value on the scale is determined by a multiplicity of factors such as the tenacity of maintaining and preserving the value, preparedness to invest energy and resources in its realization and propagation, and the attachment of high sanctions to the value (i.e., how much compliance is expected and how much reproach heaped upon the transgressor), etc. The reordering of

such a value scale by mutual re-ranking of its components in a "re-valuation of values" is among the more drastic varieties of value change.

4. *Value-redeployment:* A value is inevitably held in the context of a domain of application, the range of cases that are held as coming within the purview of this value: the objects or occasions for value-implementing action or appraisal. (Paradigm example: driving a car within the speed limit lies within the domain of application of the value *"law abidingness."*) The operative arena of the ideals of legal and political equality were gradually extended to include the American Negro and the American Indian, but this does not mean that these values as such were given a different or higher niche in the shrine of American values – simply that we began to apply them over an enlarged domain with changed boundaries. One of the most profound value-changes in Roman history was the bringing of the provincials within the precincts of Roman citizenship; for the Roman politician and jurist this was clearly a matter of redeployment of existing values – rather than turning upon the acquisition of new values, it involved redefining the area of application of old ones. (Think also of the Apostle's conception of some gentiles as being "circumcised of the spirit.") The education-for-social-adjustment cult in the U. S. in the 1920's-1950's was moderately successful in promoting an enlargement in the domain of application of society's value-requirement of *"mature, socially responsible behavior"* from young adult to teenager as starting point. (Part of the current-youth-malaise may be seen in the light of a revolt against this.)

5. *Value Restandardization:* A mode of value change that is particularly sensitive to and reflective of changes in the social, economic, and technological environment is a change in the *standard of implementation* of a value, the guidelines for assessing the extent to which a value is attainted in particular cases within its domain of application. Here there are two possibilities; the changing of existing standards, the the introduction of new ones. The airplane-passenger has not changed the high importance he places upon the values of *"safety," "speed," "reliability" and "comfort"* with respect to his mode of transportation since the 1920's, but he expects these value-desiderata to be realized in a heightened degree: he brings a different set of standards to bear in judging the degree of their attainment, especially in settling the question of whether they have been *sufficiently* or *minimally* realized. (It is in this sense that we generally speak of the "raising" and "lowering" of standards, that is, of a resetting of the "level of aspiration" in the realization of a value.) A more dramatic example is that of the *standard of* living – a century ago economists thought of a worker's earning his "livelihood" in terms of *survival* for himself and his family; today we think of it in terms of a share in "the good life" which the economy makes possible for all and the society expects for everyone. In such cases we have a restandardization of the value in question, a changed concept of the minimally acceptable degree of their attainment. Also, new

standards can be added, as in this age of pesticides we add standards of consumption safety to the usual standards of palatability in evaluating fruit.

In the course of this analysis of five, very different modes of value-change, we confront the important fact that a society's subscription to a value is a very complicated phenomenon, and that a diversified variety of change is correspondingly possible in this sphere.

One worthwhile step of terminological reunification is however possible: Upgrading/Downgrading. We may distinguish systematically between modes of upgrading and corresponding modes of downgrading in terms of the preceding varieties of value-change, as follows:

MODES OF UPGRADING		MODES OF DOWNGRADING
value-acquisition	1	value-abandonment
increase-redistribution	2	decrease-redistribution
rescaling upwards	3	rescaling downwards
widening redeployment	4	narrowing redeployment
restandardization by a raising of standards	5	restandardization by a lowering of standards

The point is that the modes of upgrading all represent diverse ways in which heightened acceptances of our emphasis upon a given value can occur: the modes of upgrading all represent higher valuations of the value, and the modes of downgrading represent a devaluation of it.

A METHODOLOGICAL FRAMEWORK FOR ANALYZING VALUE CHANGES

We must now examine in detail the basic question: How can a change in the economico-technological or the demographic sector be expected to work to induce a change in the schedule of values? Since our orientation is to the future, what we need is an essentially predictive mode of analysis. But what methodological tools are available for the study of value-change? Three sorts of predictive techniques are clearly relevant:

(i) *Extrapolation* of historical experience. This consists in the projection of current trends and tendencies, perhaps under

(ii) *Analytical forecasting models* of the sort familiar from other disciplines (especially economics).

(iii) *Questionnaire techniques* designed to elicit from well-informed persons their considered judgments about future developments – particular efforts being made (by information "feed-back" techniques or in other ways) to establish some sort of concensus results.

We defer until later any consideration of the questionnaire methodology to the study of our problem. Our present problem is: How can one best apply the extrapolation and analytical forecasting techniques (or some combination thereof) to the study of value change in a society?

One important key to this question lies in a consideration of the fact that values can come into conflict with one another, not of course, in the abstract, but in the competing demands their realization and pursuit make upon man's finite resources of goods, time, effort, attention, etc. Thus when a change occurs in the operating rationale that constitutes the operative framework within which a value is pursued in a given society, we may expect a series of stresses upon our scale of values militating for a rescaling in their ordering or a change of the value-standard, etc. But how is one to predict the character of this value response? Here key factors lie in two considerations: *cost* and *benefit*.

(1) *The cost of maintaining a value.* As was just said, the pursuit of the realization of a value requires the investment of various resources. The extent of the requisite investment will be affected by changes in the environment: *"cleanliness"* comes cheaper in modern cities than in medieval ones, and the achievement of *"privacy"* costs more in urban environments than in rural ones. The maintenance of a value will obviously be influenced by its cost. When this becomes *very* low, we may tend to depreciate the value as such. When it becomes high, we may either depreciate the value in question as such (the "Fox and the Grapes" reaction) – or rather more commonly – simply settle for lower standards for its attainment. (Think here of "peace and quiet" in this era of jet-screams, sonic booms, and auto sirens.)

(2) *The felt benefit of (or need for) maintaining a value.* Any society is likely to have a group of values that occupy a commanding position on its value-scale. These are the values to which it is most fundamentally committed in the various relevant modes of commitment, such as the tenacity of maintaining and preserving the value, preparedness to invest energy and resources in its realization and propagation, the attachment of high sanctions to the value (i.e., how much compliance is expected and how much reproach heaped upon the transgressor, and the like). These most deeply held values are viewed as unchangeable and "beyond dispute."

In most modern, Westernized societies – and certainly in the U.S.A. – these dominant values prominently include: (1) the *SURVIVAL* of the society, (2) the *WELFARE* of the society, (3) the *ADVANCEMENT* of the society, (4) and *REALITY-ADJUSTMENT* of the society. The first is, of course, not only a matter of the *mere* survival of the society, but its survival as the sort of society it is; the holding of this value is thus a matter of a kind of homeostasis. We mean the welfare of the society to be concerned largely in the manner of the economists, having to do with the standard of living in the society, the set of goods and services available to its members, but also calling for a reasonable degree of attainment of its various (non-materialistic) ideals. The third value, progress, is primarily a matter of the improvement of the state of affairs obtaining under the two preceding heads. Finally, reality-adjustment is a matter of accepting things as they are, and adjusting to them or changing them, rather than seeking security in myth or magic. If the pursuit of the realization of a value somehow becomes much more difficult or costly so that one must *(ex hypothesi)* "settle for less" one can either (1) adjust, or (2) keep the lamp of aspiration burning bright, possibly even giving this value a greater emphasis. A culture heavily committed to "reality adjustment" would, by and large, tend to the first mode of resolution, except where its dominant and basic values themselves are concerned.

Now when we speak of the "benefit of" or the "need for" maintaining a certain value in our society, we mean this to be thought of in terms of its inducing to realization of the four dominant values just indicated. Thus, for example, "pluralism," which plays such a prominent role in contemporary U.S. Catholic thought answers to a "need" precisely because it conduces to the interests of this group in helping it to adjust to the constraints of its environment. Again *"scientific and intellectual skill"* and the various values bound up with this are of late coming to be upgraded on the American value scale precisely because of society's increased need for these skills in the interests of survival, welfare, and advancement under contemporary conditions. Much the same can be said for "innovation," as witness the really very modest degree of worker resistance to technological change in recent years.

The illustrations just given have gotten us ahead of our place; before turning to such items of concrete detail we must resume our topic of predictive method. What we are proposing to do is to examine pressures upon American values in terms of the following line of methodological approach:

1. We begin with an environmental change in the operative context of a value represented by an economico-technological or a social or demographic change that increases the cost of pursuing the realization of a certain value.

2. We examine the nature of this increased cost to see what sorts of stresses and strains it imposes upon the pursuit of the value at issue.

3. We consider the likely resolution of the stresses and strains in the light of the needs of the society, construing "need" in terms of its continuing pursuit of its basic values.

We thus begin with a trend or tendency of economico-technological or social or demographic character that makes for changes in the costs of pursuing an existing scheme of values; we note the difficulties or opportunities that such a cost-change creates; and then we examine how these difficulties are likely to be resolved (or opportunities capitalized on) effectively, assuming that certain basic values provide the relatively stable centers around which the resolution of value-conflicts will pivot. Given a change in the pattern of the *costs* of the value-pursuit we ask – how most effectively can the society derive *benefits* therefrom – i.e., how best can "needs" of the society (construed in terms of an accommodation of its basic values) be accommodated? Put in a nutshell, the proposed method of inquiry is an extension into the area of value studies of the cost-benefit or cost-effectiveness approach of economic analysis.

It should be stressed that even major technological changes can be such as to have very little effect upon values. For it is important to distinguish between a *value* as such on the one hand, and the means for its realization on the other. A technological change that affects the latter may leave the former substantially unaffected. (Think of the few relevant values apart from *convenience* affected by the switch from manual to electric typewriters.)

In saying that *x* is one of *N*'s values ("Patriotism is one of Smith's values") we underwrite, *inter alia*, the inference to two conclusions:

(1) *N* is prepared to devote some of his resources (money, time, effort, discomfort, etc.) to the implementation of *x* – i.e., in furthering the extent of its realization in the world.
And moreover,

(2) He does so *in the belief* – and indeed *for the reason* – that the increased realization of *x* will benefit ("prove advantageous for," "promote the interests of") certain individuals – either *N* himself or others to whose interest he is attached.

A brief comment on each of these points is in order.

First consider point (1). When we say (seriously say) that *x* is one of *N*'s values we are prepared to claim that *N* would take his subscription to *x* into due account in making relevant choices, with the result that the outcome of these choices, viz. *N*'s actions, significantly reflect *N*'s commitment to *x*. Thus we may view *N*'s investment of resources (money, time, etc.) in those of his actions explicable in terms of his espousal of *x* as an indispensable part of this acceptance of *x*. Authentic adherence to a value implies *some* commitment to the pursuit of its realization, and this, in turn, calls for at least some investment of resources (advocacy and verbal support at the very minimum.) The extent of this requisite investment will be dependent upon – and will be affected by changes in – the working environment: *cleanliness* comes cheaper in modern cities than medieval ones, and the achievement of *privacy* costs more in urban environments than in rural ones.

As regards point (2), it is of the essence of *x*'s serving in the role of *a value* for *N* that the realization of *x* be viewed as beneficial by *N* (for someone, not necessarily himself). Moreover, this benefit will have to be of such a kind as to be a benefit ("a thing of positive value") from *N*'s own point of view. Some benefits will be more fundamental than other, subsidiary benefits, and the most basic and fundamental benefits will be associated with dominant values (including survival, security, health and pleasure in the case of individuals, and survival, security, welfare, and progress in that of modern Western societies).

This dual aspect of costs and benefits provides the key to the single most important type of stresses and strains that work upon values. For it renders them susceptible to an evaluation-procedure of the cost-benefit type familiar from economic analysis. In the case of any value we can make a kind of balance-sheet of (1) the balance of benefits – i.e., advantages over disadvantages – inherent in its realization, as contrasted with (2) the various sorts of costs that would be entailed by the endeavor to bring this realization about. The following possibilities obviously arise in the context of a cost-benefit analysis of this sort: In the circumstances of a given operating environment:

(A) N may "oversubscribe" to x, the value at issue, either because (Ai) he has an exaggerated conception of the benefits involved, and accordingly "invests" too much in the value, or (Aii) he has a correct conception of the benefits involved, but nevertheless makes a larger than proportionate investment towards securing these benefits (i.e., "overpays" for them).

(B) N may "undersubscribe" to x, the value at issue, either because (Bi) he has an unduly deflated conception of the benefits involved, and accordingly "invests" too little in the value, or (Bii) he has a correct conception of the benefits involved, but nevertheless makes a less than proportionate investment towards securing these benefits.

A survey of possibilities of this sort indicates the sort of pressures upon values that can build up from the direction of a cost-benefit point of view.

When we consider the constellation of value commitments of a person or a society, the soundness or "realism" of a value can be assessed – not abstractly, but – in context. We can test the value-economy at issue against the background of the concept of a spectrum of well-ordered modes of life, each one of which is characterized by an appropriate and viable balance of value-commitments. In extreme instances, the entire value-economy that is built into the framework of a life-history ideal can become obsolete by becoming infeasible under changed circumstances (e.g., the knight-errant, the master-craftsman).

This brings out the contextual nature of this mode of value criticism – its dependence on the setting of a complex of value commitments held under certain specific conditions and circumstances. It is clear that value criticism of this sort would never result in the verdict that a certain value (i.e., genuine value) is inappropriate as such. But it could maintain that a person, leading his life in a certain particular setting, oversubscribes or undersubscribes to a given value, given the nature of this setting. Such criticism, then, does not address itself to values directly and abstractly, but rather to the holding – and consequent concrete action upon – certain values under specifiable conditions. In the face of grounds for criticism of this sort, the value at issue becomes subject to a pressure for change.

It is important to notice that social and technological change in a life-environment can thus centrally affect the stability of values from this cost-benefit point of view. For on the one hand, such change can alter the costs involved in realizing a value (either downwards, as with air-travel *safety* in recent years, or upwards, as with urban *privacy*). And on the other hand, such changes in the life-environment can also alter the benefits derivable from realizing a value (as, e.g., the benefits to be derived from wealth decline in an affluent society).

This perspective highlights the idea of the *relevance* of values to the specific life-environment that provides the operative setting within which a value is espoused. For with a change in this setting, a certain value may be greatly more or less *deserving* of emphasis, depending on the changes in the nature and extent of the corresponding benefits in the altered circumstances. Or again, the value may be greatly more or less demanding of emphasis depending on changes in the cost of its realization in a given degree. In extreme cases, a value can become irrelevant when the life-setting has become such that the historically associated benefits are no longer available (e.g., knight-errantry, chivalry, and – perhaps – *noblesse oblige*), or it can even become malign when action on it comes to produce more harm than good (as with certain forms of "charity").

THE QUESTIONNAIRE

I should like to conclude my discussion with a brief presentation of the highlights of the results of a questionnaire on likely changes in American values over the next generation (to the year 2,000). The aim of this questionnaire was to elicit the respondents' views concerning two items:

(1) Which widely held American values are likely to change under impact of forseeable scientific, technological, demographic, and socio-economic change?

(2) What can be said about the nature, magnitude, causal mechanism, and above all, the desirability of such change?

During the Spring of 1966, roughly 75 copies of this questionnaire were sent out to various persons, a special effort being made to focus upon high-level scientists and science administrators whose interests are significantly future-oriented. It was felt that the impact of technological change on American values could be assessed most effectively and relevantly by the persons best qualified to form a vivid picture of the prospects, possibilities, and nature of technological change. Moreover, scientifically-oriented people provide in large measure the channels through which technological changes make their impact on the society in general, and how they *perceive* these effects is important.

C

Nicholas Rescher

The composition of the respondent group is as follows:

I. BY AFFILIATION

IBM Corporation Scientists	10
NSF Staff Members	14
RAND Corporation Futures Group	10
Harvard Program on Technology	8
Pittsburgh Values Project	10
Miscellaneous	6
TOTAL	58

II. BY TRAINING

Natural Scientists	29
Social Scientists	8
Humanists and Educators	15
Others	6
TOTAL	58

Various cautions must be mentioned and indeed emphasized. The sample is minute and – even within the group of scientists and intellectuals – definitely biassed in the direction of the "hard" sciences. No weighty "conclusions" can be rested on the outcome of the present round of the questionnaire. It is avowedly a *pilot project* in the study of value change by questionnaire techniques.

The following tentative conclusions emerged from the results of this questionnaire:

i. The interrelation between technology and values is thought to be reciprocal: not only do technological changes affect values by bringing about their realization or frustration, by making some more, others less important, some obsolete and others highly relevant, but some treasured values promote, others retard technological advance in general or in some particular sector.

ii. It is generally felt that great pressures will be exerted on many of our values, but that the chief factors exerting these pressures will be primarily demographic and social in origin, and only secondarily technological. The anticipated population increase is expected to give rise to a long series of social problems, such as shortage of food, housing, schooling, employment opportunities, as well as various forms of congestion and pollution and also friction, both in the social and political (national and international) realm. Certain anticipated scientific and technological developments will be aggravating, but not prime factors in causing these social problems. The developments most frequently mentioned in this connection are those in the biomedical area, such as techniques for grafting replacement organs, whether natural or artificial, arresting the process of ageing, and others designed to increase the natural life span, techniques for mechanical transfer of knowledge, acceleration of the learning process, and determination at will of sex, temperament or type of character.

iii. The chief mechanism by which such developments exert pressure on existing values is thought to be a simple rational one. The undesirability or intolerability of the conditions of life for some or most which result from such demographic and other changes become widely regarded as social problems, that is, as social states of affairs *to be remedied*. As a consequence, there is research into cures and clamor for their adoption. The case of the increasing birth rate is paradigmatic. Here four values come into conflict: sexual love, fertility, longevity, affluence. At least one has to give way. Technological advances make possible solutions conforming to people's preferences, thereby reducing the range and severity of the unavoidable sacrifices and frustrations. Some values not in this way related to human welfare tend to come under pressure and eventually to be abandoned.

iv. The respondents revealed awareness of and optimism about the new opportunities afforded by the rapid advances in technology, for improving the quality of life, i.e. for realizing to a higher degree many of our prevalent values. Here primarily two areas of technological advance were stressed: again the biomedical area and the development of the computer. Both seemed to open vistas for the realization of our most basic values to hitherto undreamed of levels of aspiration.

v. Finally one striking feature of the questionnaire responses is their clear optimism. One has grown accustomed to virtually endless diatribes on the dangers of technical civilization to human values. This point of view finds a decisive rejection by the consensus of respondents throughout the questionnaire. The point of view of those whom we may characterize as the "cocktail party catastrophists" finds little if any support in our findings.*

University of Pittsburgh

*For further details see N. Rescher, "Report on the Questionnaire for the Pittsburgh Values Project," forthcoming in K. Baier and N. Rescher, edd., *Technology and Values* (New York: Free Press, 1968).

THE EXPERIENCE & JUDGMENT OF VALUES

Arnold Berleant

I

One of the most persistent problems in modern theory of value centers around the nature and significance of judgments of value. Controversy has raged over alternative accounts of the origin, analysis, and justification of such judgments. And indeed, the failure to achieve general agreement on answers to questions about value may, more than any other reason, account for the presence of widespread cynicism toward philosophy. It may help explain the feeling among many observers of philosophical activity that it is on the one hand mere sophistry and sterile scholasticism, and on the other vapid platitudinizing or profound vagueness. At a time when increasingly rapid advances are being made in science and technology, the philosopher remains behind in his study, musing over the same "insoluble" problems that have troubled his predecessors for countless generations. We must admit, however, that society rarely looks to him for answers; it has long since realized the futility of that. Men continue to make personal choices, determine public policy, wage wars, overthrow governments, get born, marry and die – all with little philosophical assistance in determining (as opposed to justifying) their actions!

It is with questions of value that such inconclusiveness is particularly hard to bear, for, in contrast with other regions of philosophical discussion more removed from the issues of human choice and action, value theory cannot confine itself to library carrels and seminar rooms. It reaches out into the streets and forums of society. Yet a hopeful thought occurs: Might not assistance be tendered in the other direction? Might not the impossibility of being secluded work more to the advantage of the study of values than to its detriment? In fact, might it not provide direction for the discussion of value, and even offer the hope of answers? Perhaps the conduct of men can instruct him who would understand it.

There is, I think, one principal issue that underlies the difficulties and inadequacies of the philosophy of value which I have just described. It rests on a deeply rooted tendency, systematically developed by Kant and usually accepted by philosophers since him, the tendency to perceive a basic, qualitative difference between the factual statements one can establish about our physical world and the normative ones we apply to relations among men. As the distinction is usually presented, it is established and defended on the basis of a radical difference between the subject-matter about which

we can attain factual knowledge and the subject-matter of normative reference. Facts deal with the so-called objective world of external objects and
events which we can observe in common, and about which we can discourse
and formulate verifiable statements. Values, on the other hand, are quite a
different matter. They concern a region beyond the range of scientific
scrutiny, the realm of the noumenal, or they derive from intangible, in-
communicable subjectivity. Whatever their locus, values elude all attempts
at proving and establishing them as a body of knowledge to which we must
assent on the same logical grounds as we assent to factual statements.

I should like to take issue with the assumption underlying this position,
the presumption that those situations that involve considerations of value
differ sharply from those that are concerned with factual matters. This is a
difference that is claimed quite apart from the particular theory by which
values are explained. It is typically asserted that full knowledge of whatever
is the case can never tell us what we ought to do. For this we must turn in
some other direction – to authoritative sources in religious and political
doctrines and leaders, to revelation, to intuition – or, in despair, we end by
consigning values to the irrational region of emotion.

Not only does the belief in the radical separation of the factual and the
normative obstruct the rational deliberation and resolution of basic dis-
agreements of value. I am convinced that it also rests on a misleading
analysis of the normative situation. Specifically, our difficulties in dealing
with values follow from the failure to distinguish clearly and effectively
between values as characteristic kinds of human experiences and value
judgments as statements about such kinds of experiences. The first are the
actual occasions of valuing themselves and, like all direct and immediate
experience, are non-cognitive. Value judgments, on the other hand, are of a
distinctly different order. They are statements which are framed *about* our
value experiences; they offer a conceptual formulation and ordering of the
valuational mode of experience. This being the case, such statements can
be verified by placing them against the value experiences of men, and
consequently these statements take on a cognitive character.

I should like to offer here a basis on which it is possible to support this
distinction between the experience and judgment of values. In developing
this position, I shall first make some observations about the conditions of
valuing, and then examine, in turn, the place and function of the analysis
of values, the justification of judgments of value, and the implications of
this proposal for the theory of value.

II

The initial stage of any inquiry is of crucial importance, for the structuring of a problem often involves assumptions which are neither made
explicit nor justified. The more that inquiry deals with issues which have
logical priority, the more difficult it might seem to be for one to avoid

assumptions of some sort. One must begin somewhere, and surely any significant philosophy cannot be manufactured *ex nihilo.* Hence it is that in questions of value, writers often begin their discussion with the conviction of the transcendental origin and status of values: values must have their root in Being, in the Absolute, or in a divine mind. Or, in a more sophisticated form, values are separated from the natural world and thought of as non-natural qualities apprehended intuitively. And even when they are considered from an exclusively naturalistic standpoint by the emotivist theories, values, reflecting the influence of the same assumption, are set apart from the knowable realm of natural knowledge and taken as expressions of feelings and other such forms that have only subjective significance. Here, too, values are excluded from the factual order of verifiable statements that command general assent.

Thus from all sides the same assumption appears to be unquestioned. It seems commonly agreed that the goodness of a thing is a matter apart from and independent of whatever other characteristics of that thing we can designate by observing its behavior, responses, and other such ways in which it appears in our experience. So for one reason or another, one cannot claim that nations should renounce violent means of settling disputes from the fact that the failure to do so places human survival in jeopardy. Nor can one draw any normative conclusion about the rightness of capital punishment, birth control, or a social order based on narrow self-interest from any data that can be supplied about the use or consequences of these practices.

Contrary to this common view, however, I should like to argue that the separation of values from empirical facts is not an assumption that is warranted. It is not grounded in valuational experience nor in the nature and function of value theory which derives from that experience. Rather it is the outcome of dealing in exclusively conceptual terms which what is originally an empirical issue. That is to say, when we regard the value-traits we assign to objects as non-empirical or non-objective properties, we make a conceptual, not an empirically-based decision. It is a decision which therefore begs the question of whether or not values are indeed factual in nature.

But, one might object, must we not start somewhere? Either we begin by placing the values of objects and events outside of these factual things and occurrences, or we place them within. Could we not be accused in either case of being assumptive? For if we see the values of things contained in our experiences of them, then we are insuring the conclusion that such values are indeed empirical in origin.

The answer to this objection is not hard to find. In fact, the objection is itself presumptive. Suppose the value-component of objects and events were indeed independent of experience. How, but through experiencing these objects, through becoming acquainted with them under various circumstances, can we infer what values they actually possess? How can one conceivably know that democracy is good or bad, liberty desirable or not, life worth preserving and promoting or freely expendable – assuming agreement on the meaning of the terms – if one has no acquaintance whatsoever with social organization, free and restrained actions, and life itself? Indeed, the artificiality of this problem becomes obvious when we observe that it is impossible for a man ever to come to the point at which he will ask such questions without having had his interest in them generated by the conditions under which he has lived and been educated. The morality of lying would never have been considered, were it not for the social need to communicate and engage in collaborative action. Nor would liberty be prized but for restraints men have borne, trust and benevolence valued but for knowing, needing, and loving other people.

These considerations lead to an important observation. It is that the artificiality of denying the empirical origins of values follows from extrapolating them from the historical and social setting in which the lives and beliefs of men occur, and placing values in a realm quite apart from the circumstances that produce and inform them. If a distinction such as that between fact and value is to be ontologically based, the validity of this distinction must be established, not assumed.

Thus even if values should actually be transcendental or nonnatural, we could never know it, for whatever we can believe or know about values is a fact about our belief or about our knowledge. It is impossible to establish anything whatsoever about values that does not presuppose their factuality. The Kantian expedient of locating values beyond experience in a noumenal realm falls flat. We are in a situation similar to that which Berkeley developed in arguing that all ideas are mental, although we do not have to accept his idealistic conclusion. Just as Berkeley correctly observed that it is impossible by the very nature of the matter to have an idea that is not in the mind, so it is equally impossible to speak meaningfully of value which is independent of human experience. Values, therefore, can have no knowable status apart from the life of man. This means, then, that they are natural experiences of human beings. While the logical possibility of nonnatural value remains, there is little point in concerning ourselves with something that by the nature of the case we can never come to experience and thus to know, unless we obtain some perverse pleasure in attempting the impossible task of demonstrating the truth of a logical contradiction. For experiencing and knowing values means bringing them in some fashion into our lives – acting on them, becoming aware of them, feeling them, deliberating over them. Values independent of man are values which man can never experience and know, and of that which he cannot know, he cannot meaningfully speak. As soon as values are experienced and known, they are affected by those who hold them and are, in turn, themselves modified, related, and otherwise affected.

Arnold Berleant

How the belief in values that have objective status independent of man ever came about is an important and fascinating question, one whose answer would undoubtedly clarify the nature of the problem of the claim that values are independent of facts. It is likely that the influence of supernatural theology and transcendental metaphysics played a central role in promoting this belief. Yet important though it be, the origins and history of this conception do not concern me here. What I am interested in doing at this point is rather clarifying the assumptive nature of the problem, and suggesting that, once this is admitted, the claim that values are independent of experience cannot be supported. From this follows a consequence of central importance. It is that evaluations cannot meaningfully be discussed without recognizing that they are made in and from the experiences that men have. Moreover, such experiences cannot be viewed in the limited sense in which philosophers have traditionally spoken of them, that is as passive responses to perceptual stimuli. Experience must rather be taken to include the full range of human activity as it is affected by the physical, social, historical, cultural, technological and other conditions under which men live at any particular time and place.

Often when a value claim is made, such as asserting that life, happiness, or the satisfaction of human needs is an ultimate good, the questions are asked, "But is it *really* good?", "It is not enough that you value life; is life, *itself*, an ultimate value?" Yet it is now clear that such questions are misdirected. Indeed, they have little meaning. How can we speak of value without someone who values? It is a term which cannot be conceptualized without reference to the human activities of believing, striving, responding in all sorts of ways to the things and events which men encounter. Anything else is but a hypostatization, the fabrication of a product of human experience into an independent object. Thus while we may not *make* values, they *depend* upon us.

Yet in some quarters it will be maintained that this is not the issue at all. The question, so the ethical emotivists will object, is not whether or not values arise out of the experiences of man. Values indeed do occur in experience, but they are sharply removed from the range of facts because they reflect, not things about the world, but the feelings, desires and demands of men instead. Thus to value friendship, for example, is in some way to feel favorably disposed toward it, to want to acquire friends and promote this feeling and action in others. Ethical judgments, then, are deceptive; they seem to be stating facts, whereas they are actually expressing feelings, commands, and exhortations.

There is, as I have already noted, an assumption that the emotivists make which in certain ways parallels that of transcendental or objectivist ethics. This is the contention that there is a sharp distinction between factual and normative statements. Factual statements are expressed in indicative or hypothetical sentences and refer to things and events in the world about us which can be verified by the appropriate observations. Normative statements cannot be verified, however, since they have no empirical reference but refer only to the feelings, needs, and desires of the person who utters such statements.

Yet when we apply to this dichotomy between facts and values the distinction I have been urging between experience and judgment, we make a revealing discovery. We see that emotive feelings and hortatory and exclamatory expressions are indeed non-cognitive, since they are part of the *direct experience of value. Statements about such experience*, on the other hand, are capable of verification, at least in principle, and are therefore cognitive.

The belief in this kind of fact-value separation rests, in its turn, upon still another assumption, and one that is so pervasive and influential that it might appear querulous even to question it. I am speaking of the belief in the radical division of the world into things and events whose status is in the objective world around us, and internal mental occurrences whose locus is exclusively in the subjective consciousness of the human being.

This is not the place for an exhaustive inquiry into the grounds for maintaining a dualism of the subjective and objective. It is a doctrine that has predominated for so long that it often makes a subtle appearance in the arguments of those very writers who would refute it. Here, in fact, is an instance of this, for the emotivists generally agree in rejecting the Cartesian dualism of body and spirit. Still, the net effect of emotivist ethics is an ethical subjectivism in which the truth or falsity of normative propositions can never be determined, since they refer not to events that can be empirically observed but to personal states of consciousness.

Here too, however, it is assumptive to insist on an ontological dualism of subjective and objective. It is this separation which must itself be established. However we analyze them, there is no reason to assume that feelings and desires are different in kind from other modes of experience. This distinction and incompatibility between subjective and objective is not a postulate; it is a conclusion, and a conclusion which the evidence does not appear to warrant. How and why, then, must we exclude felt needs and desires as irrelevant to the truth of ethical judgments? And why must we confine ourselves to subjective evidence alone in attempting to establish such judgments? The existence of human feelings and desires occurs in relation and response to conditions in the surrounding environment, and these conditions are themselves affected by the kinds of feelings we have. All may be interpreted by the same categories.

Values, then, originate in the basic conditions under which human beings conduct their lives at different times and places. There must be things and men who relate to them for there to be goods. As the anthropologist Robert Redfield has observed, "We do not expect a people to have a moral norm that their material conditions of life make impossible."[1] In a Kantian

fashion, the very possibility of values, as well as identifying and disagree-
ing over them, presupposes conditions about human life, about society,
and about culture, along with beliefs about these conditions. Moreover,
there first must be basic values which are necessary in order for other values
– about which men disagree and dispute – to occur. These primary values
cannot be denied without denying the possibility of any value whatsoever.
Nietzsche put this neatly when he wrote in *The Geneology of Morals* that
"life itself forces us to posit values." But more of this later.

III

I turn now to the core of my argument. In the preceding part of this
discussion, I have spoken uncritically of fact and value, using these terms
in a more or less conventional fashion. Now, however, I should like to
examine the significance and role of judgments of value, by approaching
them contextually rather than linguistically. It will be illuminating to consider such judgments in their relation to the full setting of human experience
in which they play an important part.

Unfortunately, the terminology that is usual in discussing questions of
value is misleading. We speak of facts and values as if they were concepts
of the same order. I should like to suggest, on the contrary, that they are
not. Yet while both terms are troublesome, it is of small advantage to
propose, as Quine does of "fact",[2] that they be eliminated. Not only does
the problem with which we are dealing derive in part from a particular view
of the nature of fact, but the term itself is useful as long as we clearly designate its meaning.

While it is common to think of a fact as a state of affairs to which we
may refer in a statement, there are reasons why this usage is not satisfactory.
It would be unwise to become entangled in an epistemological digression
at this point, inasmuch as my terminological practice here is stipulative
and its justification heuristic. Suffice it to say that to speak of a fact in the
sense of a state of affairs involves one in certain assumptions which I am
unwilling to make. In particular, it implies that the conditions about which
we make statements are already determinate, and that these statements are
an easy and direct reflection of those determinate conditions. Certainly in
common situations there is little ambiguity in this usage. We may refer to
the strange "fact" that during the snowstorm last night there was a flash of
lightning and a peal of thunder. Yet there are other instances which are not
so clear, as when we cite the "fact" that there seems to be an uneasiness in
the air, that Jared has musical talent, that pop art is revealing but not great,
or that the stringent economic policies in Britian have helped that country's
economy. Here the states of affairs are not entirely obvious. We need
clarification about just which conditions are referred to. And when this
happens, we are no longer regarding the so-called facts as states of affairs
but rather as statements which refer to states of affairs that need to be

identified and specified. It is such statements, then, that specify, select, and identify from the press of experience those features toward which we wish to direct attention. These statements do something to the conditions around us by organizing and interpreting them. Indeed, to ascribe ontological status to our ordering of experience suggests the idealistic tenet that reality is what we know and thus what we can say about it. This misuse of the order that *we* find in experience is something the careful mind of Spinoza long ago cautioned us against.

For reasons such as I have suggested here, then, I shall take a fact to be a *statement* about experience, one that has high probability and whose truth is not open to serious question.

A similar confusion greets the notion of value. It, too, may refer to a condition in experience that is valued, or to a statement that expresses an evaluation about that condition. Here it seems most useful as well as accurate to accept the common inclination to associate a value with the conditions experienced as valuable, and to speak of statements about such values as *evaluations*.

This leads me to the main idea of this paper. It is that many of the problems with which we are beset in theory of value are the product of the failure to distinguish clearly between the existential field of human experience and the particular cognitive activity of reflective analysis by which we develop our knowledge of that field. Let me develop this point a bit further by contrasting value experience and reflection on a number of counts.

The existential field is the region within which the range of human experience, including value experience, takes place. It is, as such, non-cognitive, for the activity of knowing is a specialized one involving reflective and often manipulative techniques. Hence knowledge is always inferential, whereas experience as it is directly had is immediate. Thus, on the one hand, *valuation*, or the experience of value, is the valuing we have as directly experienced in its uniqueness and particularity. Reflection on such experience, on the other hand, is concerned with *evaluation*, with developing a conceptual framework and arriving at judgments of value which have the abstract generality of all cognitive statements. It is an activity usually called forth by the need to decide between conflicting values, but it is of a different order from the values with which it is concerned. Evaluation, then, is the product of intellectual appraisal; it is experience dealt with at one remove, so to speak. It results in the formulation of judgments of value which can be verified by reference to the existential field from which they derive. Thus specific normative situations arise in the broad context of human experience, and evaluations produce judgments about such situations.

We have, then, normative experience and normative language. Here we arrive at a crucial point. For we do not create values; we identify, describe, analyze, and deliberate about them. To apply a useful Kantian distinction, experience is constitutive of value, whereas reflection is regulative. Theories of value do not make or constitute values; they identify, analyze, and order them. Similarly with the issues with which we are beset in value theory. The "is-ought" problem, for example, is a problem in the reflective analysis of values: it is a cognitive, not a substantive issue. It is, as I have tried to show, the outcome of a faulty analysis of valuational experience, of a confusion between the experience and judgment of value. Values, themselves, are rather a feature of the existential conditions in which valuing occurs. We do, to be sure, make statements about these conditions, and these include factual statements together with their sub-class of normative statements which denote the normative conditions in experience. To explain, justify, and relate these normative statements, we are eventually led, then, to an examination not of normative knowledge but of normative experience.

IV

Let me now show how the position I am proposing can be applied to the problem of justifying judgments of value, those in particular which, in the common view, appear most to elude justification. I am thinking here of final ends or ultimate values. It is such values as these which, in naive or sophisticated ways, are most typically consigned to faith, authority, preference, or postulation. In a preliminary study such as this, a discussion of so difficult a topic can only be programmatic, but at least an approach can be sketched.

The view that I am developing here serves remarkably well to illuminate and explain some important proposals about ultimate values in the history of ethics. These are ideas that are highly suggestive but were not developed with sufficient rigor, so that they have at times been regarded as strange aberrations of otherwise important theories. Aristotle and John Stuart Mill offer good illustrations of what I am speaking of.

In his *Nicomachean Ethics*[3] Aristotle makes what is perhaps a puzzling observation when he states that while we deliberate and choose means, we rather desire and wish for ends. And the good man will wish for what is truly good. Now Aristotle has already argued that the good, in his famous phrase, is "that at which all things aim."[4] He maintains that the good of a thing follows from its peculiar nature, and consequently that man's highest good follows from his peculiar function.[5] Thus, since the good man is one who functions in accordance with his nature, he will, by that fact, desire and wish for the end which is truly good. Aristotle seems to be saying, then, that the good is the goal of things, that the good for man is man's goal, and that man's goal is based on man's nature. In other words, an accurate understanding of the conditions of human functioning (that is, the facts of man's function) will provide us with knowledge of the proper final end (that is, the standard by which goals are to be evaluated).

Aristotle's reasoning seems to resemble closely the argument I have been urging. For he is maintaining that the "is" of man's nature becomes the ground for determining the "ought" of man's good. Ends, then, are not the result of rational deliberation but rather the product of the natural condition of human life and the desires that are manifested when such conditions are most completely fulfilled. Indeed, Aristotle observes that few people go wrong when it comes to natural appetites, and when they do it is only in the direction of excess.[6] Our basic desires, then, tend to lead us aright, and they are most dependable in the proper functioning of the good man. Pleasures peculiar to individuals, however, are of greater variety and hence are more prone to error.[7] So, too, does Spinoza reason. For he holds, you will recall, that man's highest good, a good that is common to all, "is deduced from the very essence of man,"[8] and he maintains that that which we hold to be good is good "because we strive for it, wish for it, long for it, or desire it."[9]

The case of Mill is particularly interesting, for his famous proof of the principle of utility has been the object of strong attacks, attacks so vehement that his argument would seem to have been long since demolished. Yet the very fact that it has evoked so violent a response and still continues to elicit interest suggests to me that Mill has, however inadequately, hit upon something highly significant if not crucial to the problem of justifying ethical value.

Mill holds that the only proof possible, and also the only proof necessary, that something is desirable is that people actually desire it. He introduces his proof by a series of analogies that illustrate it rather than establish it. Let me quote the familiar passage:

> The only proof capable of being given that an object is visible is that people actually see it. The only proof that a sound is audible is that people hear it; and so of the other sources of our experience. In like manner, I apprehend, the sole evidence it is possible to produce that anything is desirable is that people do actually desire it.... No reason can be given why the general happiness is desirable, except that each person, so far as he believes it to be attainable, desires his own happiness.[10]

The reason why the desirability of an object may not seem to follow from its being desired, and thus make this inference falsely analogous to the previous ones, depends on the assumption that facts and evaluations are separate. For if they are, how can one infer a normative conclusion – "ought to be desired" – from a factual premise – "is desired?" If the gulf between facts and evaluations be bridged, however, the inference can be appraised in a different light.

Indeed, Mill may be interpreted as holding that the presumed distinction between factual statements and normative ones is not as absolute as his critics claim. He does distinguish, it is true, between what he calls the Method of Science which is concerned with causes and conditions, and the

Method of Art which includes ethics and which is concerned with determining and appraising ends and finally arriving at rules or precepts.[11] Yet Mill seems to be claiming that the basis for evaluations of ends and the moral percepts that summarize them, like the basis of facts, lies in the realm of nature, and that evaluations, expressing natural phenomena as they do, must be derived from the facts of human nature. Hence, knowledge of the facts of what people desire is indeed capable of providing us with knowledge of the values which people ought to desire.

Moreover, Mill may be claiming that the limitations of method restrict one to basing value judgments on the observable facts of human behavior. In other words, every assertion of value must be grounded on the fact that under conditions of fully adequate experience and knowledge, men actually do hold such values. Under these conditions, men value happiness and those material, social, intellectual and cultural goods that contribute to happiness. Hence it is the fact of valuing them that makes them valuable. For Mill, like Aristotle, grounds his argument on the constitution of human nature, and the constitution of human nature is for him an empirically determinable fact.[12] Both Mill and Aristotle hold that the good man is the source of ethical knowledge. Aristotle regards the good man who exercises practical reason as the true judge in determining which action in any particular case is in accordance with man's proper function. Mill, on the other hand, considers such a man to be one who has undergone the full range of experience, quantitative and qualitative. The validation of ethical belief is then found in the constitution of human nature which guarantees Mill's pleasurable conception of happiness as it is expressed in the principle of utility.

John Dewey's theory of value is a cognate one. He distinguishes between "appraising," which is concerned with means, and "prizing," which deals with ends. There is, for Dewey, no final end but rather what he calls "ends-in-view," that is, proximate ends which arise as ways of organizing and directing men in their transactional relationship with their environment. Both the characteristics of men and the conditions of their existence must be taken into account in deciding upon the value of particular ends for resolving difficulties and aiding in the ongoing process of developing experience. Here, too, values emerge out of the conditions of human activity.

I have not engaged in this brief foray into the history of ethical thought for the purpose of adducing authorities in support of my thesis. Their doctrines add little to the argument I have developed. My object has been rather to reveal certain of their insights, and to show how the view for which I have been contending assists in formulating openly a conception that was obscure and implicit in these historical appearances.

Final ends and ultimate values are not such because we decide so to designate them. They are neither the postulates nor conclusions of a theory of value. They grow instead out of the existential conditions in which the human animal functions and, when recognized, serve to assist men in better achieving a fuller and more complete development. Those conditions which constitute and encompass the activities of living are the context or field in which valuation appears and toward which evaluation is directed. Moreover, this existential field includes those needs, drives, and desires, whose fulfillment is necessary in order for men to live and to flourish.

Conflicts of value, then, must be seen for what they are – discordances within the existential field which may be cognized in the effort to understand and resolve them. Here is the role which value theory can fulfill. And yet in transforming the incompatibility between valuations into the conceptual order, we do not place all valuings in question. The class of values is never empty, and primary values are, so to speak, existentially given. We do not have the prerogative of accepting or rejecting them in general. The issue is only with the status of those values which are in conflict in the particular situation at hand. For example, a conflict involving the value of life, itself, deals only apparently with the ground of all value. Actually such a conflict is generated by problematic conditions *within* an individual life to which, say, suicide may be proposed as a solution in that particular case. And although under certain circumstances life may be denied, the decision, instead of placing all value in question, may be explained according to the same features of the ground and context of valuation. For one can never make an abstract judgment of the value of life in general that is a genuine evaluation. Instead, particular judgments deal only with the way in which basic values manifest themselves in the existential field under specific circumstances.

The same observations apply, with appropriate modifications, to other such fundamental and ubiquitous values. What these values are, and what the existential conditions are out of which values grow, are factual questions. They constitute empirical problems that are the fitting province of the behavioral sciences. And indeed, much has already emerged from these sciences that is highly suggestive. Kurt Lewin and other social psychologists have identified certain of the conditions under which groups function with a minimum of conflict and a maximum of personally fulfilling and socially productive consequences. Carl Rogers has developed therapeutic techniques in psychology for assisting people in freeing themselves from repressive restraints and opening themselves to experience and to their own momentum of growth. Sociologists like Morris Ginsberg and Raymond Firth and jurisprudents like Karl Llewellyn have talked about the primary experiences of value which develop into increasingly well-defined and applicable standards, and culminate in universal moral principles which emerge from the universal conditions of human living. Nor does this mean that such principles must perforce possess the sanction of eternal absolutes. In fact, as conditions change and knowledge develops, so, too, do universal values. Thus we may speak, as the anthropologist Clyde Kluckhohn does, of "conditional absolutes."[13] Indeed, it takes little insight to perceive the possibility of a correlation between the startling transformation of the conditions of human life in the modern world and the altered awareness and quality of the valuational experiences that men have, and between the rapid changes in our factual knowledge and the instability and changes in human evaluations. More particularly, it would be illuminating to study the effects that the acquisition of knowledge in the behavioral sciences has had on the breakdown in conventional morality. But all this is merely suggestive and not germane to our present purpose. What remains, finally, is to sketch the implications of the view I have developed here for the theory of value.

V

I have tried in this paper to show that by turning to the normative conduct of men, it becomes possible to resolve the age-old controversy between facts and values and to heal the breach thought to keep them separate. For factual statements are like normative ones; they are statements about objects and experiences, and thus quite a different sort of thing from what they denote. Just as events are neither true nor false but only statements about them are, events involving values are neither true nor false but statements about them are. Value statements, then, are a species of fact. They derive from the conditions of human existence rather than from values that subsist in some inexplicable way independent of these conditions. It is our failure to observe the distinction between the experience and judgment of value that has created our philosophical difficulties, for *judgments do not legislate experience; rather, experience legislates judgments.*

The conditions of human life are simply there; they are what is given for inquiry. All we can do in theory of value is to talk about those conditions that concern our wishes and needs – our values. On the basis of our discourse, we may become clearer about what these values are and what their place is in the full range and context of human experience. And surely our theoretical examination of values can aid us in identifying and systematizing them and in resolving incompatibilities and conflicts among them. The success with which we can do these things can then be tested against the experiences of values, themselves, in much the same way as observations of the results of trying out an hypothesis confirm or disconfirm that hypothesis. We must begin, then, with the conditions of human life – with the basic human needs and patterns of development and response. We do not construct them; we do not presuppose them ; we do not postulate them; we start with them. For values are already present in the existential field of human action. They precede and are presupposed by inquiry. Thus it is not necessary to justify living in order to live, nor eating in order to consume food, nor any other such fundamental condition for any other value. These come up for evaluation only when there is some conflict among our ways of fulfilling such needs, as between life with an unendurable and incurable illness, or food at the expense of the starvation of a dear one. We do not first judge the preservation of life to be a prima facie good. It emerges in the existential field and is experienced as valuable, and on the basis of such experience a judgment of its value is formulated. Judgments do not create value; they merely recognize it, and they do so in a hypothetical fashion since they are corrigible. To think that judgments confer value is a survival of idealism. Judgments cannot constitute value; they can only identify it as a characteristic already present in a human situation.

In sum, a value theory which draws from the experiences of men and can then be applied back to these experiences in order to guide human action is capable of fruitful and progressive development. By contrast, a value theory that develops independent conceptual distinctions which then obstruct its connection with experience is doomed to drown in its own verbal deluge. It is not for us to decide whether the good shall consist in satisfying human needs; it is for us to decide whether specific needs are good.

Sarah Lawrence College

[1] *The Primitive World and Its Transformations* (Ithaca, New York: Cornell University Press, 1957), p. 163.

[2] *Word and Object* (Cambridge: M.I.T. Press, 1960), p. 248.

[3] III, 2, 1111b; 4, 1113a.

[4] I, 1, 1094a.

[5] I, 7, 1098a.

[6] III, 11, 1118b.

[7] *Loc. cit.*

[8] *Ethics*, IV, xxxvi, Note.

[9] *Ibid.*, III, ix, Note.

[10] *Utilitarianism*, Ch. IV.

[11] *A System of Logic*, 8th ed., Bk. VI, Ch. XII. It is worth noting that this work was first published in 1843, two decades before *Utilitarianism*.

[12] *Utilitarianism*, Ch. IV.

[13] "Values and Value-Orientations in the Theory of Action: An Exploration in Definition and Classification," in *Toward a General Theory of Action*, edd., Talcott Parsons and Edward Shils (Cambridge: Harvard University Press, 1951), pp. 418-9.

FORMAL AXIOLOGY AND
THE MEASUREMENT OF VALUES

Robert S. Hartman

1. GENERIC VALUE AND SPECIFIC VALUE

A distinction must be made between value in general and specific values (interests, preferences, pleasures etc.). Theoretically, this distinction has been emphasized by G. E. Moore, and the confusion of generic and specific value been called by him the naturalistic fallacy. Value theoreticians have not taken it seriously; and the confusion persists in value theory. While there it does the theoretical harm that consists in intellectual confusion, in practice, especially that of value measurement, this confusion would do practical harm. Therefore, in value measurement, one has to be careful to keep strictly to the Moorean distinction.

The capacity to value in general is to specific value capacities (interests, preferences, etc.) as the capacity to see color is to specific color interests, preferences etc. Before testing a person as to his preference for, say, green or red, he ought first to be tested as to his capacity for *seeing color*. A color-blind person, obviously, cannot have a valid judgment as to his preference for red or green.

Similarly, before testing a person as to his preference for, say, religious, theoretical, economic or political values (as is done in some widely used tests), the person ought first to be tested as to his *capacity to value in general*. Since his interests are *specific* values, his capacity to distinguish them depends on his capacity to *value in general*.

In the degree that a person is more or less sensitive to color in general, his preference for this or that specific color is more or less valid and significant. Similarly, in the degree that a person is more or less sensitive to value in general, his preference for this or that value is more or less valid and significant.

There is thus need of a test which does *not* measure the subject's particular interests; but which does measure his capacity for selecting an interest, making relevant choices, pursuing his interest with a proper sense of proportion, and without confusion of fundamental valuational features. Such a test has been developed on the basis of formal axiology.[1] In the following the theoretical reasoning behind the test will be presented.

2. THE DEFINITION OF VALUE.

Formal axiology is based on the logic of value thinking. This logic analyzes *Meaning*. Value thinking identifies value and meaning. When we say that life is full of meaning we mean to say that it is full of value. When we say that life has lost its meaning we mean to say that it has lost its value. Value logic analyzes that aspect of meaning which is identified with value. The meaning of a thing is the total set of properties connected with the thing. Thus, the meaning of life is the total set of properties connected with life, its richness of features, qualities, characteristics; and the loss of meaning of life is the loss of this richness. Thus, when a beloved dies we say that we have suffered a *loss*. Our life has lost a source of richness. This loss, we say, has left "a gap," "an emptiness that cannot be filled." On the other hand, when a joy enters our life we say "our cup runneth over," our life is full of content, we are "content," we do not know how to "contain" ourselves, etc.

Value thus, may be defined both as *meaning* and as *richness of properties*. A thing has value in the degree of its richness of properties; and it has disvalue in the degree of its poorness of properties. Or, a thing richer in properties is more valuable than a thing less rich in properties and vice versa. A rich cake is a more valuable cake than a lean cake, an "easy chair" a more valuable chair than a wooden chair. The rich cake has greater richness of cake ingredients than the lean cake and the easy chair has greater richness of chair features than the wooden chair.

3. THE LOGICAL MEANING OF MEANING.

The meaning of a thing is, logically, the set of predicates by which the thing is characterized. This set of predicates is called, logically, "the content" of the thing's concept or the *intension* of the thing's concept. The definition of value, thus, may be stated logically as follows: *A thing has value in the degree that it fulfills the intension of its concept.* Thus, if the intension of "chair" is "a knee-high structure with a seat and a back" then a thing which is called "chair" will be the more valuable a chair the more of the chair properties it has, and the less valuable a chair the fewer of the chair properties it has. A chair which has no seat is not a *good* chair but a *bad* chair.

Formal axiology is based on the logical nature of meaning, namely intension, and on the structure of intension as a set of predicates. It applies set theory to this set of predicates. Set theory is a certain kind of mathematics that deals with the relationship of sets and subsets in general, and of finite and infinite sets in particular. Since mathematics is objective and *a priori*, formal axiology is an objective and *a priori* science; and a test based on it is an objective test based on an objective standard.

4. THE INTENSION AS MEASURE.

Through the notion of intension as a set of predicates, meaning assumes the form of a *measure*, and of a measure of value in particular. A standard of measuring is a set of units arbitrarily selected which is applicable to certain phenomena and by comparison with which the nature of these phenomena can be numerically determined. Thus, the standard of length is the meter composed of centimeters as units. The length of phenomena is measured by comparing the centimeters as the units of the meter, with the number of corresponding units in the thing to be measured.

To measure value by meaning means then, to use meaning as a measuring rod which fits the thing and from which the number of the value of the thing can be read off. Meaning as logical intension, or as a set of predicates, is, precisely, such a standard of measuring. Just as the units of the meter are the centimeters so the units of an intension are the predicates it contains. This set of predicates is compared with the set of properties actually possessed by the thing; and the thing has *valuè* in the degree that the set of its properties corresponds to the set of predicates in its intension; just as the thing has *length* in the degree that the units of length it possesses correspond to the centimeters contained in the measure of its length, the meter. Just as each class of things must be measured by the kind of measure appropriate to it – the circumference of a tree cannot be measured by a meter rod but only by a tape – so each class of things must be measured by the intension appropriate to it. Pears cannot be measured by the intension of "apple," and apples not by that of "tree." But any kind of intension is a set of predicates as any kind of length measure is a set of centimeters (or inches etc.).

If a thing possesses the whole set of properties given in the intension it is called a *good* such thing. It corresponds to the full measure of its value, or it corresponds fully to the measure of its value, the intension. If it does not possess them all, it is not so good a thing, or a *bad* thing – as the chair, which lacks a seat or a back or both. Words such as *good* or *bad*, then, are nothing but words of measuring meaning, logically no different from words such as *meter*, *dozen*, *score* and other measuring words. Sometimes such value words are actually used to measure number, as when we say "the town is lousy with tourists," meaning that there are very many tourists in town. We use *lousy*, which is a value word meaning "very bad," to signify "very many."

The measure of the value of the thing thus is the logical intension of the thing; and a thing is the better the more elements of the intension can be matched with the set of properties contained in the thing. In general, the possession of all the intensional properties makes the thing *good*, of half of them *so-so* or *average*, of more than half *fair*, and of less then half *bad*.

5. THE INTENSION AS NORM OF VALUE.

The intension as value measure is structured according to the theory of sets and subsets. Any set has a certain number of subsets. A set of two items, for example, has three subsets: (1) the first item, (2) the second item, (3) both items together. In general, if the set has p items, it has $2^p - 1$ subsets, e.g. $2^2 - 1 = 3$. If an intension has p predicates, then it has $2^p - 1$ subsets of predicates. Each of these subsets is a *value* of the thing. The thing therefore has $2^p - 1$ values (in combinatorial analysis the full set is also called a subset, namely, of itself). In a thing with 4 properties, such as the chair, there are possible $2^4 - 1 = 15$ subsets, or values. The chair may have all the 4 properties, and thus the value *Goodness*. It may have only 3 properties, and thus the value *Fairness*. It may have only 2 then it has the value *Average*, or only 1, then it has the value *Badness*. There are four values *Badness*, four values *Fairness*, six values *Average*, and one value *Goodness*. That is to say, the chair may be bad or fair in 4 different ways, having or lacking any one of four possible properties, seat, back, knee-height or structure (in case it wobbles). The chair may be average in 6 ways; it may be knee-high and have a seat, but lack a back and wobble; it may have a seat and a back, but not be knee-high or wobble, etc. And there is one set of all four properties. A thing can be good in only one way.

Valuation thus arranges and re-arranges the properties of things. It sees things fluidly rather than solidly, dynamically rather than statically.[2]

Things, of course, usually have more than four properties. A thing with ten properties has $2^{10} - 1 = 1023$ values. Thus, in job evaluation, if a job is defined by ten properties, the employee can fulfill or not fulfill this job in 1023 different ways; there are, in other words, 1023 different ways in which he can perform or not perform the particular job. There is one way of good performance, 385 ways of fair performance, 252 ways of average performance, 385 ways of bad performance. By dividing the possible number of performances through the possible total of *all* performances one obtains the percentage of performance expectation: 0.098 percent for *good*, 37.64 percent for *fair*, 24.64 percent for *average*, and 37.64 percent for *bad*. The difference between this theoretical expectation and the actual performance is an *objective measure* of the shop performance, or of the value of the actual performance of workers on these particular jobs.

The more expert we are at knowing certain things the more properties we know these things to have. The taste of a glass of Burgundy, for example, has been shown by experts to contain 158 properties. This means that there are $2^{158} = 3.6 \times 10^{46}$ possibilities of taste of a glass of Burgundy,[3] an astronomical figure, considering that the number of all particles in the universe is only of the range of magnitude 10^{79}.

Thus, the application of the combinatorial calculus to intensions brings about the exact measurement of value. Value sensitivity may then be exactly defined. It is the capacity of matching a set of predicates one has in mind with a set of properties one recognizes in an actual thing or situation. It is a capacity of conceptual-perceptual matching – a capacity of qualitative measuring. Formal axiology, thus, is the qualification of qualities.

There are both perceptual and conceptual sources of value errors: One can see the thing wrongly; one can believe it has another name from what it has; one can misunderstand its concept; one can wrongly apply the concept to the thing; etc. In all, since there are three elements in valuation – the perception of the thing, the conception of its meaning, and the application of the latter to the former – there are $2^3 - 1 = 7$ possibilities of error: Perception without either conception or application; perception and conception without application; conception and application without perception etc. Each of these cases of valuational misjudgment has, for all practical purposes, an infinity of subcases. A test of axiological valuation must take into consideration all the conceivable possibilities of value error.

Since, in formal axiology, the intension or logical meaning of a thing is the value standard of the thing, and this standard is objective, namely the definition of the thing in question – which is arrived at by the development of human speech and society throughout history – *the correct answers for a test based on the system of formal axiology are known from the system of axiology itself, that is, from the mechanism of value thinking.* In this respect, an axiological test is similar to a mathematical test, in which the correct answers are known from the system of mathematics, and the testee's answers are measured against the correct ones. Actually, the capacity of valuation is a talent similar to the mathematical or the musical.[4]

The items of the test have their axiological order, and the ordering by the subject has a definite and measurable relationship to that order. The items are illustrations of formulae arising from the mathematical statement of the value dimensions.

6. THE DIMENSIONS OF VALUE.

The dimensions of value – *systemic, extrinsic,* and *intrinsic* value – arise from the relation, in combinatorial analysis, between finite and infinite sets. There are possible three kinds of intensional sets, finite sets, denumerably infinite sets, and non-denumerably infinite sets (with cardinality, n, $\aleph_0$, and $\aleph_1$, respectively).[5] Each of these kinds of sets defines a specific kind of intension; and the fulfillment of each such intension defines a specific kind of value.

Finite intensional sets define *formal concepts.* The things corresponding to them are constructions of the human mind, such as geometrical circles. Such things either fulfill their concept or else they are not such things; that is to say, they either are or are not what they are said to be. A geometrical circle either fulfills the definition of the concept "geometrical circle" or else is not a geometrical circle. There are no good or bad geometrical circles. If a circle lacks a single of the properties of the concept "circle" – which is "a plane closed curve equidistant from a center" – then it is not a circle. Hence, there are, geometrically, only perfect circles or non-circles. Constructions of the human mind, thus, have only two values, which are called *systemic values:* either perfection or non-value. The world of systemic valuation is not only that of systems as in science, but also in other fields: ideologies, slogans, rituals, psychological illusions and delusions, imaginations, and orders of all kind, from monastic and military orders to the routine of a household: it is the world of any actual or ideal structure. Systemic valuation is an either-or valuation, the simplest kind of valuation there is. It sees things either black or white. Since it belongs to constructions of the mind it is obvious that when applied to actual beings it "prejudges" them. Systemic valuation is the model of dogmatism and prejudice, of rigid and schematic thinking; and of formal construction.

Denumerably infinite sets of intensional predicates define *abstract concepts*. Abstraction "draws off" properties common to at least two things. These properties are denumerable, for they must be abstracted one by one (in the process of learning to speak; a striking example is found in the Autobiography of Helen Keller); but there is an infinity of such possible properties. The things to which such concepts refer are the things of the everyday world, chairs, and tables, cars and lampposts, horses and applecakes. Each such thing has potentially an infinite number of properties in common with other such things – depending on the extension of the class in question – but in practice extrinsic valuation will turn upon only a few of these properties. But even a few, as was said above, give a great number of value possibilities, 10 give 1023, and 158 give an astronomical number. What is valued in extrinsic valuation is not the thing in itself but its possession of the intensional properties of its concept, or of the class it belongs to. Fulfillment by a thing of an abstract concept constitutes *extrinsic value*. Extrinsic valuation sees the thing in the fluidity of all its properties and in all possible contexts. It is flexible and pliant. Extrinsic valuation is the model of pragmatic thinking.

Non-denumerably infinite sets of intensional predicates define *singular concepts*. Things corresponding to such concepts are unique. They are incomparable and irreplaceable. Once they are lost, all is lost, once they are won, all is won. The intensions of such singular concepts, e.g., "my wife," "my baby" are not series of words but Gestalten. In comprehending them we are completely involved, we form a continuum with them. The mathematical form of such a continuum is that of non-denumerable infinity. (Such infinities, $\aleph_1$, are infinities *of* denumerable infinities, $\aleph_0$; $2^{\aleph_0} = \aleph_1$). The fulfillment by a thing of a singular concept constitutes *intrinsic value*. Intrinsic value is the valuation of poets and artists, lovers and mystics, magicians and advertisers, chefs de cuisine and politicians, theologians and creative scientists. Intrinsic valuation is the model of creativity, spontaneity and commitment; of emphatic – and empathic – thinking. This kind of thinking has been called, in psychology, Being-cognition.[6]

Systemic value, extrinsic value, and intrinsic value are the value *dimensions*. They constitute a hierarchy of richness, with intrinsic value richer in qualities than extrinsic value, and extrinsic value richer in qualities than systemic value. "Richer in qualities" is the definition of "better," "poorer in qualities" is the definition of "worse". The definition in use of "ought" is: "That which is worse ought to be better." Hence, intrinsic value is better than extrinsic value, and extrinsic value is better than systemic value. Also, systemic value ought to be extrinsic value, and extrinsic value ought to be intrinsic value. The hierarchy of values is a *valuation of value*. Formal axiology specifies and elaborates systematically an objective scale of valuational richness.

The test is based on this scale. Its expressions respresent hierarchical combinations of systemic, extrinsic, and intrinsic values. *The subject's ordering them, as compared to their objective order, measures the subject's value capacity.*

We shall now summarize what has been said so far:

1. Value is meaning.
2. Meaning is richness of properties.
3. Sets of properties are intensions.
4. A thing has value in the degree that it fulfills the intension of its concept.
5. There are three kinds of concepts: constructs, abstracts, and singular concepts.
6. Correspondingly there are three dimensions of value:
   a. Systemic value as the fulfillment of the construct.
   b. Extrinsic value as the fulfillment of the abstract.
   c. Intrinsic value as the fulfillment of the singular concept.
7. Constructs are of finite, abstracts of denumerably infinite, and singular concepts of non-denumerably infinite content.
8. The dimensions of value form a hierarchy with intensional cardinalities n, $\aleph_0$, and $\aleph_1$, respectively.
9. Systemic valuation is the model of schematic thinking, extrinsic valuation that of pragmatic thinking, intrinsic valuation that of emphatic – and empathic – thinking.

7. THE CALCULUS OF VALUE.

Systemic value (S), extrinsic value (E), and intrinsic value (I) can themselves be valued in terms of each other. Thus, intrinsic value can be valued either systemically or extrinsically or intrinsically. For example, my wife as an intrinsic value, may be valued systemically as my housekeeper; extrinsically as "a good woman;" intrinsically as "my one and only," "my world," "my heaven," "my life". These valuations of the value dimensions in terms of each other give rise to the calculus of value. The calculus combines the three value dimensions and their respective cardinalities n, $\aleph_0$, and $\aleph_1$.

Combinations of the three value dimensions can be either compositions or transpositions. A *composition* of values is a positive valuation of one value by another, a *transposition* is a negative such valuation (a disvaluation). Each of the three values may be either valued by the other three or disvalued by them. Hence there are $3(3+3) = 18$ value combinations, half of which are compositions and half transpositions. A composition, for example, is the valuation of a systemic value in terms of another systemic value. This composition upgrades the systemic value in the direction of intrinsic value, and so does any other valuation of a systemic value, whether in terms of an extrinsic or an intrinsic value. Value compositions raise the value in question to a higher value power, they are exponentiations of value. Transpositions are the corresponding disvaluations, degrading the value in question in the opposite direction from intrinsic value. They are negative value exponentiations, raising the value to a negative power.

The symbolization of value combinations follows that of the underlying arithmetical cardinalities. Thus, the systemic valuation of a systemic value is the exponentiation of one systemic value by another, or the raising of a systemic value to the power of a systemic value, written "S^S". This signifies, for example, the writing of a systematic treatise about mathematical logic, or jurisprudence, or for that matter, value theory. The extrinsic valuation of an extrinsic value – "E^E" – means that one extrinsic value is valued in terms of another, for example, chocolate is mixed with whipped cream. On the other hand, a transposition or disvaluation of one extrinsic value by another – "E^{-E}" or "E_E" – would be the mixing of chocolate with sawdust.

Since each of the three value dimensions S, E, or I, has a numerical value, namely n, $\aleph_0$, and $\aleph_1$ respectively, the value compositions and transpositions have themselves numerical values, and these numerical values can be ordered in a precise sequence. The 18 value compositions and transpositions, in the sequence of their numerical values,[7] are the following:

$I^I,\ E^I,\ S^I$	$\aleph_2$	1, 2, 3	COMPOSITIONS
$I^E,\ I^S,\ E^E,\ S^E$	$\aleph_1$	4, 5, 6, 7	
E^S	$\aleph_0$	8	
S^S	n	9	
S_S	$\dfrac{1}{n}$	10	TRANSPOSITIONS
E_S	$\dfrac{1}{\aleph_0}$	11	
$S_E,\ E_E,\ I_S,\ I_E$	$\dfrac{1}{\aleph_1}$	12, 13, 14, 15	
$S_I,\ E_I,\ I_I$	$\dfrac{1}{\aleph_2}$	16, 17, 18	

The 18 statements in the test[8] represent these value formulae. Thus, "E^E" is represented by "A good meal" in Test I and by "I like my work. It is good for me" in Test II; "I$_E$" by "Slavery" in Test I and "My work makes me unhappy" in Test II, etc. In general, in Test I, the intrinsic, extrinsic and systemic dimensions are represented by everyday values [Persons (I), Things (E), Systems (S)], while in Test II these dimensions are applied to the person himself [the Self or "I" (I), Work (E), the World (S)].

University of Mexico

[1] The Hartman Value Inventory (Boston:Miller Associates, 1966).

[2] Robert S. Hartman, The Structure of Value: Foundations of Scientific Axiology (Carbondale, Ill, :Southern Illinois University Press, 1967), pp.,215-228.

[3] A. L. Hilliard, The Forms of Value (New York:Columbia University Press, 1950), pp., 278f.

[4] Hartman, op.cit., pp., 258-57.

[5] For transfinite intensional sets, see Benno Erdmann, Logik (Berlin, 1923). chs. 21-24; for transfinite values, Edwin T. Mitchell, A System of Ethics (New York, 1950), pp., 123-129; for the relation between intension and valuations, Emil Lask, Die Lehre von Vrtell (Tubingen, 1912).

[6] Abraham Maslow, Towards a Psychology of Being, (Princeton:Van Nostrand, 1962).

[7] The transfinite quotients have axiological but not mathematical meaning For details see Hartman, op.cit.,pp. 272-274.

[8] [See Footnote -Edd.]

THE PHENOMENOLOGY OF FREEDOM IN THE GERMAN
PHILOSOPHICAL TRADITION: KANTIAN ORIGINS

Robert Herzstein

The treatment of an important value scheme within a philosophical tradition must avoid two dangerous pitfalls. One such approach is the viewpoint best characterized as *geistesgeschichtlich*. This attitude can be summarized as the conviction that the problems in any given philosophical tradition may best be understood in terms of their own immanent development in the world of speculative thought. Ideas are seen as logical progressions in an essentially linear development. They influence one another and evolve in a critical fashion, but are not determined by the objective conditions of the society which is the scene of their birth and transformation. By the same token, this approach to our problem – best typified by the work of men like Ernst Cassirer,[1] Friedrich Meinecke[2] and A. O. Lovejoy[3] – omits the consideration of the objective causation problem. By this latter I mean the thorny question regarding the influence that an intellectual tradition may have upon the society which is the real stage of its existence.[4]

That is one extreme, but there is another, one which errs in the opposite direction. This viewpoint sees a value scheme or a speculative tradition strictly in terms of the political, social and economic conditions of the surrounding civil framework. The forays of economic determinists into areas of concern to the historian of philosophy or the intellectual historian have not generally produced happy results. We may take the work of the Hungarian Marxist Georg Lukács as an example. His book *Die Zerstoerung der Vernunft*[5] has never received the critical and serious treatment which its purpose deserves, at least not in this country. Lukács takes entire philosophical traditions and analyzes them in terms of their deterministic dependence upon the dominant mode of production in their societies. He goes even further than Marx or Engels[6] and carries vulgar determinism to its apogee when he attacks the German intellectual tradition. Lukács argues that a value complex reflects the needs and anxieties of the "class" that develops it, and that this complex may be later used or misused to reinforce the needs of the same class in a new situation.[7] As an extremist, Lukács is often right when speaking of extremes, such as pre-fascism in German *Lebensphilosophie* after 1890.[8] But otherwise, he only succeeds in making a travesty out of both philosophy and critical Marxist analysis.

My own approach in this paper differs from the two manners of thinking described above. I am in agreement with Kant when he emphasizes the subjective freedom of the pure speculative intellect.[9] I can accept Kant's

speculative freedom as the rejection of the absurd sensationalist determinism of Condillac.[10] Yet while the freedom of the speculative intellect (or
pure reason) may well be an acceptable philosophic fact, the point remains
that the *communication* of a freely arrived at concept immediately trans-
forms it from idea to ideology. I would submit that it is in this middle-
ground between the formulation of a concept and its articulation-for-others
that objective conditions play their vital role in the history of human
"abstract" thought. A concept may arise from a spontaneous thought, one
originally provoked by an outside stimulus but not determined by it. When
formulated for others in the same society, however, this concept will take
on what the historian (but probably not the philosopher, who tends not to
be disturbed by this particular problem) might call an ideological coating.
Hence, in looking at a certain value scheme in German philosophy, I feel
that I am not being rudely deterministic if I occasionally point to the role
of objective historical circumstances in making it into an ideology that was
acceptable to many literate Germans after the end of the eighteenth century.
Historians of philosophy have too often ignored the objective role that
speculative thought has played in the social history of Western man. I have
chosen Kant as my subject, since he is particularly useful in demonstrating
how I feel historians of value inquiry should alter their approach. I am not
so bold, however, as to believe that I can explain Kant's second *Kritik* as
the intellectual result of "objective circumstances"!

By way of further definition of my work, let me also clarify my introductory terminology. I use the expression "phenomenology" in a much
more basic way than does Hegel, though my attitudes have been influenced
by the study of Hegelian dialectics. I am referring to the life-movement and
various manifestations and transformations of the word "freedom" in
the German speculative tradition. "Freedom" here has its own series of
appearances, hence the science of phenomenology as articulated in Hegel
can be of use to us. We are, as I state in my title, dealing with the origins
of a value tradition; the objective evolution of this tradition *(noumenon)*
can only be studied in terms of its contradictions, that is, dialectically,
and *via* its appearances, or phenomenologically.

We will be concerned with certain aspects of Kant's critical philosophy,
particulary those relating to freedom and the will. Kant's resolution of the
problem of freedom, accomplished in the ethical rather than the metaphysical sphere, had a colossal impact upon the German pre-romantic
generation.[11] We may almost say that the history of German speculative
thought from Fichte and Schelling through Ernst Mach, Hermann Cohen
and Ernst Cassirer is an attempt to come to terms with the Kantian
Freiheitsgedanke.[12]

Over a generation ago, Bertrand Russell, speaking as an English liberal
empiricist, expressed the view that Kant had been a "disaster" for philosophy.[13] Russell felt the same way about Friedrich Meinecke's last work

(1945). Meinecke had, let it be pointed out, urged the Germans to return to the thought-treasure of the world of Kant and Goethe.[14] In 1873 John Stuart Mill had expressed his aversion for the deductive-speculative nature of German critical philosophy,[15] and he was then referring to an earlier period in his life. (Coleridge,[16] Carlyle,[17] T. H. Green[18] and a few other "Anglo-Saxons" have felt differently about the German tradition, but they have been in the minority). Recently, an American historian has expressed his view that Kant's influence on historiography – whatever it might have been – was nefarious, for he lured historians from the empirical pursuit of historical knowledge.[19] For all of these Anglo-American liberals, the German preoccupation with Kantian freedom was an unhappy consequence of Kant's thought and its influence.

The Kantian idea of freedom inaugurated the most influential age of German philosophy. The very ambiguity of the idea only strengthened it in its later German setting. Kant's critical idealism, articulated during the years 1781-1790, would never have had such a vast influence upon German thought had it not been for its ethical teaching. Yet its ethical doctrine was, in a very real sense, a passionate addition to what was a dry, critical system. Moses Mendelssohn called him the "smasher of everything,"[20] but Kant's place in German thought is that of the "explainer" and the rebuilder, not the negativist.

About fifty years after Kant's second *Kritik*, Heinrich Heine, a poet who clearly saw both the revolutionary and conservative facets of Kant's thought, wittily remarked that Kant had let God, freedom and immortality in through the back door in order to appease his old servant, Lampe.[21] Though we may doubt the truth of Heine's anecdote, the fact remains that Kant felt he had to come to grips with the value "freedom" after 1781. Kant's Copernican Revolution of 1781 was essentially anti-deterministic in that it was concerned with the formal mechanism of the cognizing subject, rather than with the inter-action of subject and object. He criticized earlier philosophy because it turned to metaphysics and the possibility of freedom before dealing scientifically with the basic question of mind and reason.[22] Hegel was later to attack this sterile formalism of Kant, but Kant felt that he was performing a necessary scientific task in the late 1770's, the fruit of which was the first *Kritik*. Equally rejecting the "dogmatic slumber" of empiricism and the system-building deductions of the German metaphysical school, Kant had succeeded in writing a work that demolished old illusions, yet left his students wondering whether there was not room for a traditional value structure in new bindings. Kant was equal to this latter task.

The Kantian value "freedom" first makes its fully mature appearance in 1785, in the *Grundlegung*.[23] Kant starts off on a new tack. He turns from cognizing man to affective man. Not being able or willing to guarantee the objective value of freedom on the basis of epistemology, revealed religion, or physics, Kant turns to the will: "The good will is not good because of what it effects or accomplishes or because of its adequacy to achieve some proposed end; it is good only because of its willing, i.e., it is good of itself."[24] This, then, is man's quality as a rational being. His will is predisposed to goodness, and is good because it is non-determined, i.e., is free. Sensing that he is groping his ways towards an arbitrary, Pelagian, voluntaristic ethic, Kant quickly returns to his scientific first *Kritik* and tells us that "reason is...meant to have an influence on the will."[25] The reconciliation of freedom and speculative reason – the latter a scientific assumption beyond (or antecedent to) *ethical* investigation as of 1781 – will lead Kant to the full-blown "praktische Vernunft" of 1788. As an example, let us merely cite his phrase "A free will and a will under moral laws are identical."[26] Kant, like Rousseau before him, is here developing an affective value for Everyman; and, as we shall see, this value is both democratic and illiberal. But then, such was also the case with Rousseau.[27]

Kant goes from the will itself to its predisposition towards the good (a thing-in-itself), to pure practical reason (its formulation of principles), and finally to the deduced concept of freedom. There are certain dangers here. Kant deduces freedom from morality, needing the former to guarantee the latter. We need not apply the tools of psychoanalysis in order to spot Kant's own affective needs in this structure. In deducing freedom from morality, rather than from nature or social politics, Kant was treading on dangerous turf. Rejecting both neo-Epicureanism[28] and contemporary libertarian politics as the basis for freedom,[29] Kant is juxtaposing freedom to both causation in nature and decision in politics. Here we see the beginning of the fatal Kantian dichotomy: *Mensch als Freiheit* and *Mensch als Natur*.[30] Kant the moralist thus consummates a trend in German thought that goes back beyond Leibniz to Melanchthon and Luther. We will later work out the genealogy and ramifications of the Kantian *Freiheitsidee*.

And so, "With the pure practical faculty of reason, the reality of transcendental freedom is also confirmed."[31] And, going even further, God and immortality gain objective reality as concepts through the reality of the free will.[32] God and immortality are assumed *a priori* as conditions of the morally determined will.[33] It would be too cruel to ask Kant at this point whether it was for *this* that he had asked many years earlier, "How are synthetic judgments *a priori* possible?" Thus, the "smasher of everything," who had accepted the challenge of Hume the skeptic by scientifically re-asserting the rights of the synthetic intellect, now evolves from moderate idealism to extreme fideism. He tells us in 1788 that he has solved the "enigma of critical philosophy."[34] Given his premises of 1781, God, freedom and immortality had to be renounced as categories of rational and metaphysical speculation. Though originally given no place in the realm of pure speculative reason, they are let into the kingdom of critical philosophy *via* pure practical reason. The rigorous investigative techniques of the first "critical period" are relaxed in order to make allowances for a holy trio. Kant even states proudly that while freedom is the stumbling-block for empiricists, it is the sublime key for critical moralists.[35] And here we come to a key problem, namely Kant's dichotomizing of will and intellect.

Kant had stated in 1785 that reason influences the will[36] (and the practical reason/categorical imperative syndrome was the dialectical synthesis of speculative reason and the autonomous will), but he was eventually to come up with an important new formulation. He declared that in a combination of pure (speculative) reason and pure (practical) reason in one cognition, the latter has the objective primacy.[37] Cruder nineteenth century "Kantians," men like Schopenhauer and the prophets of fin-de-siècle *Lebensphilosophie*, would seize upon Kant's *Primat des Willens*. They would distort it in such a way as to overlook the fact that Kant described the will in terms of a moral system rather than as a biological affect.

But what were the deeper implications of the Kantian value "freedom" in the German idealist philosophical tradition? For one thing, let us note Kant's differentiation of the autonomous and the heteronomous will. The autonomous will is truly free in that it wills something for its own sake.[38] This will shows man as *noumenon* or thing-in-himself, since man-as-freedom is beyond the causal structure of nature and desire *(Causalitaetsgesetz)*. This is Kantian transcendental morality in its purest delineation; it is not an irrational conception, but, in Kantian terms, is merely non-natural. Universal principles grow out of the marriage of the autonomous will and pure reason, and hence Kant's moral transcendentalism is not the *Schwaermerei* that New England Transcendentalists were later to take it for.[39] All principles, however, which have a material object are empirical and hence mere maxims at the very most.[40] Here we come to Kant's "radical evil," a concept that should not be confused with Pauline-Augustinian-Lutheran concepts of "original sin." Kant was referring to the fact that men have a pre-disposition towards the good, but are easily misled by their sensuous sides. This, in turn, relates to that other Kantian man, man-as-nature, Man the Phenomenon, man as part of the endless chain of causation. Kant the moralist dislikes this man, though, as we shall see, he views him as the very stuff of historical evolution.

What are the implications of all of these Kantian oppositions? First of all, I would say that ethical universalism in Kant becomes a function or correlate of a transcendental will. Secondly, nature is opposed to freedom, and is placed beneath it on the scale of realities. Thirdly, man as subject achieves his highest purpose when freely developing laws consistent with the moral will. It is this latter view of the aim of subjective man that the Marx of 1845[41] was to revolt against. He was to attack Kant as having downgraded sensuous-subjective man by making freedom an expression of the moral will. I would thus say that Kant's break with the *Aufklaerung* in the area of morality is more significant than his much discussed epistemological attack on vulgar sensationalism in 1781.[42]

When I said earlier that Kant was both democratic and illiberal, I did not mean this in a flippant way. Eighteenth century libertarian philosophy, from Locke down to Paine, Jefferson and Condorcet, had been liberal because it studied ethics from the viewpoint of the happiness of man, taking this latter concept as the *aim* of human life.[43] Kant breaks with this idea in a most violent way. He tells us that individual happiness in its broad psychological sense cannot be the basis of man's generalizing moral sense. "If a rational being can think of its maxims as practical universal laws, he can do so only by considering them as principles which contain the determining ground of the will because of their form and not because of their matter."[44] Matter is a synonym for sensuous pleasure or happiness here, and it is hence logical that the concept *duty* should be introduced by Kant after his rejection of sensuous happiness as a norm. This insistence upon the sole principle of morality being an anti-sensuous, anti-materialistic sense of *duty* is socially suspicious, to say the very least. Early nineteenth century conservative thought, that of de Bonald, de Maistre and Mueller, was to stress constantly the ancient hierarchical concept of duty over the seditious liberal (and modern) concept happiness. Hence, paradoxically, though Kant sympathized with the French Revolution right down to 1804, he undermined the libertarian premises of natural law that had gone into the declarations of 1776 and 1789. This was to have dangerous consequences in German thought and practice.[45] Kant's theory of pure practical reason was certainly democratic – and Kant gave Rousseau much credit in this area[46] – but his ultimate conclusions reinforced all of the conservative tendencies in contemporary East Prussian and North German society. Kant, for instance, reflected the main concern of the Pietists when he described holiness – the highest good – as the complete identity of personal intentions and the universal moral law.[47] Kant, like Plotinus and the whole school of later classical neo-Platonists, speaks of such a state as impossible in a world of sensuous beings, a world where man is phenomenon as well as *noumenon*. Hence, we arrive at a theory of ascent that takes us to the immortality of the soul. The whole psychic structure of the *ancien regime*, from universalized duty to the priestly promise of immortality is restored by a man who later hailed the fall of the Bastille as the opening of a new era in the history of man.[48] This was one of the tragedies of Kant's legacy, his refusal to go along with the implications of his own critical intellect, his constant restoration of the outmoded. In this way, I believe that Kant foreshadowed and reinforced the major contradictions in post-1804 German society. At the very most, Kant, the revolutionary, will only grant us that "morals is not really the doctrine of how to make ourselves happy, but of how we are to be *worthy* of happiness."[49]

Yet what is the specific role of the Kantian value "freedom" in all of this? It is no less than the key to our understanding of vital aspects of the

German intellectual tradition down to the 1930's. How does freedom "appear" in the Kantian system? It became, after all, an ideology in the Germany of the post-Kantian period. I might add parenthetically that we are not referring to any "German idea of freedom" in the political sense, such as Ernst Troeltsch discussed it fifty years ago.[50] We are speaking of freedom as a phenomenon in German philosophical speculation. And it is in the realm of nature and history, areas dominated by phenomena and causation, that the real ambiguity of Kantian freedom comes to the fore. Ernst Cassirer has pointed out that this concept of freedom reflected the new German culture of the late eighteenth century and also influenced the entire later history of the German spirit.[51] I would go even further and say that this Kantian idea of freedom, with all of its corollaries, was the major factor in the unique course that German philosophy pursued from Schelling to Heidegger.

Kant's concept of freedom as an inner value of the self-conscious will, rather than as the objective expression of *homo faber*, had its roots in the German intellectual past and the social and political circumstances of the present. Both Cusanus and Luther had made this "inner" freedom the essential expression of man's being, though Luther[52] was tormented by the conflict between divine omnipotence and man's freedom to close his heart to faith. Leibniz attacked this central dilemma. *Mens non est pars, sed simulacrum divinitatis, repraesentativum Universi.* His monads are in one sense a reflection of the completeness of God, and of this completeness the human essence partakes.[53] The realm of phenomena in space and time bows to necessity in the usual causal pattern, but not man's soul as window and mirror. As a mathematician Leibniz accepted causation in the created *Weltall*. As a metaphysician, however, he taught the total freedom of the ego. Hence, German speculative philosophy in the eighteenth century, departing from the main empirical and skeptical currents of France and England, was faced with a Leibnizian dichotomy that the metaphysical-mathematical school of Christian Wolff merely repeated rather than resolved.[54] In terms of transcendental logic, Kant solved Luther's problem by having the certainty of the free will precede the certainty of God. The knowledge of God was assumed *a priori* on the basis of moral freedom. Yet Kant, who epistemologically had insisted upon the totality of conditions by which thinking completes the phenomenal object,[55] left a legacy of an idea of freedom that was anything but clear and whole. I want to analyze this problem for a moment before demonstrating the confusion that Kantian freedom caused its author when he tried to make some room for man as history in his "system."

Kant certainly hoped that the moral will, guided by pure speculative reason into the realm of universal principles, would bring man-*noumenon* into a position and a world where nature and man-*phenomenon* were premeated and used by this moral consciousness. Yet failing such a world,

E

Kant (perhaps gleefully?) had to admit that inner moral greatness, even if it had no causal effect in terms of transforming the world, was more valuable than the sensuously affected heteronomous will.[56] An entire German generation lapsed into stupified quiescence during the French Revolutionary epoch (1790-1806), largely vindicating its lack of action on these Kantian premises. Friedrich von Schiller is a good example.

The pre-Kantian Schiller showed traits of political and social rebellion that were reflected in both his dramas and earlier historical efforts.[57] Schiller's study of Kant, begun in 1791, coincided with and reinforced his new tendencies towards a merely aesthetic and inner-escapist concept of freedom. This quietism reflected the glorified impotence of the German middle classes, along with the concomitant retarded political and economic development of the German people after the late sixteenth century. Schiller, along with many others, spoke of the "German mission" to create a new idealistic *Kultur* based on a cosmopolitan ethic of the dignity and inner moral freedom of man: "If the Empire falls, the German has created a unique, new sense of dignity and value."[58] Thus Schiller in 1801 on the immanent collapse of the only existing national German political structure.

I would agree with Cassirer that the primacy of practical reason is the foundation of mature Kantian speculation.[59] One must go further, however, and see that this, in turn, led to a schema furthering cultural consciousness based on "pure" (as opposed to social) thought, and the cosmopolitan cultivation of the moral and intellectual capacities of the apolitical individual. When Schiller wrote,

> Into the sacred, quiet realm of the heart
> Flee before the ceaseless pressures of life;
> Freedom only exists in the world of dreams
> And beauty only flourishes in lyric and song,[60]

he was merely going one logical step beyond Kant. After all, Kant had implied that "The free individual differentiates himself from the slave in that he asks, 'Is it right?' not, 'What are the consequences?'"[61] On this basis, Kantian philosophy gave to the German intellectual tradition – and not merely in philosophy – that value of *Innerlichkeit* which was later used as a refuge before the onslaught of a gruesome reality. And let us never forget that pure idea becomes ideology when systematically articulated. We will return to Schiller as philosopher, but let me give two examples to support my thesis here.

Kant's claim that man's autonomous will entitled him to the position of *noumenon* in a world of phenomena led him to the universal imperative that we never treat another human being merely as a means, but always as an end in himself.[62] Now the moral basis of this imperative belongs to the purely philosophical study of Kantian ethics. Nevertheless, the thought itself must be examined in terms of yet another factor, namely the objective spatial and temporal framework in which Kant the man of flesh and blood (to borrow an expression from Unamuno[63]) lived and worked. The Koenigsberg of 1788 was the most highly developed commercial city in East Prussia, largely due to the mercantile efforts of the Hohenzollern dynasty. Yet its remoteness from more advanced centers of German intellectual and economic development, and its location in the midst of a socially backward, overwhelmingly agrarian area all served it poorly in terms of industrial capitalist development.[64] Its traditions as a frontier city, as a university town, as the former residence of the Hohenzollerns (and their crown city) were to be more important to it than the potential application of science to industrial production. It is doubtful if Kant could have enunciated his imperative regarding man as an end in himself if he had written in the Manchester of 1820. But living in a society that was remote from *Hochkapitalismus*, was paternalistic, and did not yet see large scale industrial exploitation of man by man in the name of profit, such a formulation still had some meaning. It is in this sense that we can learn much regarding the transmogrification of philosophical conceptualizations if we study the words of a National Socialist writing some hundred and thirty years after Kant's death. This individual, Otto Dietrich, discussing the "philosophical foundations of National Socialism,"[65] declared that the Kantian imperative concerning the universalization of the individual desire was a "National Socialist thought." What I believe Dietrich meant was that there was an ideological affinity with Kant due to the fact that both his imperative and Dietrich's claim that National Socialism was post-capitalistic met on common non-capitalist, *voelkisch* German ground. I am certainly not suggesting intellectual or moral affinities between the Kantian concept of freedom and National Socialism. Yet, I want to show that Kant's *articulation* of a law or imperative based on an abstract idea gave it a certain coloring that might serve another ideology in an entirely different context.

A second example of the role of idea, reality and ideology in Kant is suggested by the work of Houston Stewart Chamberlain (1855-1927). Chamberlain regarded Kant as the German philosopher *par excéllence*. He wrote a two volume study of the Sage of Koenigsberg,[66] a work which is usually neglected today but is, in my opinion, still worth reading for its methodology and approach. Yet I am not interested in telling you about a dead Anglo-German's sixty-year-old study of Immanuel Kant. Chamberlain was truly a man of his time in Germany. He attempted to forge a synthesis out of racialist science, Prussianism, modern nationalism and the German intellectual tradition. In this synthesis he made much use of Kant, especially in certain essays written during the Great War.[67] Western literature and propaganda had been hurling bitter charges at the German intelligentsia, decrying its lack of democratic initiative, its poorly developed idea of political freedom, its surrender to a series of *Machtmaenner*, ranging from Bismarck to Ludendorff. Chamberlain attempted to answer these charges by pointing to "German freedom" – as exemplified by the work of

Immanuel Kant. Chamberlain was particularly bemused by the Kantian trichotomy of pure reason, practical reason, and faculty of judgment. He took Kant's analysis of man-as-nature and man-as-freedom and used these to explain why, 1.) The German nation was free in will and spirit even if it did not have responsible cabinet government; 2.) The Prussian-German penchant for scientific organization did not contradict the German ideal of freedom.[68] Here was another case of unconscious Kantian ideology being used as a conscious political weapon, albeit in exaggerated and distorted form.

When Kant enunciated his view of man as *noumenon* and as *phenomenon* he did so for many reasons, and his concept attacked both Humean *skepsis* and sensationalist optimism. Yet when we review the objective circumstances of his life, we are forced to conclude that Kant's relationship with both his time and his government led him to the articulation of an intellectual framework for his philosophy that can only be construed as ambiguous. As one example of this, we can cite Kant in 1784, that is, between the first and second *Kritiks*. He tells us that free thought and speech denote and cause the progress of the human race, but that enlightened despotism was acceptable in that it made the people "capable of managing freedom."[69] Despite a few minor brushes with Prussian authority, Kant was never the rebellious subject. He stayed *intellectually* loyal to the French Revolution through thick and thin. Never a rebel, this progressive soul articulated a view of man and society that could accommodate almost any situation. In this he was both farsighted and typical of later German abstract speculation. Even looking at his contemporaries, drenched in his ethical formulations, we see Schiller, the Kantian escapist, putting the following words into the mouth of his dying heroine in the play *Die Jungfrau von Orléans*:

> Upwards – upwards – the earth fades away –
> Brief is the pain, and eternal is the bliss![70]

Now, temperamentally Kant was no romantic. He had no feeling for the type of romantic apotheosis that Schiller portrayed. When we think of the dry methodology of the first *Kritik*, or the pedantic attacks on Herder in the 1780's, I think that we will realize how far Kant's disposition – hostile, let me note, to genius, a characteristic he felt he did not possess – differed from that of a "sentimental" Schiller. We may even go back to the young Goethe in the early 1770's (in Kant's pre-critical period), who sang that "Only in heaven will you find freedom; this world is a prison."[71] Thus, I am admitting that the concept of freedom as a transcendental rather than as a cognitive-objective value antedates Kant in Germany. Kant, however, codified it as part of a broader philosophical system. His critical idealism gave it permanent prestige in Germany.[72] Therein lay his influence on future German generations. The same man who destroyed for all time the illusions of both deism and a divinely revealed morality put in their place a transcendental concept of freedom and an *a priori* proof of God's existence.

Kant's ambiguity will be found in a different guise in both Hegel and Mach, that is, in the post-Kantian currents stemming from both objective and empirical idealism (1806-1918).

"Freiheit ist Menschenwerk": These stirring words tell us that Kant had an abstract pattern which he wished to see realized in his contacts with historiography. In this, his approach to history was in harmony with the prevalent attitudes of the *Aufklaerung*.[73] Yet history could never be the main stage of the realization of human freedom, at least not for Kant. Kant, like Goethe, was influenced by the historical irony of men like Gibbon and Hume; for him the violent and the accidental played too great a role in human history.[74] The study of history led one to surfaces, *accidentiae*, grist for the mill of the mere empiricist. Yet the Kantian value "freedom" was affective-subjective, not cognitive-objective. For this reason, Kant remained a dualist until the end of his life. I would agree with Menzer[75] that the dichotomy of freedom and nature dominated Kant's *Weltanschauung*, but particularly after 1790. As late as 1798, Kant was very careful to dissociate the progress of mankind from the advance of human morality – and of freedom, as Kant understood this term. "... It is only as a moral being that man can be the final purpose of creation." (1790)[76] Kant was, then, quite ambiguous in his attitude towards evolution in history, and this ambiguity foreshadowed and influenced late nineteenth century anti-Hegelian, anti-developmental German philosophy. This reinforcement of conservatism on the philosophical plane can be seen in Nietzschean vitalism and *Verstehen*-addicted historicism. In this respect, Kant's acceptance of *telos* in nature and history must be treated with some skepticism. It must be seen as aprioristic rather than inductive. Obviously, Kant dreamt about a world in which man-as-freedom and man-as-nature would be acting in unison.[77] Kant actually foresaw an ideal society in which moral man rationally governed both nature and himself: this was at the root of his admiration for the substance of the French Revolution.[78] Yet, in the end Kant always takes us back to a concept of freedom that is more akin to a modern *Heilsgeschichte*[79] than to the secular actualization of total human liberty. In separating man from nature, Kant divorced his idealistic view of free, moral man from the often violent conflicts that have marked the progress of the human race.[80] And this divorce in turn marked his path to dualistic escapism, an escapism perhaps best symbolized by the surrender of Heidegger in 1933. Like all true Christian apologists from Augustine to the early Karl Barth, Kant refused to escape from his dualism by opening a door to pantheism or panentheism. Hegel discovered this door and smashed it down in his amalgamation of history and freedom.

Kant was the first German philosopher to make that baneful dichotomy of *culture* and *civilization*.[81] This bifurcation passed from the realm of German philosophy to that of historiography and finally, in the work of Troeltsch, Toennies, Dilthey and Spengler, to that of historical sociology.[82]

As early as 1784, Kant associated practical morality with culture, and "mere" material graces and comforts (nature as re-worked by man) with civilization. Here he was borrowing a page from the Rousseau of 1755.[83] Insofar as rationality in history reflected man's growing moral awareness, the product was human culture. Basing his value "freedom" upon the supposed reality of the individual will, Kant was forced to view the *works* of man in a dualistic fashion. What stemmed from the autonomous will, at least potentially, was both rational and good; what stemmed from the "radical evil" to which we all at times succumb is less purely rational and certainly not as good. Hence, an inquiry into the nature and value of freedom led Immanuel Kant to a sociology that was quietistic if not philistine in its implications.

The influence of Kant on the German intellectual tradition is nowhere better demonstrated than by a concluding reference to Friedrich von Schiller. Schiller was to become one of the gods of German literature. An historian with the title "professor of philosophy," Schiller changed his view of philosophical history during the period 1789-1792. Originally, Schiller was the typical teleological *Aufklaerungshistoriker*, seeing history as man's progress towards freedom and happiness.[84] "The summit of all of his ideas was the 'Idea of Freedom' as this was understood in his 'philosophic' age."[85] He related happiness to a eudaemonic concept of freedom, one that was both cognitive and affective. A change comes about, however, particularly after 1793. Schiller, now to some extent under the influence of the Kantian *Freiheitsbegriff*, turns away from his earlier concept of progress in history. He gives up his historical *a priori* of the advance of happiness and freedom, and turns instead to what I would call two other values. These were the portrayal of colossal figures in drama, and the celebration of cosmopolitan, Kantian inner freedom in the individual.[86] I am aware that the third *Kritik* can be used against me at this point: Kant certainly provides for the dialectical interaction of pure (speculative) reason, pure practical reason and the *Urtheilskraft*. Yet, although Kant insisted that his critical system rested "on a perfectly sound basis, forever fortified,"[87] we should know better. Kant's view of man, despite this seeming intellectual unity that he had achieved by 1790, was firmly anchored in the Christian worldview summarized by the names Pelagius, Erasmus, and Spener. He had advanced beyond Augustine and Luther, but his innate conservatism kept him far from La Mettrie and d'Holbach. He questioned everything except the existence of a self-moving Will. This acceptance led him to the solipsism that man is indeed morally and intellectually free. And this solipsism, rightfully contemptible in Hegel's eyes, had as its social origin Kant's commitment to the social and value structure that surrounded him in Koenigsberg.

The Kantian value "freedom" was the most influential part of the entire critical system. Wrenched out of its broader philosophic context by Schiller,

Fichte, Stirner and Burckhardt, Kantian freedom became the father of the crudest romantic solipsism in philosophy. And all the work of the great neo-Kantians – Cohen, Lange, Cassirer – could not put the critical system back together again. Kantian freedom enabled its exponents to rebel inwardly against the prevalent relationships in society – without attempting to change them. This, I believe, tended to increase the inner psychic tensions of the German middle classes. Given the nature of nineteenth century German society, this is not at all surprising, particularly after 1848. One should not be surprised at the spate of books lauding Kantian freedom that appeared in Germany after things had gone so badly in the phenomenal world during the years 1918-1923. In this manner, the Kantian idea of freedom became a poetic ideology, one that Kant himself would have rejected as only part of a total *Wahrheit*.[88] Yet in rooting freedom so firmly in the "inner" affective syndrome of man, rather than in the dialectical interplay of man-in-nature, Kant himself prepared the way for the *reductio ad absurdum* of his own concept. His fideism and his formalism betrayed him in the end: this Hegel clearly grasped.

Around 1825 Goethe brilliantly recaptured the appearance of freedom that Kant had given to German philosophy when he had the blind and aged Faust cry out,

> Allein im Innern leuchtet helles Licht
> (Only within us does the truest light glow).

Massachusetts Institute of Technology

[1] Cassirer's intellectual history generally took on the appearance of a brilliant escape into the world of *Ideengeschichte*. More on this anon, but Cassirer's elective affinity for Cusanus, Leibniz and Kant is relevant here.

[2] I would, however, agree with Hajo Holborn that Meinecke was more willing to allow for the influence of the "mode of production" upon ideas, so long as the ideologue was foreign, e.g., Voltaire and the French bourgeoisie.

[3] For a classical statement of this approach, cf. Lovejoy's "The Historiography of Ideas" (1938), in *Essays in the History of Ideas* (Baltimore, 1948).

[4] Hajo Holborn's "Der deutsche Idealismus in sozialgeschichtlicher Beleuchtung," *Historische Zeitschrift*, 174 (1952), represents an attempt to overcome the abstractions of *Geistesgeschichte* and demonstrate this influence. I have translated it for a forthcoming book on German intellectual history in its political and social context; and the translation will also appear in a collection of Mr. Holborn's essays (Doubleday).

[5] Berlin, 1955. There is also a French translation of high calibre.

[6]Engels was most subtle when it came to demonstrating the role of speculative philosophy (e.g. Hegel and Feuerbach) and literature in modern history. He was far from vulgar determinism regarding the origins of ideas, and was not hesitant about admitting that they could occasionally have an autonomous influence upon social history.

[7]Cf. Lukács, *op. cit.*, pp. 417-431 as an example of this interpretation.

[8]*Ibid.*, in particular the discussion of Dilthey.

[9]I am, of course, referring to conceptualizations theoretically devoid of *Wertmaesse*. So was Kant – in 1781.

[10]Ernst Cassirer (who wrote of the Enlightenment as if it was the prelude to Kant's critical philosophy) is outstanding in his discussion of Condillac. Cf. *The Philosophy of the Enlightenment* (Boston, 1955), pp. 18-19, 102, 117-118. Diderot remarked that Condillac "adopted Berkeley's principles, but tried to avoid his consequences." Kant's first *Kritik* is what I would call an epistemological *Freiheitslehre* that came to grips with Diderot's dilemma. On Kant's revolt against sensationalism, cf. Wilhelm Windelband's acute point in *Lehrbuch der Geschichte der Philosophie* (Tuebingen, 1903), p. 440, note 4.

[11]Cf. H. A. Korff, *Geist der Goethezeit: Versuch einer ideellen Entwicklung* (Leipzig, 1964), I, 49.

[12]This was implied by Cassirer fifty years ago. Cf. *Freiheit und Form: Studien zur deutschen Geistesgeschichte* (Berlin, 1918), pp. xi, 224.

[13]Russell enunciated this view in many ways and many times. For an example of Russell on Kant's "deflection" of empirical philosophy, see, *inter alia, A History of Western Philosophy and its Connection with Political and Social Circumstances from the Earliest Times to the Present Day* (New York, 1945), p. 759.

[14]*Die deutsche Katastrophe: Betrachtungen und Erinnerungen* (Wiesbaden, 1955), pp. 160-177. "Wird es gelingen, den deutschen Geist zu retten?"

[15]*Autobiography of John Stuart Mill* (New York, 1960), pp. 157-158. "The German, or *a priori* view of human knowledge, and of the knowing faculties, is likely for some time longer (though it may be hoped in a diminishing degree) to predominate among those who occupy themselves with such inquiries, both here and on the Continent."

[16]Cf. John Stuart Mill, *On Bentham and Coleridge* (New York, 1962), pp. 107-111, *et passim.*

[17]The influence of the German intellectual complex upon Carlyle is best discussed in Eric Bentley, *A Century of Hero-Worship* (Boston, 1957), Part One.

[18]For a comment on the place of Green's neo-Hegelian liberalism, cf. Guido de Ruggiero, *The History of European Liberalism* (Boston, 1959), pp. 148-149.

[19]Bruce Mazlish, *The Riddle of History: The Great Speculators from Vico to Freud* (New York, 1966), p. 123.

[20]Quoted by Carl J. Friedrich, ed., *The Philosophy of Kant* (New York, 1949), p. xi.

[21]Heinrich Heine, *Werke* (Berlin, n.d.), IX, 247 *(Zur Geschichte der Religion und Philosophie in Deutschland)*.

[22]"Vorrede," in *Kritik der reinen Vernunft*, in *Werke*, ed. E. Cassirer, III (Berlin, 1913), 5-9.

[23]The edition I am using is in *Kants gesammelte Schriften* (Berlin, 1903: ed. *Koeniglich Preussische Akademie der Wissenschaften*), IV.

[24]*Ibid.*, p. 394. The translation is that of Lewis White Beck in his edition of *Foundations of the Metaphysics of Morals* (Indianapolis, 1959), p. 10.

[25]*Gesammelte Schriften*, IV, 396. Emil Hohne's *Kant's Pelagianismus und Nomismus* (1881) was not available to me, but I believe that Kant's "Pelagianism" bears investigation.

[26]*Ibid.*, 447.

[27]See, for instance, Ernest Barker's brilliant discussion in *Social Contract* (New York, 1962), pp. xxxii-xl; for a viewpoint more favorable to Rousseau, see Alfred Cobban's summary in *Rousseau and the Modern State* (Hamden, Connecticut, 1964) pp. 166-170.

[28]Such as was later to be embodied, for example, in the eudaemonism of Heinrich Heine or Ludwig Boerne.

[29]Prof. Peter Gay has brilliantly demonstrated the role of his Genevan experience in the formulation of certain of Voltaire's libertarian concepts. Cf. *The Party of Humanity: Essays in the French Enlightenment* (New York, 1964), pp. 65-96. Gay sees Voltaire as a conscious *Erlebnispolitiker;* what Kant rejected was, in effect, *Erlebnisphilosophie*. This became clear in 1785.

[30]Paul Menzer, *Kant's Lehre von der Entwicklung in Natur und Geschichte* (Berlin, 1911), analyzes this dichotomy and emphasizes its significance. Cf. pp. 301, 376. "Das Uebersinnliche wurde zum gemeinsamen Urgrund von Natur und Freiheit" (p. 378).

[31]Cf. *Kritik der praktischen Vernunft*, in *Gesammelte Schriften*, V, 3.

[32]*Ibid.*, 4.

[33]*Loc. cit.*

[34]*Ibid.*, 5.

[35]*Ibid.*, 8.

[36]Cf. *Gesammelte Schriften*, IV, 396.

[37]*Kritik der praktischen Vernunft*, in *Gesammelte Schriften*, V, 121.

[38]*Grundlegung*, in *Gesammelte Schriften*, IV, 394; *ibid.*, V *(Kritik der praktischen Vernunft)*, 27-29.

[39]Octavius Brooks Frothingham, *Transcendentalism in New England: A History* (New York, 1959), well described this enthusiasm in his Preface.

[40]*Kritik der praktischen Vernunft*, in *Gesammelte Schriften*, V, 21.

[41]I am referring in particular to one of Marx' notes on Feuerbach: "Feuerbach, mit dem *abstrakten* Denken nicht zufrieden, will die *Anschauug;* aber er fasst die Sinnlichkeit nicht als *praktische* menschlich-sinnliche Taetigkeit." *Marx-Engels Gesamtaugabe*, One, V, 534. The *form* of the Left Hegelian (*i.e.*, Bruno Bauer and colleagues) consciousness cult was Kantian, though its *content* and meaning stemmed from Hegel.

[42]John H. Randall, Jr. asserts that the German tradition ("where Kant has been gospel") baffles Anglo-Saxons largely due to the role it assigns to "duty" in its ethical constructs. *The Career of Philosophy* (New York, 1965), II, 156 ff.

[43]Of course, this happiness need not be devoid of a continuing element of struggle:
> Nur der verdient sich Freiheit wie das Leben,
> Der taeglich sie erobern muss.
>
> (Goethe)

[44]*Kritik der praktischen Vernunft*, in *Gesammelte Schriften*, V, 27.

[45]Cf. Holborn, *op. cit.*, 377-379; Ernst Troeltsch, "The Ideas of Humanity and Natural Law in World Politics," in Otto Gierke's *Natural Law and the Theory of Society, 1500-1800* (Boston, 1957); Leonard Krieger, *The German Idea of Freedom: History of a Political Tradition* (Boston, 1957), pp. 86-88, 124-125.

[46]Lukács, it might be mentioned, castigates Schelling, Dilthey *et al.* for what he calls their "aristocratic, élitist epistemology." That Kant had more respect for the common man was largely due to his reading of Rousseau. Cf. Harold Hoeffding, *A History of Modern Philosophy* (New York, 1955), II, 72.

[47]*Kritik der praktischen Vernunft*, in *Gesammelte Schriften*, V, 122.

[48]Cf. William Wallace, *Kant* (Philadephia, 1882), p. 40.

[49]*Kritik der praktischen Vernunft*, in *Gesammelte Schriften*, V, 25, 130.

[50]"Die deutsche Idee von der Freiheit," in *Deutscher Geist und Westeuropa: Gesammelte kulturphilosophische Aufsaetze und Reden* (Tuebingen, 1925).

[51]*Freiheit und Form*, p. xi.

[52]Cassirer made many suggestive statements in this area. Cf. "Deutschland und Westeuropa im Spiegel der Geistegeschichte," in *Inter Nationes. Zeitschrift fuer die kulturellen Beziehunger Deutschlands zum Ausland*, 1, 3 and 4 (1931), p. 84.

[53]Cf. Frederick Copleston, *A History of Philosophy* (Garden City, New York, 1963) IV *(Modern Philosophy: Descartes to Leibniz)*, 304 *et passim.*

[54]In addition to Cassirer, cf. Friedrich Ueberweg, *Grundriss der Geschichte der Philosophie* (Berlin, 1924), III, 454.

[55]I believe that this concept of the "organic totality" of a perceptual situation deeply influenced German historiography, and later, German historical sociology. One might recall von Ranke's comment in 1859, that he viewed events in their "political and religious totality," rather than allowing an abstract doctrine to atomize his approach to the past.

[56]Cf. *Kritik der praktischen Vernunft*, in *Gesammelte Schriften*, V, 21-22.

[57]Cf. Johannes Janssen, *Schiller als Historiker* (Freiburg, 1879), pp. 29-30, and Eduard Fueter, *Geschichte der neueren Historiographie* (Munich, 1911), p. 400.

[58]Quoted by Cassirer in *Freiheit und Form*, p. 476.

[59]*Ibid.*, p. 229.

[60]My translation of Schiller's poem as quoted in Cassirer, *op. cit.*, p. 475.

[61]*Ibid.*, p. 235.

[62]*Kritik der praktischen Vernunft*, in *Gesammelte Schriften*, V, 131.

[63]Cf. *Das tragische Lebensgefuehl* (Munich, 1925), pp. 4-5.

[64]Cf. Wallace, *op. cit.*, pp. 1-7.

[65]*Die philosophischen Grundlagen des Nationalsozialismus: Ein Ruf zu den Waffen deutschen Geistes* (Breslau, 1935), p. 23.

[66]*Immanuel Kant: Die Persoenlichkeit als Einfuehruug in das Werk* (Munich, 1905).

[67]See, for example, "Der Mensch 'als Natur'" in *Politische Ideale* (Munich, 1915) and "Deutsche Freiheit," in *Kriegsaufsaetze* (Munich, 1915). On p. 17 of the latter we read that "Freiheit ist ein gar zartes Wesen und flieht oft erschreckt das oeffentliche Leben, um sich im still-energischen Dasein des Einzelnen zu behaupten." A classic statement of the uses of Kant for German escapism.

[68]Cf. "Der Mensch 'als Natur'", p. 22.

[69]Beantwortung der Frage: *Was ist Auflkaerung?* in *Gesammelte Schriften*, VIII, 40-41.

[70]*Werke* (Stuttgart, 1855), I, 724.

[71]These words are to be found in *Goetz von Berlichingen* (1774), *Werke* (Insel Verlag, n.d.), II, 160.

[72]Cf. Ernst Cassirer, *Freiheit und Form*, pp. 486-487; and Ernst Troeltsch, "Die deutsche Idee von der Freiheit," *op. cit.*, p. 103.

[73]Cf. Preserved Smith, *A History of Modern Culture* (New York, 1962), II *(The Enlightenment*, 1687-1776), 202-211.

[74]On Goethe's misgivings about history as his age understood it, see the profound and relevant essay by Friedrich Meinecke, "Goethe: Das negative Verhaeltnis zur Geschichte," in *Die Entstehung des Historismus* (Munich, 1959), pp. 504-525.

[75]*Op. cit.*, p. 301.

[76]*Kritik der Urtheilskraft*, in *Gesammelte Schriften*, V, 436.

[77]Cf. Lewis W. Beck, ed., *Kant on History* (Indianapolis, 1963), p. xviii.

[78]Kant's concept of the citizen and his famous *Zum ewigen Frieden* should be approached in the light of this vision.

[79]I use this term in the fashion of Karl Loewith. Cf. his *Meaning in History* (Chicago, 1957), p. 225, note one of the Preface.

[80]*Idee zu einer allgemeinen Geschichte in weltbuergerlicher Absicht*, in *Gesammelte Schriften*, VIII, Vierter Satz, esp. 20-21.

[81]*Ibid.*, 26. Bruce Mazlish deals with this problem from a different viewpoint in *op. cit.*, p. 109.

[82]Thomas Mann's *Betrachtungen eines Unpolitischen* (Berlin, 1920) is a classic statement of this dichotomy. Its Kantian origins have too seldom been recognized. Cf. my forthcoming "German Intellectuals and German Reality, 1789-1933," *Art and Sciences* (New York University, Spring, 1967).

[83]Cf. *Discours sur l'Origine et les Fondements de l'Inégalité parmi les Hommes* (1755), in Jean Jacques Rousseau, *The Political Writings*, ed. C.E. Vaughan (New York, 1962) I, especially 177 ff.

[84]Cf. Benno von Wiese, *Schiller: Eine Einfuehrung in Leben und Werk* (Stuttgart, 1955), p. 41. "Geschichte ist fuer Schiller – darin bleibt er dem Zeitalter der Auflkaerung verhaftet – Universal-geschichte, Entwicklung des Menschengeschlechtes... zu einem hoeheren Ziel."

[85]Janssen, *op. cit.*, p. 29.

[86]Von Wiese, *op. cit.*, p. 47 on the former, and Cassirer, *Freiheit und Form*, p. 475 *et passim* on the later.

[87]Quoted in Wallace, *op. cit.*, p. 82.

[88]Friedrich, *op. cit.*, p. xl.

THE FACT-VALUE QUESTION
IN EARLY MODERN VALUE THEORY

J. Prescott Johnson

Modern value inquiry took its rise in Germany and Austria during the last quarter of the nineteenth century and the early years of the present century. The discussions in which the inquiry engaged centered around the antithesis of fact and value. Accordingly, my purpose here is to elicit the structure of that discussion so as to indicate the directions which the discussion took.

In the tradition, the value question stood before the forum of metaphysics, and this because the principle of end, or telos, was espoused as the principle of explanation. With the advent of the genetic principle, according to which things are understood in causal terms, the value question was brought to the forum of empirical science. To be sure, this change took considerable time. The genetic principle was first applied to the physical world, with the result that value was extruded from nature. The world of Newtonian physics tended to become a value-free world void of ends and purposes. While Kant accepted Newtonian physics and provided a justification for it, nevertheless the larger burden of his thought was the retention of value in the world. In all his works, even in the *First Critique*, there are considerations of value which are directed to this end. The only observation that I have time to make here is this: that Kant was able, in his terms, to retain value within and alongside the world of nature because he refused to apply the genetic principle to man himself. On the contrary, man is a value-laden being, possessed of a dignity and excellence untouched by the genetic principle. Man is thus the fulcrum which secures value in what otherwise must be a value-free world. It remained for Darwin to extend the genetic principle from physical nature to life, thereby opening its further application to mind and its conventions. Under the aegis of this way of thinking, the first and foremost condition of the origin and development of values lies in human desires and feelings, and ultimately in the impulses, interests, and tendencies which they presuppose. And the value ideas and judgments merely describe the conditions of their emergence and development in consciousness and function as instruments in the service of natural life and existence. They do not sustain any objective import bearing upon a metaphysical order of value and man's relation to that order. All this, for example, Nietzche saw, and saw consistently.

Value theory emerged as a philosophical discipline out of the tensions created by the application of the new genetic logic to man. The early value theorists believed that values were indeed bound up with organic and psychical phenomena, yet they tried to find a place for value and the validity of value as independent of its conditions in experience. It is this two-fold thrust in their thinking about value which I wish to present here.

Hermann Lotze introduced a line of thought which was destined to be of considerable significance. For our purposes here it is sufficient to observe that Lotze assigned to perception the task of intuiting the immediately given facts of reality, and to reason the task of formulating the necessary truths expressed in the science of logic. Now reason and its necessary formulations cannot be explained in terms of any facts, including those facts of empirical consciousness which admit of a mechanical explanation. The necessary truths of reason are completely independent of existence, cannot be explained or justified by an appeal to existence or causally ordered processes of existence. Here any genetic or causal consideration is wholly irrelevant.[1] What, then, is the status of these truths? They possess a peculiar status of their own, that of "validity" (Geltung). What is validity? Validity is a unique form of reality which is absolutely independent of being or existence, and accordingly cannot be understood in any terms of fact. In more modern language, the realm of validity is the realm of autonomous value. Thus Lotze says:

> .... We must not ask what is meant by validity, with any idea that the meaning which the word conveys to us can be described from some different conception; .... the conception has to be regarded as ultimate and underivable, a conception of which everyone may know what he means by it, but which cannot be constructed out of any constituent elements which do not already contain it.... This conception of validity (is) a form of reality not including being or existence....[2]

Although he insisted that validity is independent of fact, at least as viewed from outside from the perspective of science, Lotze could not bring himself to give it a wholly free-floating status. Thus he constructed a metaphysical synthesis which finally anchors value, as well as finite fact, in a spiritual reality. But since that synthesis raises precisely those difficulties which occasioned the dominance of the scientific understanding of the world, the details of the synthesis are not germane at this point.[3]

In the attempt to acknowledge simultaneously the claims of fact and value, the Baden School of Neo-Kantianism placed increasing emphasis upon the notion of validity. In many respects the founder of the school, Wilhelm Windelband, was close to Lotze. Windelband ties values, including the cognitive values, to the psychological conditions of experience. He says of value that it

> .... is never found in the object itself as a property. It consists in a relation to an appreciating mind, which satisfies the desires of its will or reacts in feelings of pleasure upon the stimulation of the environment. Take away will and feeling and there is no such thing as value.[4]

When faced, however, with the question of the evaluation of values, Windelband requires a standard which transcends individual appreciations. This standard according to which some of our values are over individual and absolute cannot be, obviously, a product of individual minds, yet it cannot, on the hypothesis that values are products of mind, be wholly unrelated to mind. Thus, Windelband requires the postulation of an absolute mind to effect this synthesis. For example, he says that truth, or the truth-claim, is entirely an affair of the formative act of judgment. Yet truth is validity, that which ought to be affirmed, and constitutes a norm for judgment.[5] Thus it is required that the validity which is immanent in judgment and yet transcendent to individual judgments be a function of the divine mind. In sum Windelband remarks:

.... our conviction that for human valuation there are absolute norms, beyond the empirical occasions of their appearance, is based upon the assumption that here also we have the sovereignty of a transcendent rational order. As long as we would conceive their orders as contents of an actual higher mind, on the analogy of the relation we experience of consciousness to its objects and values, they have to be considered contents of an absolute reason – that is to say, God.[6]

The resort to analogy for the purpose of aligning the descriptive and normative problems of value appeared questionable to Windelband's successor in the Baden School, Heinrich Rickert. Rickert very well insists that, however it be related to psychological phenomena, value cannot be restricted to these phenomena. On the other hand, it cannot be grounded in a spiritual metaphysics. Instead, value sustains a unique status of its own. Just what this status is can be brought to view by a brief consideration of Rickert's analysis of the structure of cognition.

He observes that the cognitive judgment, which is a psychological act, involves more than just that act. The judgment asserts a content and in so doing makes a claim to truth. Now, this content, which cannot be reduced to act, is not merely an immanent content within consciousness. Perhaps we might say, in more contemporary language, that it is not merely a phenomenological object bound to the intentionality of some consciousness. It is something transcendent. As transcendent to both act and immanent content, it is not, however, a real existent. This is evident, Rickert says, when we realize that a judgment of existence, that something exists or exists as such and such, sustains a meaning content which does not have the existential status that characterizes the referent of the judgment. For the same kind of reason, the content does not have ideal existence, the existence which the referent of a judgment of an ideal object, say a mathematical object, possesses.[7]

However, Rickert argues, the transcendence of meaning over empirical reality neither requires nor warrants a metaphysical synthesis, such as those resorted to by Lotze and Windelband. On the contrary, the content of the judgment is objective and transcendent purely as a value, or validity.

To be sure, when the cognitive judgment is considered subjectively as act, it is seen to involve valuation or appreciation, the acceptance of meaning and truth as value. That is, theoretical knowledge presupposes *a priori* that we place value upon knowledge, that we esteem knowledge as a value. But, he continues, this appreciation in no sense constitutes the value. When the judgment is viewed objectively, it is seen to sustain a meaningful and true content which is a value in this sense, that meaning and truth are validities which ought to be affirmed. Such imperative values which devolve upon us in our judgments and appreciations are not our own creations. Nor are the values existing things, because existing things are, for us, the referents which cognition brings to view and are as dependent upon and subsequent to value as is cognition. Accordingly, value is absolutely prior to and beyond all being. The objectivity and transcendence of value is precisely its *validity*.[8]

After Rickert proposes the concept of negation as the criterion by which value as autonomous validity is distinguished from being, thereby showing that meaning is such a value, he sums up his position:

For that a value is valid without any consideration of existence
....is precisely what we understand by its transcendence. The science of theoretical values is concerned with that which is conceptually prior to all sciences of reality, with that which is prior to their material which is assumed as "real" or "actual."....As understood in this way, the much debated concept of the *a priori*....is a form of meaning, a theoretical value, which is transcendentally valid. Apart from such validity, there would not only be no experience, but no "perception," or any other *"a posteriori"* knowledge.[9]

The last school of thought which I shall mention in this discussion is the Second Austrian School of value, which included Franz Brentano, Christian Ehrenfels, and Alexius Meinong. These men had breathed deeply of the scientific atmosphere of their day and, rejecting any purely speculative or metaphysical resolution of the value question, demanded that the question be brought to the forum of empirical science, in particular the science of psychology. Yet, with the possible exception of Ehrenfels, after their elaborate psychological analyses, they ended up by projecting value beyond natural fact. I propose to treat the Austrian school very briefly, merely to indicate this line of their thought.

Brentano develops implicitly a theory of value on the basis of his "new empiricism," which in turn rests upon an act psychology. He argues that the emotions of love and hate, one class of psychological phenomena, have their intentional objects. In distinction to its being a property of objects, value is a product of these phenomena. Value is founded in the attitude of the subject which qualifies the presentational content as pleasant. Value is therefore amenable to psychological analysis.[10]

However, if value is a product of emotional acts, it becomes subjective as relative to those acts. Brentano attempted to avoid this "psychologism of values" by arguing that certain emotional phenomena are so characterized as to confer a measure of validity and objectivity upon the values which they sustain. Analogously to self-evidence which evinces the truth of certain judgments, such as the principle of contradiction, there are certain emotions which evince a rightness with a comparable self-evidence, for example, the pleasure which men take in knowledge. From this basis, Brentano defines value in normative terms: "That which can be loved with a right love, that which is worthy of love, is good."[11]

Thus, Brentano's implicit claim is that value is founded in an emotion which possesses an objectively valid character. But he did not, perhaps, show clearly or adequately either the foundations or implications of the fact that such psychological phenomena possess the character of rightness. Certainly his extension of the criterion of self-evidence beyond the sphere of the analytic tends to vitiate his argument. Hence, he was not too successful in his effort to combine the descriptive and normative in a unified concept of value.

Ehrenfels was almost exclusively preoccupied with the descriptive side of the value question, while Meinong went on to address the normative side as well. Ehrenfels defined value in terms of desire. "We do not," he said, "desire things because we perceive a mystical, intangible essence called 'worth' in them, but on the contrary, we ascribe 'worth' to them because we desire them."[12] As the object of desire, value is personal and relative. And since, for Ehrenfels, judgment is not an internally constitutive factor in the formation of desire, but performs only a collateral function as the enhancer of the idea of the object of desire in consciousness, value is deprived, ultimately, of any objectivity which the intellectual judgment might bring to it. On the other hand, some measure of uniformity is brought to desires and valuations, hence to values, as a result of pre-established behavior patterns – "feeling-dispositions," as Ehrenfels calls them – and, finally, the unconscious mechanisms of evolution. This, however, is quite consistent with his thesis that value is a function of desire. For him, value always consists in the fact of desire; in nowise is it, or does it issue in, an extra-factual or extra-psychological element.[13]

Meinong begins his value analysis by bringing value to the forum of psychology. Here he differs from Ehrenfels in two significant respects: 1) he interprets value in terms of feeling rather than desire, and 2) he makes the judgment an integral part of the value feeling, rather than a collateral accompaniment of it. Thus, he says that "...with respect to value, it is sufficient to designate value experience as essentially emotional in nature."[14] Again, he remarks: "...the value-object does not cause the value-feeling. The cause of the value-feeling is a judgment of the existence of the value-object. The judgment provides the connection between the value-feeling and the value-object."[15] Meinong's basic point is that a judgment, or at best an assumption, of the existence of an object is necessary to occasion the sort of feeling – an "existence-feeling" or "judgment-feeling" – which, in distinction to a merely hedonic feeling, constitutes the value emotion and thereby qualifies the object as valuable, i.e., institutes the value. Although value is personal and relative, the fact, however, that a reference to existence *via* judgment or assumption is an integral part of the value emotion brings, in principle, an element of objectivity to value meaning.

There is yet a further and very important respect in which Meinong secured an element of objectivity in value so as to complement the subjective element. He does this in connection with his theory of objectives. According to Meinong, the objects which we may experience fall into two great classes, which may be designated as *objecta* and *objectives*. In distinction, however, to both objecta and objectives, the *content*, e.g., of an idea, is grasped in the wholly passive and non-intentional experience of presentation. The reference of the content to an objectum, so that the presence of an object is acknowledged or the nature of an object is recognized, is accomplished by the active and intentional experience of assumption or judgment. However, while the judgment, for example, is about an object or the properties of an object, the judgment grasps directly and primarily, not the object or its properties, but a certain "that" which is judged to hold for the object. In the judgment that there is snow, or that snow is white, what is given is neither the object snow nor the property white, but the complex circumstance that, or that it is the case that, snow exists or is white. The class of those entities, of which some are and others are not the case, is given the name of *objectives*. And the mode of being which is peculiar to objectives is that of *subsistence* rather than existence. Objectives which are true, as $2 + 2 = 4$, have *factuality* over and above their mere being. And the factuality of an objective is a genuine property of the objective, in a way in which existence is never a property of an objectum, and it is given to us by a peculiar, luminous quality of experience known as "evidence."[16]

We have seen that for Meinong value meaning involves the assumption or judgment of existence. And both assumption and judgment signify objectives, which, even when they concern existence, are ideal and possess the property of factuality – a property disclosed in the experience of evidence. Accordingly, value meaning, which is an emotion to which assumption and judgment are integral, is ultimately ruled by purely idea entities, objectives, whose factuality is certified in the experience of evidence. The point I am making is this: Meinong insisted that value be given a psychological interpretation in terms of feeling. But when he requires an element of assumption or judgment to be integral to the value emotion and insists that this element involves objectives whose factuality is given in the experience of evidence, he has introduced considerations which transcend a strictly descriptive, naturalistic account of value. Implicated in the value situation are not only states of feeling and assumptions or judgments of existence, but, finally and definitively, ideal entities, objectives, and the inner experience of evidence in which the factuality of objectives is disclosed.

F

So far forth Meinong has argued that the content of ideas presents *objecta* and that the content of judgments and judgment-like assumptions presents objectives. In line with this direction of thought, he was led to the view that the emotions, feeling and desire, involve contents which present objects of a higher order than either objecta or objectives. There are emotional experiences of feeling and desire in which certain properties of objects come before us without appearing to have anything to do with ourselves and with our attitudes and experiences. These are the *dignitatives*, presented by feeling, and the *desideratives*, presented by desire. Thus, for example, the value feelings, the earlier analysis of which had implicated the psychology of feeling and the epistemology of judgment, now present the good, or value, as an ideal object which is independent of the conditions of experience. It should be observed here, however, that while value is emotionally presented as a dignitative having phenomenologically objective status, the question as to whether the value qualifies objecta and objectives, i.e., has being, is a question of fact and involves a new objective whose factuality is evident in the same manner which holds for any objective. In sum, then, Meinong's early theory which finds value to consist in feeling as internally qualified by assumption or judgment, and therefore amenable to psychological analysis, has changed to an impersonal and objective theory, according to which value, although cognitively occasioned by emotion, is an ideal entity enjoying a unique status beyond experience and existence, but capable of a real and normative implication in reality.[17]

In this discussion I have shown how, with the increasing disaffection with metaphysics, the value question was brought to the forum of scientific description. At this forum value became a natural fact of psychological experience. I have further shown that, nonetheless, there was instituted a powerful counter-movement in the attempt to sustain the validity and normative objectivity of value over the facts of existence, including those of psychological experience. Value then became an autonomous validity or ideal entity whose unique status is that of independence of, or transcendence over, being. From this opposition of the descriptive and normative ways in value philosophy, there has come the hiatus which has brought such disarray in modern value theory. On one side of this hiatus stand the various forms of naturalism, while on the other side stand the various forms of non-naturalism. Deeper, perhaps, and underlying this schism is the *horror metaphysicus*, the repudiation of that vision in which reality and value are fused in metaphysical synthesis, and apart from which, in some form, we may not expect to bring order and meaning to our value thinking.

Monmouth College

[1]Hermann Lotze, *Microcosmus*, translated by Elizabeth Hamilton and E. E. Constance Jones, 4th edition (Edinburgh: T. & T. Clark, 1885), II, 575ff.

[2]Hermann Lotze, *Logic*, translated by Bernard Bosanquet, 2nd edition (Oxford: At the Clarendon Press, 1887), II, 209-11.

[3]Lotze, *Microcosmus*, II, Bk. ix.

[4]Wilhelm Windelband, *An Introduction to Philosophy*, translated by Joseph McCabe (New York: Henry Holt & Co., 1921), p. 215.

[5]*Ibid.*, pp. 166-175.

[6]*Ibid.*, p. 216.

[7]Heinrich Rickert, *Der Gegenstand der Erkentniss*, 4th and 5th editions (Tubingen: J. C. B. Mohr, 1921), pp. 221-8.

[8]*Ibid.*, pp. 219-20, 228-9.

[9]*Ibid.*, pp. 236-8.

[10]Franz Brentano, *The Origin of the Knowledge of Right and Wrong*, translated by Cecil Hague (Westminster: Archibald Constable & Co., Ltd., 1902), pp. 13-15.

[11]*Ibid.*, p. 19.

[12]Christian Ehrenfels, *System der Werttheorie* (Leipzig: O. R. Reisland, 1897), I, 43.

[13]*Ibid.*, 116-31, 146-65, 195-207.

[14]Alexius Meinong, *Zur Grundlegung der allgemeinen Werttheorie* (Graz: Leuschner and Lubensky, 1923), p. 35.

[15]Alexius Meinong, *Psychologisch-ethische Untersuchungen zur Werttheorie* (Graz: Leuschner and Lubensky, 1894), p. 21. See also pp. 14-35.

[16]Alexius Meinong, *Ueber Annahmen*, 2nd edition (Leipzig: Barth, 1910), pp. 59-73, 88, 285-6.

[17]Alexius Meinong, *Ueber emotionale Präsentation* (1917), pp. 33-42, 113, 120-2, in J. N. Findlay, *Meinong's Theory of Objects and Values* (Oxford: At The Clarendon Press, 1963), chap. x.

ACTIONS, CONSEQUENCES
AND
ETHICAL THEORY

Ruth Macklin

Several writers have claimed recently that a sound theory of action and intention is a necessary condition for any ethical system. Miss Anscombe has made such a claim[1], as has Stuart Hampshire, who writes:

> One must in philosophy consider human beings simultaneously as observers and as agents and as language-users. If one considers the theory of mind and ethics separately, both are apt to be falsified.[2]

In his book, *Thought and Action*, Hampshire examines the concept of action and the concept of intention, holding that nothing else in ethics and the philosophy of mind can be made comparatively clear unless the notion of intention is comparatively clear. And, as one recent writer has put it: "Current philosophical interest in the notion of action is at least partly motivated by a sense of its fundamental role in ethics."[3] If these and other writers who make similar claims are correct, it seems that an analysis of the concepts of action and intention is crucial to the development of any ethical theory. Accordingly, I should like to examine some recent accounts of the concept of action which have special relevance to ethics, and to indicate the directions future inquiry might take.

The search for a proper basis for evaluating human actions has played a primary role in moral philosophy. A distinction is maintained between teleological theories of ethics which stress ends, goals or consequences, and deontological theories which take the notions of duty and rules for acting as central. Recently the teleological-deontological distinction has been challenged, and called a false dualism which has contributed confusion to moral philosophy.[4] The basis for this type of objection, as well as for much that has been written currently on the topic of action, lies in the ability to provide alternative descriptions of the same action or piece of behavior. Recent accounts by a number of writers[5] focus on the question of how to describe and classify actions. How we classify and describe actions seems to be of crucial importance for any evaluation of such actions and hence, for any moral theory which attempts to justify one or another scheme of evaluation.

In this paper I shall concentrate on the much discussed distinction between actions and their consequences, with special attention to the importance of this issue for ethical theory and the problem of evaluation of human actions. Among the questions underlying this issue are the following:

If several alternative descriptions of the same action are possible, is there one uniquely applicable description for the purposes of moral evaluation? How important, for the purpose of moral evaluation, are descriptions which an agent gives of his own action? What counts as "the same action" when several alternative descriptions are said to be given of the same action? I shall not attempt directly to answer these and other questions. Instead, I shall concentrate on the action-consequence distinction in examining some recent views of writers whose interests fall in the area of ethics, philosophy of mind, or both. The issue encompasses at least two problematic alternatives. The two following assumptions seem to be true:

(a) We can redescribe an action in such a way as to include consequences of the action in a fuller description of the action.

(b) The various alternative descriptions which can be given are true of the action in the sense that the action does in fact have the characteristics attributed to it in the description.

Given these assumptions, we can state the alternatives as follows: If it makes no difference where we draw the line between action and consequence, then consequentialist views are surely misconceived, since the same action may be evaluated as good or bad, right or wrong, or morally neutral, depending on what is to count as consequences. If, on the other hand, it does make a difference for moral theory where we draw the action-consequence line, then we are faced with the problem of coming up with a set of criteria for making the distinction which can be applied in a non-arbitrary fashion to different cases of human action. The consequentialist faces two distinct but related objections: (1) There is the problem of just which events or states of affairs are to count as consequences of a particular action. For example, at what point do events which are temporally removed from an action cease to be consequences of that action? Furthermore, given multiple consequences of an action, what principle is to be used to select the consequences which are relevant for moral evaluation of the action? (2) Even if objection (1) can be met, there is the additional problem raised by our ability to redescribe actions so as to include the consequences. There is a sense in which this difficulty is prior to the first, since the consequences of an action must be stipulated or selected *under some description or other.* Thus, either we cannot make a plausible distinction between action and consequence, for the above reasons, and consequentialist views turn out to be arbitrary or counterintuitive; *or* we can make a distinction but no one has yet provided necessary and sufficient conditions for such a distinction.

To opt for the first alternative seems counterintuitive, since we often appeal to what are loosely called "consequences" in deciding between two courses of action which seem themselves morally neutral or at least of equal moral weight. The reply to this is that under another description – one which includes the consequences in the description of an action – those actions cease to be morally neutral or to have equal moral weight. For example, Jones may face the alternative of remaining in his job or taking a new position in another city which involves an increase in salary and prestige. He knows that his wife is not materialistic and that she always becomes unhappy when moving to a new city and that his children become insecure. These, then, are the consequences of Jones's action of changing jobs. Can we plausibly redescribe Jones's action as uprooting his children and making his wife depressed? That the answer to this question is not simple is shown by the following factors. Jones *knows* that these will be the consequences of his action; moreover, the probability that these consequences will ensue is very high: the same thing occurred three times in his married life with these unhappy consequences. These factors lend credence to the view that we can redescribe Jones's action in the way indicated. On the other hand, Jones is not undertaking the action with the *aim* or *purpose* of uprooting his children and depressing his wife. In fact, he is displeased with that prospect of his action. Just which factors are central in determining whether we may include or exclude consequences in our description of an action will be examined below. Meanwhile, suffice it to note that it makes little difference in our moral assessment of Jones's action whether we include the consequences in our description of the action or appeal to consequences as lying outside the action. Such a result strikes a blow at consequentialist ethical theories. For if an action can be redescribed so as to include at least some of its consequences in a broader description of the action, and we praise or blame the agent for his action for the same reasons in either case, then what is the point of an ethical theory which bases the evaluation of human actions on the consequences of those actions? If the action-consequence distinction is dubious, this casts some doubt on a consequentialist view, such as utilitarianism, which seeks to evaluate actions in terms of their consequences (although perhaps not solely on this basis). Allowing for a latitude of redescription, the further removed a state of affairs is from an action (perhaps at the end of a causal chain of events), the more it qualifies as a consequence of the action rather than as part of the action itself. But then, the farther removed a state of affairs from the action, the less we are likely to consider the agent responsible for such a state of affairs and hence, the less likely are we to assign praise or blame. So on these considerations, consequentialist theories appear arbitrary or counterintuitive. Let us examine some recent controversies over the action-consequence distinction with an eye to the second alternative.

On one side of the controversy Andrew Oldenquist attacks the distinction between action and consequence. He asks, "How are we to separate an action from its consequences with clarity and finality sufficient to support the importance of this distinction? Any attempt to specify what a person did involves reference to what happened, in other words, to what could be called consequences, however direct and immediate they might be ... It is plain that this kind of analysis can be carried to the point where all we can say that the man 'actually did' were certain trivial and individually meaningless bodily acts and, perhaps, the intending of these acts".[6] On Oldenquist's view, the sole cost of calling an occurrence an action or the consequence of an action, in any given case, will be stretching certain conventional ways of speaking. He claims that "If, as seems certain, it is of no moral significance whether or not we let a given event count as part of the action or instead as a consequence of a simpler version of the action, then whether we appeal to rules or to consequences to determine the rightness or wrongness of a particular action is of no moral significance."[7] On the face of it, Oldenquist's account seems plausible, but he has failed to provide reasons why the distinction is usually made, with one exception: "It is a person's lack of knowledge of the later events in a series he has started which accounts for one of the practical reasons why he designates some of these events part of his 'action' and others of them 'consequences'."[8] Lack of knowledge is only one factor which enters into the rationale for making the action-consequence distinction. But on Oldenquist's view, there is only a "practical" reason and never a "moral" reason for making the distinction. He concludes: "Insofar as the [deontologist] formalist and teleologist each notices that certain events are 'wrong-making' it makes no difference whether these events are taken to be part of or instead external to the action."[9]

Directly opposed to Oldenquist's view is that of John Ladd, in a paper entitled "The Ethical Dimensions of the Concept of Action."[10] Ladd's view can be summarized in an extended quotation from his article:

> Ethically it makes a great deal of difference whether a certain segment of the act – consequence series is to be put under the category of action or under the category of consequences. This is because these categories function quite differently in ethical discourse. Ethical discourse, and moral evaluation in particular, focuses on action, and what it has to say about consequences is relevant only through the concept of action. In other words, moral good and evil are properties of actions as such, and hence, whenever we whittle down an action to its bare minimum or, on the other hand expand it to encompass various consequences, we directly affect the moral evaluation of the action thereby.... The ethical effect of incorporating consequences into an action is to accentuate its moral quality – either positive or negative. By whittling it down, on the other hand, its moral quality is reduced, perhaps even to zero. This is not because one is ignoring or denying the consequences; it is because the moral significance of the consequence depends on the act.[11]

There is something peculiar in the claim that "moral good and evil are properties of actions as such." What is an action *as such?* If it is true that we can give alternative descriptions of an action, must it follow, on Ladd's account, that we can give one correct description of the action *as such?* What are our criteria of selection for the action as such? Or for the correct description of an action as such? Ladd seems to be conflating the notions of action and description which can be given of an action. It is not *actions* which we whittle down to their bare minimum or expand to encompass various consequences, as Ladd claims. Rather, it is the *descriptions* of actions which can be whittled down or expanded in this manner. When Ladd speaks about ethical discourse as focusing on action he should be talking about actions *under a given description.* He recognizes indeed that the same action can be given fuller or narrower descriptions, ones which are expanded to encompass consequences and ones which are whittled down. But he offers no selection criteria for picking out the "action as such," of which moral good and evil are held to be properties. Nor does he indicate whether or not this notion of an action as such presupposes that there is a uniquely applicable description which can be given of the action as such. Although there is a ring of plausibility in Ladd's attempt to show that it matters where the action-consequence line is drawn, he has failed to provide any suggestions as to how we can go about drawing it properly.

The following are true descriptions of what might be called the same action:

(1) Jones tenses his forefinger
(2) Jones pulls the trigger
(3) Jones shoots the gun
(4) Jones kills Smith
(5) Jones murders Smith
(6) Jones avenges his brother's death
(7) Jones widows Smith's wife

and here are some consequences of Jones's action:

(8) Smith's wife commits suicide
(9) Smith's six children are orphaned.

(1) describes a bodily movement (a physiologist could give another description of the micro-movements involved). (2) is a simple description of an action, perhaps "whittled down," which is not subject to moral evaluation without knowing more of the story. Similarly with (3); Jones might be shooting at a target. (4) is a fuller description of the action but we must suspend moral judgment even at this point since Jones may have killed Smith by accident or in self-defence. (5) already characterizes the killing as a killing of a certain sort; (6) gives the motive or intention in the description of the action. (7) begins to sound like a consequence of the action, yet it is certainly true that if we know that Jones widows Smith's wife, we know that Jones kills Smith. Yet widowing Smith's wife was not Jones's primary intention or aim in killing Smith. But he knew this upshot of the killing would be an inevitable result of his success. As for (8) and (9), these are clearly not descriptions of Jones's action, but rather of consequences of his action. The fact that Smith's wife committed *suicide* logically precludes it from being Jones's action. (8) and (9) cannot be considered as descrip-

tions of Jones's action, yet Jones may have known these upshots of his action, or at least believed them with a high degree of belief. For Smith's wife may have written Jones a letter threatening suicide if Jones murdered her husband (since she knew Jones wanted to avenge his brother's death), and Smith's wife's psychoanalyst may have corroborated the fact that she was suicidal. Yet this knowledge of the highly probable results of his action is not sufficient to enable us to consider (8) and (9) as descriptions of Jones's action.

This example shows us that there are clear cases of a break in the chain of action and consequence such that we cannot recast certain consequences as redescriptions of the action. As noted earlier, Oldenquist holds that there is only a "practical" reason for making the action-consequence distinction. But we have seen in our example that there may also be a logical reason: it is logically impossible that Smith's wife committing suicide can be Jones's action. Moreover, Oldenquist's suggestion that it is a person's lack of knowledge of the later events in a series he has started which accounts for one of the practical reasons why he designates some of these events part of his "action" and others of them "consequences," fails to apply in this case. For in our example, Jones *knew* the probability of the consequence and the further result that Smith's children would be orphaned. It should be noted that the inability to count (8) and (9) as descriptions of Jones's *action* does not mean that Jones is not at least partly *responsible* for these consequences. If Jones knew that Smith's wife would commit suicide if he killed her husband, and he committed the deed anyway, he is partly to blame for the suicide and orphaning of the children. What this shows is that a person *can* be blamed for consequences of his action which cannot plausibly be counted as descriptions of *his action*. In any case, we are hard put to pick out the action *as such* from our list.

Following some suggestions by Jonathan Bennett in his paper "Whatever the Consequences," I should like to consider a set of conditions which must obtain if A's action is to be described in terms of the consequences of the action so as to support a moral judgment.

(A) A must know, or entertain a high degree of belief that the upshot would ensue.
(B) The upshot of the action must be inevitable or highly probable, whether or not A expected it to ensue; if he did not expect it to ensue, he *ought* to have done so.
(C) A's action must have been committed partly or wholly with the aim, intention, or purpose of achieving that upshot.
(D) There must be a high degree of immediacy between A's action and upshot, consisting in spatial and temporal proximity, simplicity of causal connections, and absence of intervening physical objects.

(E) A description of the consequence of A's action must not logically preclude its being a description of the action.
Several points can be made about this set of conditions. (E) is a formal
condition which must be satisfied in every case where we wish to redescribe
an action in terms of its consequences. (D) seems like a plausible require-
ment, but Bennett raises the following question: "Why should a difference
in degree of immediacy, unaccompanied by other relevant differences, be
taken to support a moral discrimination? I cannot think of a remotely
plausible answer which does not consist solely in an appeal to an authority."[12] Conditions (A), (B), and (C) are jointly sufficient but no one of them
seems to be sufficient, although any two of the three seem to be sufficient.
The work remaining to be done is that of supplementing the above list of
conditions and ascertaining any connections which may obtain among
them. I shall not attempt that task here, but I think such work needs to be
done before we can decide with finality the relevance of the action-consequence distinction for ethical theory. The knowledge and intentions of an
agent in performing an action are certainly crucial for our moral assessment
of the action. But as has been pointed out amply, an action may be intentional under one description and unintentional under another. Therefore,
although conditions (A) – (D) may not be necessary for every redescription
of action in terms of consequences, they are necessary where a *moral*
judgment of the action is at issue. Cases can be imagined in which (A) – (D)
fail to obtain and we still redescribe the action in terms of its consequences.
But it has been noted as far back as Aristotle that certain forms of ignorance
are exculpating, and we do not censure a man as severely for an act that
was unintentional as we do for the same act if done intentionally. It seems,
at the very least, that these criteria serve to distinguish those consequences
of actions which can be recast into a description of the action from those
consequences which cannot be considered as descriptions of the action, for
the purpose of moral evaluation.

However, it is worth noting that in certain cases an appeal to consequences is of no relevance in our moral assessment of an action, as, for
example, when a person performs an action which we consider wrong or
evil, yet which inadvertently has some good consequences. It may be that
in such cases the consequences cannot enter into a redescription of the
agent's action in accordance with the application of the above criteria. In
addition, as has been pointed out recently,[13] we do not administer as severe
a punishment for an action which a person fails to achieve through accident
or lack of opportunity, as we do for a successful attempt (e.g., murder
versus attempted murder). Here the *intended* consequences did not ensue,
yet the action is redescribable in terms of the intended consequences. Perhaps more attention needs to be paid to the role of intended consequences,
apart from actual consequences, in our moral evaluation of actions.

I began by setting forth two alternatives, about which I have the following concluding remarks. Due to our ability to redescribe actions by includ-

ing their consequences in a redescription, as well as the problem of *identifying* consequences in the first place, it seems that the burden is on those who wish to stress the importance of the action-consequence distinction for moral evaluation of actions. If our above criteria are at all correct, they show that we can make a plausible distinction in some nonarbitrary fashion. But the crucial relevance of making the distinction has not yet emerged, as I have tried to show. Even if we can render plausible the action-consequence distinction in some systematic way, it does not follow that the distinction is important for ethical theory in the ways it has been used traditionally. And certainly, if we cannot plausibly make the distinction, then consequentialist theories are misconceived. It should be noted that similar problems arise for deontological theories which attempt to eschew consequences and which concentrate on rules or maxims of action. For a "whittled down" description of an action (e.g., "tensing one's forefinger") cannot plausibly be subject to any moral rule or maxim, while a very full description is too highly specified to be subsumed under a rule. It is not the distinction between action and consequence which is important for ethical theory, but rather the selection of those features of the action or circumstances which are to be incorporated into a description of the action. Finally, it cannot be that our entire moral evaluation rests on those consequences which can be considered descriptions of the action. For, as we saw, we are inclined to hold Jones partially responsible and to blame him for Smith's wife's suicide, even though that consequence of his action cannot be recast as a redescription of *his* action.

Case-Western Reserve University

---

[1]Miss Anscombe makes the point in connection with her discussion of the practical syllogism: "So what can the practical syllogism have to do with ethics? It can only come into ethical studies if a correct philosophical psychology is requisite for a philosophical system of ethics: a view which I believe I should maintain if I thought of trying to construct such a system; but which I believe is not generally current." *Intention* (Ithaca, New York: Cornell University Press, 1963), p. 78.

[2]Stuart Hampshire, *Thought and Action* (New York: The Viking Press, 1960), p. 67.

[3]David Sachs, "A Few Morals About Acts," *Philosophical Review*, LXXV, No. 1 (January 1966), 95.

[4]Andrew Oldenquist, "Rules and Consequences," *Proceedings of The Aristotelian Society*, LXV (1964-65). Griffin writes: "[The consequentialist and intrinsicalist] misconceive what is at issue;...they present us with a false dichotomy" (182).

[5]Hampshire, *op. cit.;* Anscombe, *op. cit.;* Donald Davidson, "Actions, Reasons, and

Causes," *Journal of Philosophy*, LX, No. 23 (7 November 1963); Eric D'Arcy, *Human Acts* (Oxford: The Calrendon Press, 1963); Oldenquist, *op. cit.;* Jonathan Bennett, "Whatever The Consequences," *Analysis*, XXVI, No. 3 (January 1966); Griffin, *op. cit.;* Y. N. Chopra, "The Consequences of Human Actions," *Proceedings of The Aristotelian Society*, LXV (1964-65); Daniel Bennett, "Action, Reason, and Purpose," *Journal of Philosophy*, LXII, No. 4 (1965); John Ladd, "The Ethical Dimensions of The Concept of Action," *Journal of Philosophy*, LXII, No. 21 (1965).
[6]Oldenquist, *op. cit.*, 180-181.
[7]*Ibid.*, 183.
[8]*Ibid.*, 182.
[9]*Ibid.*, 184.
[10]Ladd, *op. cit.*
[11]*Ibid.*, 644.
[12]Bennett, *op. cit.*, 92.
[13]Gerald Dworkin and David Blumenfeld, "Punishment for Intentions," *Mind*, LXXV, No. 299 (July 1966).

I am indebted to Bruce Miller and Samuel Gorovitz for their helpful suggestions and their criticisms of an earlier draft of this paper.

PART II

Value Theory in Social Science

PHENOMENOLOGY AS A "GENERAL THEORY" OF SOCIAL ACTION

ROBERT W. FRIEDRICHS

The renewed interest in Husserl evident within contemporary philosophy and the recent translation and publication of Alfred Schütz' *Collected Works* [1] together with the vivid and sociologically sophisticated efforts of such younger social theorists as Peter Berger, Thomas Luckman, and Edward Tiryakian [2] signal an important new turn for "general theory" in sociology and one that promises to raise the discipline's contextual awareness considerably.

Husserl, trained in mathematics, physics, and philosophy, set out to confront both the inter- and intrasubjective phenomena of consciousness immediately and directly by the systematic, ordered rhetoric of cognition. His goal was none less than a completely reliable "science" of the subjective. Aware that natural science was burdened by a set of largely unrecognized assumptions, he claimed that through a technique of self-conscious "phenomenological reduction" – the apperception of the impact of phenomena upon one's consciousness devoid of reference to the actual presence or absence of external objects – he had framed an epistemology freed of presuppositions. The phenomena abstracted were in turn seen to structure themselves within a format of universally present and relatively invariant *Ideen* and found to relate themselves, in the life histories of individuals in society, to an inverse "suspension of doubt" in the "reality" of "everyday life" on the latter's part. Needless to say, the self-evident nature of the posture was questioned by many – with perhaps Husserl's most promising student, Martin Heidegger, breaking away to become philosophy's leading exponent of existentialism and succeeding to his chair at Freibourg. Rather than claim

---

[1] Alfred Schütz, *Collected Papers I: The Problem of Social Reality*, ed. Maurice Natanson (The Hague: Martinus Nijhoff, 1962), *Collected Papers II: Studies in Social Theory*, ed. Arvid Brodersen (The Hague, 1965); *Collected Papers III: Studies in Phenomenological Philosophy*, ed. I. Schütz (The Hague, 1966). Also see Alfred Schütz, *The Phenomenology of the Social World* (Northwestern University Press, 1967).

[2] Peter L. Berger and Thomas Luckmann, *The Social Construction of Reality* (Doubleday, 1966); Edward Tiryakian, "Existential Phenomenology and the Sociological Tradition," *American Sociological Review*, XXX (October 1965), 674–688; Communication between Berger and Tiryakian, *American Sociological Review*, XXXII (April 1966), 259–264; also see Tiryakian, *Sociologism and Existentialism* (Prentice-Hall, 1962); Berger and Stanley Pullberg, "Reification and the Sociological Critique of Consciousness," *History and Theory*, IV, 2 (1965), 196–211; and Luckmann, *The Invisible Religion: The Transformation of Symbols in Industrial Society* (Macmillan, 1967).

either the certitude or the freedom from assumptions that Husserl was wont to do, Heidegger focussed upon the element of risk that adheres to an existence that must confront, as its primary datum, the threat of "non-being." Instead of projecting a set of systematically interrelated and quasi-Platonic *Ideen*, the latter drew a portrait of the concrete individual forced to accept the responsibility of making choices in a setting of substantive freedom. Rather than painting experience in the neutral hues of an invariant structure of consciousness whose appeal would be to man's search for rational order, his canvas was colored by a call to the commitment necessary for "authentic existence." In place of the cool bracketing out of all but the impact made by phenomena upon the consciousness, Heidegger reclaimed for philosophy dimensions of human experience which had been abandoned as idiosyncratic by both science and philosophy. In other words, instead of seeking to grasp the phenomena of both inter- and intrasubjective experience, via introspection, within the web of an essentially "scientific" epistemology, Heidegger renounced the value of the scientific "lens" for an understanding of the human condition that was available to it through the depth of the intrasubjective alone.

Still, a social theorist such as Alfred Schütz who sought a firmer cognitive base than that provided by the metaphors of existentialism and yet who would not abandon the subjective dimension of human experience could find much that was attractive in the phenomenological stance. For one thing, he saw it sharing with existentialism the conviction that the knowledge that one must die and the fear of that death stand as primordial data of human existence – though seen as presenting itself within the phenomena of the threat of death is consciousness rather than as the direct threat of "non-being" to "being" as is the case with Heidegger. It is Schütz' interpretation of man's reaction to that threat, however, that provides the key to his larger posture. Following Husserl, man is seen as inverting the phenomenologist's doubt of all but the phenomena of consciousness: in order to cloak his anxiety, he *suspends doubt* in the paramount reality of "everyday life." The "phenomena of consciousness" is thus seen linked to the reality of "everyday life" as accumulated sediment is to the actual process of sedimentation. "Everyday life," together with the "natural attitude" with which it is associated, then become the foci of analysis. They in turn are characterized as "action" oriented – that is, the meaning reflected by the "natural attitude" toward the world of "everyday life" originates in and is instituted by chosen, motivated "acts." The individual, though confronting a world that is largely a shared world of *typical* images and meanings (whose genesis is explicated in terms akin to those of Cooley and George Herbert Mead), discovers his "projects" – his purposiveness – confronted by unique constellations of events that demand choice. Whether his "act" (the outcome of his choice) is identical with his "action" (his preconceived project) he alone knows: others may only approach certitude through sharing in the common definitions of "everyday life." Even the failure to act is choice, for it is an explicit or implicit decision *not* to act. Still, the desire to change one's environment is seen to be such a central factor within the "natural attitude" that Schütz considered "work" the archetypal image of human reality.

Only when the individual is confronted by a problem for which no resolution is proved by the range of typical meanings available in "everyday life" is the "natural attitude" threatened. He is forced at that point – if he would seek a solution – toward a Kierkegaardian "leap or faith" from the "natural attitude" to an alternative "finite realm of meaning" – one which fails to share a common cognitive frame with the "natural attitude." One such realm is that of sociology. Man as sociologist is to accept the former world of "everyday life" as his subject matter – his *only* subject matter – but in doing so he is to superimpose an additional layer of typicalities that are justified by the aims of the new province. He does so by constructing ideal types through the method of *verstehen* in the manner of a Max Weber, especially models of "rational" actions. To these he applies the logic and standards of verification common to the larger community of natural science, except that Schütz would not limit the term "empirical observation" to sensory perceptions of the "outer" world, but would extend its meaning to include that experience "by which common sense thinking in everyday life understands human actions and their outcomes in terms of their underlying motives or goals." [3]

The aim of such a social science, Schütz tells us, is to reconstruct, in a simplified manner, the fashion in which "healthy, wideawake adults" interpret their world. Yet it does not purport to be identical, even in principle, with that world: it self-consciously distorts the "natural attitude" by abstracting from it those aspects which fit the fully systematic model appropriate to the ends of science. The result is an image of social man as but a puppet of the typicalities of sociation and in reference to which such terms as "motive," "action," or "project" – immediately appropriate to the realm of the "natural attitude of everyday life" – should always, when confronted within the province of science, be interpreted as if in quotation marks. It is a distortion that must be justified by the systematic understanding – and thus predictive utility – afforded by the latter realm of meaning.

Though much of this is compelling, it is startling to discover that Schütz could then go on to portray the sociologist *qua* sociologist as aloof, detached, and completely uninvolved in "action"; as impinging only upon the cognitive dimension of existence; as *merely* an observer and not an actor in the world about him. Indeed, he goes so far as to state that his theoretical activity may not even be considered "work" – a crucial clue to the status he would grant sociology – and, apparently, all of the pure sciences – when one recalls that "work," to Schütz, served as paradigm for human reality. Indeed, scientific activity is viewed as a point of refuge where, having made the "leap" into disinterestedness, the sociologist and his bretheren may somehow now find themselves freed even of that existential anxiety that was posited as the source of the suspension of doubt in "everyday reality." It is clear that he has, with relative accuracy, described the "natural attitude" reflected in the everyday

---

[3] Schütz, *Collected Papers I*, p. 65.

G

life of the *sociologist of his day*; yet his naive acceptance of that self image places the utility of Schütz' entire effort in question.

The phenomenological task draws its fundamental attractiveness from its claim: the assertion that it is able to deal cognitively, systematically, and reliably with the *intra*subjective as well as the intersubjective. Added to this has been its appreciation of existentialism's fundamental point of reference (the threat of "non-being") and the genetic and dialectical relationship which the two philosophic postures have demonstrated over the years; the manner in which man – even "social" man – is viewed in his primal form as "actor" rather than as "respondent"; its corresponding emphasis upon change rather than stability; its provision for fundamentally discrete realms that are incapable of containment within a common *cognitive* schema; the awareness of the manner in which the product of a science is limited by its assumptions; and the sophisticated manner in which Weber's *verstehen* sociology and the interactionism of Cooley and Mead are interwoven. Yet the cost would appear too great for either the author or the larger discipline of sociology, moving as it is into a period of epistemological self-awareness, to bear.

The root of the trouble lies with Husserl's explicit – and Schütz' implicit – point of departure: the conviction that there was a *presuppositionless* mode of confronting experience which would be amenable to systematic, cognitive and – thus – *reliable* explication; that there could indeed be a "science" built upon a base that included experience that was in principle private in its immediate givenness. In other words, the phenomenological reduction became the twentieth century's peculiar contribution to the perennial quest for certitude that would escape the net of implicit commitment accompanying any presumptive context. That it must instead accept the lable of philosophic predisposition is self-evident from the manner in which it shifted its complexion from a radical psychologism through a "neutralism" to a transcendental idealism even at the hands of Husserl himself and, upon the latter's death, was splintered into a wide variety of disputatious "schools" by those who survived to claim his mantle.

The pretention of freedom from substantive assumptions manifested by the phenomenological reduction was carried over immediately to a comparable pretention regarding the suspension of doubt that is the *epoché* of the "natural attitude": the world that is "everyday life" is treated as self-evidently an "ultimate" or "paramount" reality and becomes the center of Schütz' attention. Some have been tempted to identify such a "natural attitude" with an acceptance of the reality of the immediately given within the full range of man's inter- and intrasubjective experience. This is the tack taken by Gibson Winter's recent and provocative *Elements for a Social Ethic: Scientific and Ethical Perspectives on Social Process.*[4] Unfortunately, it is quite clear that this was *not* Schütz' intention. The latter would restrict such a "natural attitude" to the *typicalities* that frame a "wide-awake" and doubt-

[4] Gibson Winter, *Elements for a Social Ethic: Scientific and Ethical Perspectives on Social Process* (Macmillan, 1966).

free apprehension of "everyday life": it is not designed to encompass all of experience, even all of social experience. Rather it is self-consciously limited to a single "province of meaning" which is reputedly shared socially as the "natural" one in the routines of the adult workaday world. It is this "world" from which the individual is seen to turn only when confronted with a "problem" which is unresolvable within it – with a "shock "that breaks the limits of the "natural attitude" and forces one to leap into another "finite province of meaning."

One of the latter is, as we noted earlier, the realm of social science. But even sociology, according to Schütz, must limit itself to second-order typologies of the first-order typifications that form the content of the "natural attitude". The appropriate empirical referent of one's sociological conceptualization, then, is doubly narrowed thereby – a renunciation that is not likely to be accepted by a discipline that has often exhibited an even more voracious appetite for the socially atypical than for the typical. And when one notes the substantive nature of those areas that must be ruled out because they fall outside the realm of the "natural attitude of everyday life" – those social phenomena which reflect unresolved conflict or are in response to atypical crisis situations on the one hand or which depart radically from the archetypal image of "work," as "play" would appear to do, on the other – one is forced to conclude that the limitation not only will not do but should not do.

The phenomenological tradition, as it is mediated by Alfred Schütz, then, is unsuited in its present form for either the immediate or contextual needs of sociology. It founders initially in its claim to be both presuppositionless *and* reliable; its attempt to escape a positivistic realism on the one side and a naive idealism on the other results for sociology in a methodological reification of a mundane and doubly typified "everyday life" drained of the leven of both fundamental anxiety and play; and it perceives the sociologist *qua* sociologist not only in the discredited and simplistic "value-free" terms that dominated the sociology of the forties and the fifties but goes further to deny him even the active quality denoted by "work". As impressive as its aim to safeguard the subjective, purposive dimension of experience may be, the price asked cannot help but be deemed unrealistic by a sociology approaching epistemological sophistication.

This is not to say that fruitful revisions of the phenomenological lineage represented by Schütz may not be forthcoming. Indeed, one of the most intriguing would appear in process of development at the hands of Peter Berger. Though acknowledging major debt to Schütz – as his works to date clearly testify – Berger adds an accent that is decidedly his own. Rather than penning sociology within the narrow boundaries of a scheme of second-order typifications and perceiving its aim as but the reconstruction of the commonsense world of man living his everyday life among his fellow men, he would allow its subject matter to encompass both the broad range of "social facts" of a Durkheim and the empathetic sensitivity of a Weber and seek to shake man free – even if but for the moment – of the fictions that he himself has constructed quite unselfconsciously into an "everyday reality" that in fact serves to imprison and manipulate him. Though Schütz, too, recognizes "commonsense reality" as a human product, he treats it with almost sacred regard – as all of us tend to treat that which we view as of paramount reality. Berger, however, would *de*sacralize it as our larger tradition would desacralize all that is but the product of man himself. The "natural attitude" toward "everyday life" becomes, in Berger's hands and those of his associates, not the be-all and the end-all of the entire sociological enterprise but rather an exceptionally fruitful focus for an enlarged exercise in the sociology of knowledge.[5] Where Schütz would have sociology simply seek to "understand" that "commonsense world" – to reproduce its typicalities in a second-order, determinate frame – Berger conceives our discipline as a medium by which we are able to transcend the determinate forms and meanings we ourselves as men have given it. In other words, through a process analogous to the manner in which the psychoanalyst assists his patient in uncovering and thus apprehending the compulsive routines and meanings he himself had fashioned in response to the felt need for security, the sociologist may, through the format of an expanded grasp of the sociology of knowledge, portray to the layman the manner in which society – or one of its sub-systems – routinizes its own structures and meanings in the name of "reality" or "the natural" and so subjects men to a socialized prison of their own making or, when those norms have been unselfconsciously internalized (as they are typically held to have been), to the unauthentic life of the puppet. When the genesis of a particular social compulsion, cognitive or behavioral, has been carefully and accurately described – and apprehended as such – the conditions necessary to transcendence are at hand. One then becomes capable of "standing outside" the internalized norm, the prescribed role, the cultural expectation, or the structural niche for a shorter or longer period. Indeed, the cognitive norms of the language of contemporary sociology itself – role, system, generalized other – are themselves seen as socially derived fictions equally capable, in principle, of transcendence.

The attractiveness, then, of a phenomenologically *informed* format for the sociology of the 1970's may be quite formidable. It will have to take the general direction of the Berger modification, however, if it would seek paradigmatic stature, for the posture of Alfred Schütz – following hard upon that of Husserl – might be termed essentially a *priestly* one: satisfied with proximate communication of that which is deemed to be of paramount reality rather than motivated by the claim of transcendence. And there is considerable evidence to suggest that sociology is now edging – and can be expected in the immediate future to move – back toward the *prophetic* posture which was its original seedbed. That Berger has built up abundant momentum in the latter direction is self-evident.

But the strength of Berger's posture is also its weakness – at least *vis a vis* its acceptability as paradigm for the many within the discipline who continue to view sociology as a science related to the larger domain of natural

---

[5] Berger and Luckmann, *op. cit.*

science. As influential as his *Invitation to Sociology* has been, it was greeted – when reviewed in the profession's major official journal by one of the discipline's less conservative minds – with undisguised hostility as an attempt to transform an even-tempered science into a "debunking" exercise.[6] Perhaps the subtitle Berger gave the volume – *A Humanistic Perspective* – provides the crucial clue. The larger body of sociologists in America, though they are becoming aware of the manner in which the social sciences may begin to serve as a bridge between the "two cultures," will not in the immediately forseeable future be willing to renounce their image of sociology as a science nor return to the *Wissenschaft* definition traditional to the continent, encompassing as it does *any* systematic cognitive endeavor. Yet the latter represents, by and large, the intellectual context out of – and in terms of – which Berger speaks. This is not to say that it is wrongheaded. Such a return may well be our appropriate destiny in the longer run and Berger, again, one of those who will prepare the way. At the very least it represents a spring to which the more segmented, specialized inclinations of the New World have periodically returned for creative insight and the breaking of parochial linguistic habits and which gives every appearance of maintaining the strength necessary to play a similarly liberating role in the future. But from the evidence that is the state of contemporary sociology it is quite clear that such a frame places too great a burden on the undeniably attractive vision that Berger has begun to share with the larger profession and makes his imagery incapable at the moment of winning a clear cut victory in the battle for paradigmatic supremacy or even for serving as the basis for a collaborative ceasefire.

The test of the Berger version of the phenomenological posture, then, must await the passage of a decade or more by which time he and his associates and students will have blocked out more fully the range of its implications and resolved those apparent inconsistencies that are the price of any major new theoretic departure. By that time, too, those generations of graduate students who returned during the 1960's to the "prophetic" sensitivity abandoned by their predecessors in the late forties will be an increasingly dominant factor in the discipline's corporate life. Among those issues that one would expect by that time to have been resolved would be Berger's apparent reluctance, in the midst of an insistence that sociology be seen as a "debunking" dialect aimed at establishing conditions which would make transcendence of a given social reality possible, to in fact give up the traditional "value-free" characterization of the discipline;[7] the related legacy of

---

[6] Philip Selznick, "Review of *Invitation to Sociology*," *American Sociological Review*, XXIX (April 1964), 285–6.

[7] "... our conception of sociology ... does not imply ... that it cannot be 'value-free.'" Berger and Luckmann, *op. cit.*, p. 173. Berger had spoken to the issue in a more positive manner earlier when he argued, in *Invitation to Sociology* (Doubleday-Anchor, 1963), that there was nothing ethically reprehensible in ethical neutrality as such. That the issue may lie simply in the breadth of his image of ethical- or value-neutrality is suggested, perhaps, by his further observation that "Machiavellianism, be it political or sociological, is a way of looking, in itself ethically neutral" (*ibid.*, pp. 152–3).

Husserl and Schütz which argues that the sociological enterprise appropriately strives to be but "an act of pure perception";[8] a clarification of the essential difference, if any, between his expanded image of a sociology of knowledge and sociological theory, humanistically conceived, in general; and his apparent unwillingness to assign the processes involved in the structuring of a given "reality of every day life" ontological status equivalent to those that contribute to its transcendence – in other words, his inability to date to grant those forces that would guarantee stability to the flux that is human social experience the same stature he would give the disjunctive.

Drew University

---

[8] *Ibid.*, p. 5.

SOCIAL-PSYCHOLOGICAL THEORY AS A BASIS FOR A THEORY OF ETHICS AND VALUE: THE CASE OF CHARLES HORTON COOLEY †

JOHN W. PETRAS

The volume is somewhat of an anomaly in sociological literature, but it is none the less welcome for its very non-conformity.[1]

The above statement by George E. Vincent in his 1903 review of Charles Horton Cooley's *Human Nature and the Social Order* can serve to give the reader some indication of the nature of Cooley's ideas relative to the mainstream of early American sociology. In combining the study of social organization with an interactionist social psychology, Cooley was implementing the psychological works of John Dewey and George Herbert Mead at the social level. The effect of this combination was to establish the social group as something more than a mere aggregate of individuals. Besides adding a new dimension to American sociology, Cooley became one of the founders of the approach later to be named "symbolic interaction theory."

Whereas the interactionism which characterized the works of John Dewey and George Herbert Mead had contributed mainly to an understanding of the processes of human behavior, Cooley expanded upon this aspect and complemented it with a structural component making the social psychological theories of Dewey and Mead applicable to the study of society. In his application of these theories, Cooley hoped to establish a new framework for the study of man in society. To this end, he emphasized the need for both a new theory of society and a new methodology.[2]

---

† I would like to thank Floyd Dotson, Jerold Heiss, Walter Wardwell, and especially Joseph Zygmunt for their criticisms and suggestions on this paper. Special thanks are due to Herbert Blumer, Gisela Hinkle, and Roscoe C. Hinkle, all of whom took the time to offer suggestions and criticisms of an earlier draft of this paper.

[1] From George E. Vincent's review of *Human Nature and the Social Order, American Journal of Sociology*, VIII (1903), 559.

[2] Concerning the development of his own thought, Cooley writes, "I resorted to writers of little system but great wisdom, to Emerson, chiefly as a young man, then to Goethe, and, in lesser measure, to Bagehot, William James and many others" – "The Development of Sociology at Michigan," in *Sociological Theory and Social Research* (New York: Henry Holt and Co., 1930), p. 4. Regarding Dewey, "The chief thing I now recall from his lectures is a criticism of Spencer, in which Dewey maintained that society was an organism ... and language its 'sensorium.'" – p. 6. He also notes that before writing *Human Nature and the Social Order*, James Mark Baldwin's two major works were reviewed – p. 9. Although

In the pragmatic tradition of Dewey, William James, and Mead, Cooley developed an interest in the future of civilization, and much of his work became directed toward the end of understanding the role and function of democracy in modern industrial society. The impression is clearly gained from these writings that this interest played a crucial role in refining the concept of the small group which became the cornerstone of Cooley's sociological theory. My purpose in this paper is to point out the relationship between the social psychological and social philosophical theories of Cooley, and to demonstrate how Cooley utilized his theories in social psychology to provide a framework for the development of a theory of ethics and values as related to behavior.

Throughout his works, Cooley reiterated his belief that any valid explanation of society had to account for its two characteristic properties. These were its organic nature, and, on the other hand, its mental nature. As structure, society was to be conceived of and analyzed in terms of its organic form. As social organization, society exists in the minds of individuals, and this is what makes it real for its members. Cooley points out, however, that any unification of a social mind exists not through agreement among the members, but through the reciprocal influence of their being mutually dependent elements within a society.[3]

One of the implications of this view was that the so-called problem areas of the city did not represent an absence of moral values, but a different interpretation of the values which was based upon one's own interactional situation. For Cooley, the role of interaction between the individual and the environment is uppermost because it mediates between an interpretation based solely upon social determinants and one based solely upon individualistic determinants. Cooley is quick to point out that the social environment need not be bad in itself in order to have a bad effect upon the individual, and he uses the analogy of two persons, neither of whom is bad in himself, yet each having a bad influence upon the other.[4] Any degenerate side of the social environment is as natural a part of it as the "normal" side, and tends to appear when the better influences are relaxed. Any study of social problems, therefore, has to develop a frame of reference in which the concept of "cause" gives way to the concept of organic development. This, in turn, becomes the principle upon which the control of the future of civilization through intelligent planning is based.[5] At this point, it is well to take note of

Cooley claims to have had "already arrived at a somewhat similar view" by the time he studied under Dewey, I must agree with Charles Ellwood who writes that "... there can scarcely be any doubt about Dewey's influence upon Cooley. Any one who is familiar with the thought of both man can hardly fail to notice this. Indeed, Cooley's sociological thought seems ... to have been built upon the philosophical perceptions of Dewey" – "Charles Horton Cooley," *Sociology and Social Research*, XIV (1929–1930), 4–5.

  [3] *Social Organization* (New York: Charles Scribner's Sons, 1909), p. 4.

  [4] *Social Process* (New York: Charles Scribner's Sons, 1918), pp. 155–156.

  [5] *Ibid.*, p. 164. Floyd House characterizes this position as Cooley's greatest contribution to sociology, "... The thesis that formalism and disorganization are not opposite condi-

the fact that many of the examples which Cooley chooses in order to clarify his theories seem to be directly influenced by his concern for the intelligent social planning which is deemed necessary for the survival of a democracy. I shall refer back to this point later in the paper.

While society in the course of everyday interaction is seen as an organism, the ultimate source of the organization of its institutions is to be traced to the individual members, a point which Cooley treats as self-evident.[6] The point to be emphasized is that the only solid facts of social existence, the only tangible ties which people have with one another, are the ideas they have of one another, built up in the course of daily interaction. Two postulates follow, in turn, from this point. First of all, society and its members must be studied by the imagination. Secondly, the imaginations we have of one another become the primary objects of study. The sociological methodology, therefore, becomes that of "imagining imagination," whether the study is to focus on values as an organized system of ideas, or values in relationship to behavior at the individual level.

As the individual's contacts within a society increase over the span of his life time, his ideas or imaginations of the other members of the social order increase. This "evolution of awareness" indicates for Cooley a growing power of sympathy, *i.e.* the ability to enter and share in the minds of other individuals.[7] Sympathy refers to the sharings of any mental state that can be communicated, not to an emotional state. It is sympathy, as sub-vocal communication, not emotion, which bonds the separate individuals of a society into living groups and this moral order, then, presents the content of data for the sociologist.

The logical conclusion of this type of approach can be stated as follows. If the immediate nature of society is to be found in the bonds which exist because of the ideas individuals have of one another, an understanding of society must be directed toward the source of these bonds. The method of sympathetic introspection provides the principle method for the study of man and society. In view of Cooley's ideas concerning the nature of relationships between men, it can be seen that sympathetic introspection allows the social

---

tions but are closely related." – *The Development of Sociology* (New York: McGraw-Hill Book Co., 1936), p. 323. Read Bain takes the position that Cooley's conception of organization saved sociology from the perils of particularism toward which it was heading at the time – "Trends in Sociological Theory," in *Trends in American Sociology*, edd. George A. Lundberg, Read Bain, and Nels Anderson (New York: Harper and Brothers, 1929), p. 81.

[6] See *Human Nature and the Social Order*, p. 84.

[7] *Ibid.*, p. 136. Cooley saw sympathy as a much more complex phenomenon than it appears to be in its definition. In fact, so much enters into this concept as to suggest that by the time we understood one sympathetic experience we should be in a way as to understand the social order itself – *Ibid.*, p. 133. "Sentiment is ... feeling which has been raised by thought and intercourse out of its merely instinctive state and become properly human. ... Thus love is a sentiment, while lust is not .... Sentiment is the chief motive-power of life, and ... lies deeper ... and is less subject to essential change than thought, from which, however, it is not too sharply separated." – *Social Organization*, p. 177.

scientist to approach the core of society. While those non-mental factors which impinge upon society are not unimportant, they are not as important as those which constitute the raw material of social structure. The former are referred to as the material facts of society, the latter as the social facts of society. While the material elements are important because they are essential in the organic whole of life, they are certainly no more so than the ideas and institutions of the group.[8] Knowledge, however, is constituted by awareness in both realms. It is, for the most part, both behavioristic and sympathetic, "the perception or imagination of the external traits is accompanied by sympathy, with the feeling, sentiment or idea that goes with it." [9] The differences of degree which exist between the two types of knowledge can be seen in that Cooley's theories appear to trace the development of human knowledge as moving from the external to the internal. The life process represents a growing facility to enter the minds of individuals while at the same time there is less dependence placed upon material factors of behavior.

While Cooley's methodology introduced a new dimension into the sociological tradition, his lasting influence has been due to many of the concepts which grew along with his proposed techniques. In turning his attention to the smaller groups of society, Cooley popularized the concept of the primary group in the sociological literature.[10] While the importance of this concept has traditionally been restricted in sociological literature to the role which the group plays in the development of the child's sense of self, Cooley himself appears to have formulated the concept within a much broader context. In actuality, the relationship of the self to the primary group appears to be only one element involved in a *triadic* relationship which runs through the writings of Cooley. The second element connects the primary group to an under-

---

[8] "We are too complaisant ... to that prejudice of the physical scientist which identifies the personal with the vague, and wishes to have as little to do with it as possible. Even psychologists are sometimes guilty of this, which for them is a kind of treason" – *Social Process*, p. 168. "An institution is simply a definite and established phase of the public mind, not different in its ultimate nature from public opinion, though often seeming, on account of its permanence and the visible symbols and customs in which it is clothed, to have a somewhat distinct and independent existence" – *Social Organization*, p. 313.

[9] "The Roots of Social Knowledge," in *Sociological Theory and Social Research*, p. 295.

[10] Cooley was not the first to use the term. As S. C. Lee notes, it was first used in the Small and Vincent text – see "The Primary Group As Cooley Defines It," *Sociological Quarterly*, V (1964), 23. Cooley first used the concept in *Social Organization* which was published in 1909. A student, F. R. Clow writes that it was in 1900 that Cooley began mentioning the concept in his lectures – "Cooley's Doctrine of Primary Groups," *American Journal of Sociology*, XXV (1919–1920), 326. Cooley denied that the concept was a very major contribution and claimed to have added it to *Social Organization* after he had read the first draft and there seemed to be something missing. He expressed the hope that if he were to be remembered for anything it would not be this concept – see E. C. Jandy, *Charles Horton Cooley: His Life and His Social Theory* (New York: Dryden Press, 1942), p. 179. At his death, an editorial in *Sociology and Social Research* proclaimed, "The concept of primary groups is ... Professor Cooley's leading contribution to sociological thought" – XIII (1928–1929), 503.

standing of what constitutes human nature. Related to this and the development of the self is the third component, *i.e.* Cooley's concern for the future of
democracy and the future of mankind as embodied in the idea of freedom.
All three elements are bound up in the concept of the primary group, and the
writings of Cooley convey the impression that this is the way in which each
of the items is to be understood; all as part of the larger relationship. The
remainder of this paper concerns itself with that triadic relationship.

Chapter III of *Social Organization* begins with the following well-known
statement:

> By primary groups I mean those characterized by intimate face-to-face association and
> co-operation. They are primary in several senses, but chiefly in that they are funda-
> mental in forming the social nature and ideals of the individual.[11]

The result of the early intimate association characteristic of such groups is
the development of a feeling best described as "we." There are several spheres
of this intimate association, but one can single out the most common as being
the family and the play-group of children. It is essential for the social scientist
to recognize, however, that the characteristics of intimate association and
co-operation do not necessarily signify the existence of harmony and love.
Being part of an organic system, the group is always differentiated to some
degree and, therefore, the unity involved becomes best described as a competi-
tive unity. How, then, are such groups primary? First of all, they give the individual his earliest and fullest experience of unity with a larger social order.
Secondly, although they do change, the change is not to the same degree as
that which characterizes more extended social relations. It is not unicharac-
teristic then, for one's own self to become an integral part of the purpose of
the group.

It is of interest at this time to point out that in *Human Nature and the
Social Order*, which was published seven years prior to *Social Organization*,
Cooley spoke of human nature as existing on three different levels. He spoke
of human nature in the sense of a strict hereditary nature of man; a nature
which changes very slowly, and is manifested as uniform impulses and capacities. This nature of man has changed but little from its form in our ancestors
of a thousand years ago. There is also a nature more social in character which
develops in the primary groups found in all societies. Here, for example, one
learns an awareness of his self in relation to others and a moral sense of right
or wrong which is always relative to the standards of a particular group.
Finally, Cooley speaks of a human nature which has reference to more
specific forms of behavior. As examples, Cooley mentions the identification
of such behavior as liberalism or conservatism, pacifism or belligerancy, *etc.*,
as being identified as an aspect of human nature. As the type of human nature

---

[11] *Social Organization*, p. 23. Ellwood sees this book as a convenient starting point for
categorizing modern sociological theory. "The Development of Sociology in the United
States Since 1910" – *op. cit.*, 26.

moves from the first to the third level, it becomes more and more changeful, the latter being especially so because of its high degree of susceptability to social influences. Incorporating all three levels, human nature is used to refer to the phenomenon of "teachability."

By the time of the publication of *Social Organization*, human nature was emphasized only in terms of the second level, and it was identified exclusively with the primary group:

> It is the nature which is developed and expressed in those simple, face-to-face groups that are somewhat alike in all societies; groups of the family, the playground, and the neighborhood. In the essential similarity of these is to be found the basis, in experience, for similar ideas and sentiments in the human mind. In these, everywhere, human nature comes into existence. Man does not have it at birth; he cannot acquire it except through fellowship, and it decays in isolation... What else can human nature be but a trait of primary groups.[12]

We may say, then, that human nature is characterized by a plasticity which is embodied in the primary group. In any attempt to institute successful social reform in society, *i.e.* change the values of people, the social scientist must direct his efforts at the primary groups of society. Cooley is most emphatic on this particular point because it is in these groups that the individual acquires the ability to adapt himself to changing social conditions, an ability which is indispensible if civilization is to survive.

Although the importance of the primary group cannot be denied with regard to the development of a sense of self and social intelligence in the child, Cooley did not take a deterministic position with regard to its influence. His interest in these matters probably began in the late 1800's when he entered the debate surrounding Galton's *Heriditary Genius*. Referring to an earlier article by William James on the relationship of genius to heredity and environment, Cooley makes note of the role of the social group and ends with the following vivid analogy:

> On the whole it seems to me that the relation between genius and fame is fairly well represented by the comparison... of a farmer sowing mixed seeds in a furrow which traverses a great variety of ground. Here many come up and flourish, there none, and there again only those of a certain sort. The seed-bag is the race, the soil historical conditions other than race, the seeds genius, and the crop fame.[13]

This perspective of viewing behavior and intelligence in terms of interaction processes was systematically stated by the time Cooley published *Social Process*. In this work he was quick to caution against the entire dismissal of hereditary factors in discussing particular forms of behavior. There has, to the present time, he notes, not yet been established any reasonable doubt that

---

[12] *Ibid.*, 30.

[13] "Genius, Fame, and the Comparison of Races," in *Sociological Theory and Social Research*, p. 158.

differences in natural capacity may enter in an explanation of such factors as social problems and poverty.

Perhaps no one notion summed up the idea of interaction between individual and social elements in the social situation better than the famous concept of the "looking-glass self." The "reflections" which the individual received from the group were of such a nature that no individual ever became an exact copy of the group. In an article which preceded his famous exposition of the Looking-Glass self by three years, Cooley remarked:

> The moral standards which the individual applies to his own conduct are always the reflection, more or less individualized, of those of his social environment, of the group, or complex of groups, of which he forms a part....[14]

In setting forth the principles for his own theory of self-development, Cooley acknowledged his debt to the earlier works of the psychologist James Mark Baldwin, especially as the latter's thoughts were contained in *Social and Ethical Interpretations in Mental Development*.[15] Cooley's theory, however, was a definite advance over the theory of Baldwin in that he did not tie the notion of self-development in the child to the idea of recapitulation and the process of imitation – both of these being factors which led to the eventual disrepute of Baldwin's theories in social-psychological circles. On the other hand, while this concept in the theories of Cooley represented an advance over the ideas of Baldwin, he provided no attempt at an explanation as to how the individual and social processes operated in the development of a self. On this particular problem, therefore, the approach of Cooley stands mid-way between the approaches of Baldwin and George Herbert Mead. Mead's greatest contribution was to provide a satisfactory explanation of the genesis of self in terms of a particular process. Baldwin had attempted an explanation of a particular type of process, but failed. Cooley cannot claim to have attempted or accomplished either.

For Cooley, the distinguishing feature of the child at birth is his large capacity for social learning. This capacity is not a specific thing, but of a general nature which is characterized by plasticity, defined by Cooley as "sociability." At this stage the child is little more than a collection of impulses and his sole purpose of activity at this level of existence is to obtain satisfaction of these impulses. Social experience, as mediated through the primary groups, begins to shape the child into a moral entity and gives a particular slant to the development of his self. The actual "feeling" of a sense

---

[14] "Personal Competition," in *Sociological Theory and Social Research*, p. 194.

[15] Cooley acknowledges his debt to Baldwin in "Personal Competition," *op. cit.*, p. 201. Richard Dewey does not see very much difference between the approach of Cooley and the earlier theory of Baldwin, and he suggests that the best way of seeing their relationship is one where Cooley's approach complements that of Baldwin because it was approached from the sociological, rather than psychological perspective – "Charles Horton Cooley: Pioneer in Psychosociology," in *An Introduction to the History of Sociology*, ed. Harry Barnes (Chicago: University of Chicago Press), 1948, p. 847.

of self appears to develop from a growing sense of power or control, *i.e.* the idea that the individual himself is a cause. Paralleling the ability of control, is the progressive unfolding process of the self, analogous, according to Cooley, to the processes of evolution which are manifest throughout nature. Finally, reality is given to the self through the gaining of an identity. The individual obtains the identity when he becomes represented in the minds of others.[16] The self becomes referred to as primarily an "imaginative fact." [17] To understand the self and its processes, therefore,:

> Persons and society must be ... studied primarily in imagination. It is true, *prima facie*, that the best way of observing things is that which is most direct; and I do not see how we can hold that we know persons directly except as imaginative ideas in the mind.[18]

In the process of child development, it is the primary group which plays the most important role in the fostering of intelligence, a sense of morality, and the development of human nature. Its function in the genesis of the self and its corresponding processes can be stated as its playing the primary role in *teaching the child how to realize his selfhood:*

> The meaning of "I" and "mine" is learned in the same way that the meanings of hope, regret, chagrin, disgust, and thousands of other words or emotion or sentiments are learned; that is, by having the feeling, imputing it to others in some kind of expansion, and hearing the word along with it. As to its communication and growth, the self idea is in no way peculiar that I see, but essentially like other ideas.[19]

In 1908 Cooley published his now famous observations of his own children which verified the theoretical statements made earlier in *Human Nature and the Social Order.*[20] Some thirty years later, Read Bain utilized Cooley's method in the observation of his own children and reached the same conclusion, *i.e.*, "The child knows other selves before he knows his own. It is out of his responses to theirs that his 'consciousness of self' arises, together with the appropriate verbal symbols for naming it." [21] Social-psychological well-

---

[16] *Human Nature and the Social Order* (1902), p. 89. When the "I" of the individual's self incorporates other persons, there arises a "we" or group self – (Revised Edition), p. 209.

[17] *Ibid.*, p. 210.

[18] *Ibid.*, p. 86.

[19] *Ibid.*, pp. 160–161. The role of language is important because its use always includes the thought of other persons. Language cannot be disassociated from personal intercourse in the mind. Higher thought demands language, and therefore, is a kind of imaginary conversation. This, of course, is identical with the statements of Mead and Dewey on thought – see, Revised Edition, pp. 130–131, and 92.

[20] "A Study of the Use of Self-Words by a Child". *Psychological Review*, XV (1908), 339–357.

[21] "The Self-And-Other Words of a Child," *American Journal of Sociology*, XLI (1935 1936), 767–775. It might be noted that G. Stanley Hall, in so many ways ahead of the

being refers to the ability of the individual to maintain an equilibrium between the plasticity of his human nature, and the stability which is afforded him by the development of his ideal self as an inducement to betterment. This, then, represents the relationship between the primary group and the genesis of the self as handled by Cooley, and this portion of his theories remains the best known to the present day. In conclusion, let me point to the completion of the relationship as envisioned by Cooley, *i.e.* the triadic relationship between primary group, self, and democracy.

Intertwined with the concept of democracy is the concept of freedom which follows very closely the framework as laid down by John Dewey and his circle of social philosophers. In *Social Process*, for example, Cooley wrote that freedom exists within the social organization of society and not in isolation from it:

> Instead of restricting individuality, as many imagine, civilization, so far as it is a free civilization, works quite the other way.[22]

If it is the social order that offers freedom, it follows that the opportunity for freedom will grow as the social order grows in complexity, and this is the line of thought pursued by Cooley:

> It is only in a larger and complex social system that an advanced degree of it is possible, because nothing else can supply the multifarious opportunities by means of which all sorts of persons can work out a congenial development through the choice of influence.[23]

The process which Cooley defined as "sociability" (the diffuse capacity for learning) was essential to the exercise of freedom as epitomized in the democratic society. The ability to learn sympathy must be fostered at the primary level. Facing the problem of change head-on, Cooley points out the complexity of the relationship between man, values, and society. As society grows and develops in complexity, social change itself accelerates, one

developments of his day, published a similar study in 1897. His study was carried out over a three year period and was based upon the idea of self in small children as observed by their teachers. "Some Aspects of the Early Sense of Self," *American Journal of Psychology*, IX (1897–1898), 351–395.

[22] *Social Process*, p. 95. "The notion of an opposition between organism and freedom is a phase of the 'individualistic' psychology which regarded social unity as artificial . . ." – p. 29.

[23] *Human Nature and the Social Order*, p. 397. This view became popularized through Mary P. Follett's *Creative Experiences* (New York: Longmans, Green and Co., 1924), and *The New State* (New York: Longmans, Green and Co., 1918). The reception which these works received in sociology was contingent upon the theoretical commitment of the particular sociologist. Thus, her approach was either "totally unrealistic" – R. C. Smith, "Review of Mary P. Follett's Creative Experience," *Social Forces*, IXI (1925), 540–542 – or exhibited "a closeness to reality" – Arthur E. Wood, "The Social Philosophy of Mary P. Follett," *Social Forces*, IV (1926), 759–769.

of the consequences being the loss of moral control over the individual by
the fading primary group sources. For example:

> The relaxation of the family is due ... to changes progressive on the whole, but in-
> volving much incidental demoralization, being in general those arising from a some-
> what rapid decay of old traditions and disciplines and a consequent dependence upon
> human impulse and reason.[24]

In attempting to formulate a solution to this problem, Cooley suggested an
approach remarkably similar to the one proposed by the French sociologist,
Emile Durkheim:

> We need, then, a system of social groups, corresponding to the system of functions in
> society, each group having *esprit de corps*, emulation and standards with itself, and
> all animated with a spirit of loyalty and service to the whole. To achieve this would
> call for no change in human nature, but only in the instigation and direction of its
> impulses, it would mean chiefly finer association and clearer ideals of merit among
> those pursuing the several functions ... Freedom, self-expression, and the competitive
> spirit would be cherished, but would not degenerate into irresponsible individualism.[25]

If security is one of the by-products of freedom, then the greatest threat to
freedom comes from the danger of rigidity in the social order. Social change,
therefore, becomes viewed as necessary and not condemned as many of Cooley's critics would have it. Cooley writes that:

> There is nothing more democratic than intelligent and devoted nonconformity, be-
> cause it means that the individual is giving his freedom and courage to the service of
> the whole. Subservience, to majorities, as to any other authority, tends to make
> vigorous democracy impossible.[26]

Through the rational application of his knowledge to the social order, man
can enhance the possibilities for freedom within the social order. In strong
opposition to those who adhered to an older psychology which equated freedom with individuality, Cooley remarks:

> Intelligent social prediction is contradictory to determinism because instead of ignor-
> ing the creative will, it accepts it and endeavors by sympathy to enter into it and fore-
> see it working. If I predict an artistic or humanitarian movement, it is partly because
> I feel as if I myself, with whatever freedom and creative power is within me, would
> choose to share in such a movement.[27]

---

[24] *Social Organization*, pp. 370–371. The low moral level of the economic motive is due,
in large part, to the doctrine of "economic man," which teaches ... that society functions
best when each man strives after what *he* considers gain – *Social Process*, p. 135. "The
idea that the right is social opposed to the sensual is, it seems to me, a sound one, if we
mean by it that the mentally higher more personal or imaginative impulses have on the
whole far more weight in conscience than the more impersonal" – *Human Nature and the
Social Order*, p. 347.

[25] *Social Process*, p. 143.

[26] *Ibid.*, p. 381.

[27] *Ibid.*, p. 401.

Cooley's vision of a "creative freedom" and the future of democracy lie in early education in order that the spirit of co-operation, the sense of organic belonging, may begin in the formative years. The future of democracy lies with the primary groups of society which function to develop this sense of consciousness in the child. As the child expands from an individual self-realization and consciousness to a social consciousness, he becomes part of the larger political order, because the general or public phase of the larger consciousness is, according to Cooley, what we call democracy. The school, while not a primary group in itself, has an important role to play because it is at school that "... the children learn group forms of play, in which they are accustomed to strive for a whole and to put success above their private aims ...." [28] In sum, Cooley postulates a direct relationship between democracy, freedom, and the primary group because:

> The guiding force back of public will, now as ever, is of course, human nature itself in its more enduring characteristics, those which find expression in primary groups and are little affected by institutional changes. This nature, familar yet inscrutable, is apparently in a position to work itself out more adequately than at any time in the past. [29]

In concentrating upon what I see as a triadic relationship in the theories of Cooley, I have attempted to point out several features of his thought. First of all, it is important to recognize the total context in which the concept of the primary group was utilized. Secondly, this utilization has been only partly emphasized in present day discussions of Cooley. Finally, I have attempted to demonstrate that many criticisms of Cooley, such as the following one by Rosenberg and Humphrey, are rooted in the mistaken latter-day interpretation which constitute the second point. This statement is representative of the most general criticism levelled at Cooley in modern sociology:

> By his "selective inattention" to the seemy [sic] side of human nature, Cooley romanticized the primary group.... He also closed his eyes to the characteristic features of modern social life, in which mankind realizes itself but little and seldom gratifies its primary needs .... This is a sample of Cooley's thinking. Even those who pay homage to it make certain reservations in the interest of consistency. They have thrown progress over-board. Nostalgia remains. It can be seen in the "professional ideology of social pathologists," in every dichotomy that begins with the enoblement of "folk culture" whose priority is contrasted with the horrors of civilization ....[30]

---

[28] *Ibid.*, p. 421. Whereas Mead emphasized the value of play in terms of self development, Cooley is also concerned with its value in preparing individuals for life in a particular type of social order. "Without healthy play, especially group play, human nature cannot rightly develop, and to preserve this, in the midst of the crowding and aggressive commercialism of our cities, is coming to be seen as a special need of the time" – *Social Organization*, p. 49.

[29] *Social Organization*, p. 419.

[30] Bernard Rosenberg and Norman D. Humphrey, "The Secondary Nature of the Primary Group," *Social Research*, XXII (1955), 35 and 38.

H

To say that Cooley "closed his eyes to the characteristic features of modern social life" undermines the very rationale which Cooley emphasized in his calling for the establishment of *new* primary groups – a point which escapes critics. As has been stated, Cooley did not believe that the traditional primary groups of family and neighborhood would remain the most influential controls upon the individual's behavior. This mistaken conception has, in turn, contributed to the belief that his theory was implicitly anti-progress. But, progress and the ability to adapt oneself to a changing and complex social order are the defining characteristics of human nature. In actuality, it appears that the emphasis Cooley placed upon the role of the primary group in the life of the individual was in large measure due to his recognition of the passing of the folk culture mystique in modern American society. In short, the stabilization process which many critics see as the essential characteristic of the primary group takes the form of adaptability to change. It is upon this foundation that the moral systems of both the individual and society are to be based in modern society. The "horrors" of civilization result from a lack of fulfillment of human nature, and human nature is plasticity.

Discussion

In the above presentation, I have attempted to demonstrate how Cooley based his social philosophy upon a foundation provided by his social psychology. In this respect, Cooley's approach to questions of ethics and value can be seen as an extension of the organic and mental principle which he believed governed all social life. Thus, it is out of the organic relationship with society that the individual learns sentiments which serve to counter-act and to re-direct the impulsive aspect of his personality. Since sentiments are learned only within the context of the social group, questions of value can arise only in relationship to a particular social order. In order for social acts to take on a valuational nature, the key defining characteristics of the act must become located in sentiments and not impulses. For example, all acts involving a moral or value decision involve a consideration of the possible responses of others at an overt or covert level. Simply stated, all problems of value are problems of conscience, and all problems of conscience are problems of social reality. There is, then, no sharp difference between acts of value and other social acts. The heightened mental conflict which may appear at the time of value decision arises from the fact that acts of value are, by definition, removed from the impulsive level and, taking place solely at the level of sentiments, simply foster an illusion that greater conflict is present. Illusion best describes this process for it represents not a greater conflict, but a greater awareness of the conflicting alternatives from which a choice is to be made. Moral choices, therefore, are part of the total range of choices which confront the individual during his lifetime. Accordingly, as individual psychologies will differ on the basis of the society in which they are found, so too will individual consciences differ. To the extent that we can speak of psychological differentiation between individuals, we can also speak of an ethical differentiation.

Now, the question arises as to whether or not society provides us with an ultimate criterion of value. Cooley's answer is an emphatic "no," and again he falls back upon his interactionist psychology as an explanation. All moral decisions involve the thoughts of others. But, all decisions are made by the unique individual. This position on values is the logical outcome of a social psychology which stresses that the individual and the society merely represent different sides of the same coin. The implication of this for the question of the universality of values becomes obvious. There can be no universal values, because values, as all facts of social life, are products of the individual's interaction experience in the society. The closest that Cooley comes to expressing an affinity for the concept of the universality of values is with regard to his idea that the primary group, in some form, is a universal to all societies. If they are universal, then the types of responses which are characteristic of the primary group may have a universal existence. Thus, Cooley singles out loyalty, kindness toward members of the same group relative to members of other groups, and adherence to the customs of one's group as probable universal values. It must be pointed out that in each case the universality of the values is relatively defined. That is to say, the degree to which the values affect the behavior of any individual will depend upon the emphasis which is given to these values in the daily interaction processes. The moral principles which stand out in the mind of the individual represent social habits at the level of conscience. In summary, the relationship between Cooley's social theory and theory of values is one where the latter is simply an extension of the former. Cooley offers no particular solution for dealing with the problem of values because, to his mind, they do not represent a particular problem. Moral values fall within the total range of human interaction experiences.

Central Michigan University

THE "GIVENS" OF CLAUDE LÉVI-STRAUSS

Larry T. Reynolds
Janice M. Reynolds

1. *Introduction*

Recently, sociologists of knowledge and philosophers concerned with epistemology have been asking anew this basic question: Once the structural source of any ideology has been located, or even more generally, once the structural basis of all cultural values and explanations within a particular society have been located, what tasks remain for the sociologist of knowledge?

From its inception the sociology of knowledge has attempted to discover the particular social sources of particular systems of knowledge. The systems of knowledge analyzed within the general framework of the sociology of knowledge have included theological, magical, ideological, and scientific systems of knowledge.

In the analysis of the latter type of knowledge, sociologists of knowledge have often raised questions concerning the scientific validity of certain explanations of phenomena in the social sciences. At this point sociologists of knowledge are divided in their opinions concerning the relevance of the sociology of knowledge for assessing the validity of a given system of knowledge. Those who feel that the sociology of knowledge is useful in assessing the validity have taken one of the three following stances:

I. The first and perhaps most popular stance taken is this: once the link between a given ideology or explanation and either a specific position within one society or a position particular to one type of social organization from whence the ideology or explanation emanates has been established, the explanation can be dismissed as false (invalid). While this position is frequently attributed to Marx it is actually the Durkheimian stance. Durkheim employed this criterion of validity in *The Elementary Forms of the Religious Life*. Once Durkheim located an ideology, totem, concept, myth, or belief within only one culture, he considered this ideology to be culturally limited and hence invalid. This position, although employed by Durkheim at the cross-cultural level to attain the highest level of generality, differs only minorly from the approach used by more recent sociologists of knowledge. A number of these, in analyzing theories of human behavior, have pointed out that behavioral scientists are particularly prone to generalizing their observations of the behavior of the persons of one society to the species *homo sapiens*, without stating the conditions in the structure or social organization of that society which are conducive to the type of behavior observed. Thus by scientific canons the imputed generality of the proposition is invalid, and the limited proposition is often little more than description.

II. Apart from considerations of scientific validity sociologists of knowledge with a historical bent are quick to point out that science and ideas of scientific validity are particular types of knowledge. The scientific type of knowledge also derives from a particular type of social organization. Therefore in assessing the validity of ideas, more general criteria of validity are employed (*i.e.*, M. C. Cornforth in his *Dialectical Materialism*). If the system of ideas lead to the acquisition of additional knowledge which enriches the human condition, then that ideology is not only "good" but valid regardless of where in the structure or in what structure it happens to emanate from.

III. Particular structural positions may produce valid systems of knowledge and others may not or are not likely to. This position was on occasion taken by Marx, *i.e.*, the assumed validity of class-conscious knowledge among the proletariat and Mannheim's recommendation of creating a special position in society for intellectuals.

Not everyone, however, appears to be enthralled at the prospects of ascertaining validity *via* the sociology of knowledge route. There are a number of philosophers and sociologists who argue that the sociology of knowledge has either no relevance or very limited relevance with respect to the assessment of validity. Hinshaw, for example, contends that there is, and can be, no epistemological branch of the sociology of knowledge, and hence epistemological inquiry concerned with the problem of validity is beyond the realm of sociologists of knowledge.[1] Werner Stark likewise feels that sociology of knowledge should not concern itself with validity.[2] Others have attempted to limit the "types of knowledge" to which the perspective is applicable. Zollschan, for instance, feels that the sociology of knowledge cannot properly analyze science as a system of knowledge.[3] He contends, rather, that a special sociology of science should be developed. Actually he assumes the evaluative criteria of science itself and utilizes this criteria to analyze that same science and its practitioners. Simply stated he wishes to use an ideological creation of the bourgeoisie, that is to say science, and apply that standard to analyze bourgeois scientists. A somewhat separate view of the general applicability of the sociology of knowledge exists which states that over and above considerations of validity and the structural sources of

---

[1] Virgil G. Hinshaw, "The Epistemological Relevance of Mannheim's Sociology of Knowledge," *Journal of Philosophy*, XL, No. 3 (February 1943).

[2] Werner Stark, *The Sociology of Knowledge: An Essay in Aid of a Deeper Understanding of the History of Ideas* (London: Routledge and Kegan Paul, 1958).

[3] George Zollschan, *Is Scientific Sociology Possible? – A Disquisition on the Sociology of Science and the State of Art of Sociology* (Proposal for the Research Committee on Sociology of Knowledge, chaired by Kurt Wolff; Washington, D.C., June 1966).

ideology, there remains a vast reservoir of phenomenon which is within the range properly treated by the sociology of knowledge. Among the proponents of this view are Werner Stark and Claude Lévi-Strauss.

Stark, while denying considerations of validity to the sociology of knowledge, holds that there should be a more general sociology of knowledge approach capable of both directing its attention to and analyzing all forms of human understanding.[4] He feels that what now passes for sociology of knowledge is in fact merely sociology of ideology. Stark's own "general" sociology of knowledge is both well known and readily understood. Stark's approach is an elaboration on and combination of the sociology of knowledge perspectives of Max Weber, Emile Durkheim, and Max Scheler.

Claude Lévi-Strauss also supports a general sociology of knowledge, but feels that the framework for such an endeavor already exists in a modification of Marx and Mannheim which needs to be extended and applied to a larger range of "knowledge phenomena" than it has traditionally dealt with.

The remainder of this essay will consist then of a presentation of the analysis of systems of human understanding as presented in *The Savage Mind*, his recently translated treatise. From there, an analysis of Lévi-Strauss in terms of the possible social sources of his concerns and conclusions will be presented.

Prior to a presentation of the basic theses of *The Savage Mind* it is necessary to make explicit to the reader a number of basic assumptions that Lévi-Strauss takes as 'givens'. Some of these basic assumptions are alluded to in *The Savage Mind*[5] but are more strongly elaborated in *Totemism*[6] and *Structural Anthropology*[7] as well as in Rodney Needham's *Structure and Sentiment*.[8] A concise explanation of these 'givens' are listed lest the reader misinterpret the thesis presented in *The Savage Mind*.

The following constitutes a list of Lévi-Strauss' *givens*:

I. That structure is the basic determiner of relevant human behavior. If this given is not remembered, Lévi-Strauss, in the first half of the book, can easily be mistaken for a cultural determinist; however, if one perseveres through the entire book this misconception will probably be erased. One purpose of *The Savage Mind* is, however, to illustrate the impact that culture itself, even though it is structurally produced, can have on the creation of human classificatory systems (we find this a somewhat strange distinction since classificatory systems are part and parcel of culture). Lévi-Strauss is formulating a theory of "superstructures" (culture) because the Marxian perspective to date, in his terms, has "scarcely touched on (it)." Lévi-Strauss, himself a Marxist, gives no credence to culture, ideas, or ideology as the

---

[4] Stark, *op. cit.*

[5] *The Savage Mind* (Chicago: University of Chicago Press, 1966).

[6] Claude Lévi-Strauss, *Totemism* (Boston: Beacon Press, 1963).

[7] Claude Lévi-Strauss, *Structural Anthropology* (New York: Basic Books, Inc., 1963).

[8] Rodney Needham, *Structure and Sentiment* (Chicago: University of Chicago Press, 1962).

basic determiners of man's actions. His general stance is perhaps best seen in the following quotations:

"Here again I do not mean to suggest that social life, the relations between man and nature are a projection or even a result of a conceptual game taking place in the mind." [9]

"'Ideas', Balzac wrote, 'form a complete system within us, comparable to one of the natural kingdoms, a sort of bloom whose iconography will be traced by a man of genius who will pass perhaps as mad'? But more madness than genius would be required for such an enterprise." [10]

". . . superstructures are faulty acts which have 'made it' socially." [11] And lastly, "I do not at all mean to suggest that ideological transformations give rise to social ones. Only the reverse is in fact true." [12]

II. That different positions (either material positions, such as class, or categorical positions such as totemic groups) within a given society produce different ideologies in spite of the fact that all members of that society share the same system of knowledge due to the general structure of that society.

III. That the validity of a given ideology within a given society can be determined in terms of the dialectical criterion: while several types of general knowledge schemes, though separate and distinct from each other, which are products of the total societal structures, can lay equal claim to validity. These latter claim validity because they simply constitute general systems which, while taking particular forms because of the structure of the society from which they emanate, arise out of the universal human need for intellectual creativity and the universal demand to order and classify all things into species and kinds.

Having briefly discussed Lévi-Strauss' 'givens', we may now proceed to describe the internally consistant, general sociology of knowledge which manifests itself in *The Savage Mind*.

2. *The Savage Mind*

A central contention of *The Savage Mind* is that there are systems of knowledge (classification) characteristic of entire societies. These total systems of knowledge or cosmological classificatory schemes are of two distinct types, although they both arise out of and are founded on a *demand for order* which inheres in the human condition. These two cosmologies are termed by Lévi-Strauss the Science of the Concrete and Theoretical Science. These reasoning patterns are both characteristic of and produced by particular types of societies, that is to say the nature of the relationships between men gives rise

---

[9] Lévi-Strauss, *The Savage Mind*, p. 130.
[10] *Ibid.*, p. 130.
[11] *Ibid.*, p. 254.
[12] *Ibid.*, p. 117.

to patterns of reasoning whose structure corresponds to the structure of these social relationships. Simply put, social structure produces culture.

The Science of the Concrete arises in what Lévi-Strauss labels "Cold" societies while Theoretical Science is the pattern of reasoning typical of the "Hot" society. Cold societies are societies whose social institutions are geared to mitigate or lessen the impact of historical events on their own structure. Those societies do not deny historical process but rather they admit it as a form devoid of content. The past is conceived as a timeless model. Cold societies constitute cultural representations of nature. They are societies fitting the synchronic model; their constituent elements are coexisting in time. In essence, cold societies are not stratified in terms of limiting or enhancing different members or groups chances at the material means for sustaining life.

"Hot" societies are societies which internalize historical process and utilize it as a force in their development. Hot societies side with history and hence "... classification into finite groups (is) impossible because the derivative series, instead of reproducing the original series merges with it to form a single series ...." [13] In other words, hot societies fit a diachronic model; they are natural representations of culture. These societies are stratified societies.

The Science of the Concrete is a pattern of reasoning which is based on direct perception, tends to be inductive, and is primarily qualitative. It resembles a patterned rather than a hierarchical type of reasoning. It is a system of thought close to immediate sensation yet it also utilizes intuitive sensing. Its emphasis is on secondary qualities, and it utilizes events to create structure.

The Science of the Theoretical is above all a system of knowledge wherein knowledge itself is cast in hope of a return. This system stands in marked contrast to the method of "savage" thought (Concrete Science) which Levi-Strauss characterizes as undomesticated thought of no specific use. The latter constitute "wild thinking." The difference between Concrete and Theoretical Science is that the former is engaged in without consideration for a return on the thinking to be done. That is, while Theoretical Science claims for itself validity on the grounds that it supposedly explains many things with few propositions, Concrete Science or "savage" thought runs wild with no such considerations hindering its development. Theoretical Science, in addition, is quantitative, basically deductive, and hierarchical. It lays emphasis on primary qualities and is characterized by a high level of abstraction. It proceeds from structure to event.

Although Lévi-Strauss does not go far enough to make it explicit, we take one prime thesis of *The Savage Mind* to be that stratified societies produce stratified systems of knowledge and nonstratified societies produce non-hierarchical knowledge systems – *i.e.*, "hot" societies produce Theoretical Science and "cold" societies give birth to the Science of the Concrete.

---

[13] *Ibid.*, p. 233.

The Science of the Concrete is not to be conceived of as a mere forerunner of Theoretical Science. It is not only a separate and distinct form of science; it can lay claim to being equal. This rests on the following set of facts: All classificatory systems arise out of man's demand for order. The type of classificatory system which arises is determined by the structure of the society in which its "builders" live. Classificatory systems are indeed erected through the actions of real men, however, it is the types of interests these men have which determine the form the classificatory system takes. However, the particular types of interest men have are a product of the particular social structures they live under. As one is hard put to say that one set of interests is better than another, then both sets are separate but equal to the interests they are based upon. Because of a diversity of interest, in Lévi-Strauss' terms, "... the properties to which the savage mind has access are not the same as those which have commanded the attention of scientists. The physical world is approached from opposite ends in the two cases: one is supremely concrete, the other supremely abstract; one proceeds from the angle of sensible qualities and the other from that of formal properties. But if ... these two courses might have been destined to meet, this explains that they should have both, independently of each other in time and space, led to two distinct and equally positive sciences ...." [14]

The last major contention in *The Savage Mind* is that the process of human knowledge is now beginning to possess the properties of a closed system. As Lévi-Strauss states: "We have had to wait until the middle of this century for the crossing of long separated paths: That which arrives at the physical world by the detour of communication, and that which as we have recently come to know, arrives at the world of communication by the detour of the physical. The entire process of human knowledge thus assumes the character of a closed system." [15]

This latter contention constitutes the novelty of Lévi-Strauss' sociology of knowledge, and it likewise makes *The Savage Mind* not only a macro or general, as opposed to a micro, sociology of knowledge but makes of it a *super-general* or *cosmic* approach. The implications of the contention that the process of human knowledge is coming to form a closed system is not taken up by Lévi-Strauss. Neither does the book contain a sociological-historic analysis of exactly why these two forms of science are *now* crossing paths. Those latter topics not only constitute worthwhile points of focus for future general treatises dealing with the sociology of knowledge, they would also serve as a logical extension of the thesis presented in *The Savage Mind*. Unfortunately such endeavors are beyond the scope of the present paper.

Having attempted to briefly delineate the parameters of Claude Lévi-Strauss' work *The Savage Mind*, the following comments will attempt to describe the particular structural-historical context from whence these ideas emanate. In effect the attempt made here is to subject a particular sociology

---

[14] *Ibid.*, p. 269.
[15] *Ibid.*, p. 269.

of knowledge to a sociological analysis. It must be remembered that the reaction to Lévi-Strauss' work, including *The Savage Mind* has been tremendously favorable, in the U.S. perhaps a somewhat bemused and mystified reaction, but in France, for an anthropologist, his popularity is unparalleled. He, now surpassing Sartre, is *the* leading French intellectual today.

3. *French Sociology and Anthropology*

In order to ferret out the structural basis of Lévi-Strauss' ideas, the general nature of French sociology and anthropology, as it has come to be affected by French national politics, character structure and world outlook, will be examined.

French sociologists and anthropologists, nearly to the man, have made two basic assumptions concerning human nature and the human condition. The first of these assumptions is that mankind has a propensity for order, that is, a passion for classifying and systematizing in attempts to force closure on its dealings with nature and with its fellow men. The second assumption is that the Parisian is the epitome of humaness and that, in reality, all men are at heart Parisians. "Primitive" man is conceived as a "diamond in the rough," a Parisian whose current culture is not attuned to that of contemporary France. This condition superficially masks the fact that he and his cohorts are, beneath this crude exterior, Parisians.

This latter contention is not restricted to French sociologists and anthropologists but is made by many Frenchmen and in particular by those who occupy positions of power in the economy and the body politic. This assumption, which is a secondary assumption arising out of the assumption of a demand for order, has greatly influenced France in its relationships with colonial people, and subsequently French anthropologists' relations with the people they study, rendering these relations markedly different from those of Germany and England with their colonies.

Returning to the first assumption, the demand for order, French social scientists themselves seem to reflect a greater zeal for order than many of the preliterate people they claim to understand. Having a passion for order themselves, as well as assuming that a demand for order inheres in the human condition, French anthropologists and sociologists are greatly concerned with the sources of social solidarity. It is not without reason that Saint Simon, as a Frenchman, pleaded for solidarity while, in search of a model, pointed backward in time to those features of Feudalism which he thought produced stability and order. Saint Simon likewise sought, although at a different period in his life, a new society based on the ordered principles of science. It is also worth noting that Saint Simon was among the first to concern himself with the unity of science. He was also, at one time, a socialist, and his stance during this period of his life was not too unlike that of many contemporary French socialists and communists who preach communism while rejecting anarchism, which many Marxists see as a logical extension of Marxian doctrine.

August Comte likewise stressed the unity of science but saw sociology, and French sociology in particular, as its queen. Comte shared with Saint Simon, as Durkheim later did with Comte, a great concern for an ordered way of life and the disruptive, and hence harmful, effects which ensue when man is unable to force such order on nature and social life through the use of his systematic classificatory schemes. As Lévi-Strauss states of Comte " . . . he has roughly gauged the importance in the history of thought of a classificatory system, whose organization and tenor he understood better than ethnologists of the present day." [16] Comte's great concern for *order lost* is seen in the following quotation (in which he contemplates the effects of both the French and industrial revolutions, social phenomena whose disruptive effects seems to have given rise to the French asssumption of men's demand for order and subsequently the assumption of the common motivation of all human intellectual activities):

"Never since that epoch (the Feudal epoch) have human conceptions been able to recover to a degree at all comparable, that great unity of method and homogeneity of doctrine which constitutes the fully normal state of our intelligence, and which it had then acquired spontaneously . . . . [17]"

This same overriding concern for order may be seen in the works of Emile Durkheim. Suicides were seen as increasing both during societal wide periods of transition and during periods in which individuals are not, to use what is rapidly becoming a mere sociological cliché, able to maintain status consistency. The concern is likewise seen in *The Division of Labor in Society*, especially in the hope Durkheim attaches to organic solidarity as a replacement for the older mechanical form; and in the last analysis Durkheim still sees the older, and to him dearer, form underlying the "new solidarity." In *The Elementary Forms of the Religious Life*, and particularly in his discussion of totemism, his concern for order manifests itself in his definition of classification and ordering as feats which constitute ends in themselves.

These men are the French intellectual predecessors of Lévi-Strauss and he consequently shares many of their assumptions and concerns. But Lévi-Strauss is also a sociological Marxist, and hence one would expect not only his assumptions but many of his prime concerns to be vastly different from those of Comte and Durkheim and to a lesser extent from those of Saint Simon. While some of his concerns and assumptions are different, many are not, and this is particularly due to the nature of French communism.

4. *French Marxism and Communism*

French Marxism is a bastard, a two headed beast. One head is a traditional Marxist head; it is filled with ideas of internationalism, a world communistic economic order, and other time-honored Marxian concerns. In the mind of the French Marxist sociologist and anthropologist, who is also a political

---

[16] *Ibid.*, p. 218.
[17] *Ibid.*, p. 218.

animal of French Marxist persuasion, lie all those ideas and perhaps a host of finer points relating to the science of social economics, social structure in general, and other conceptions which were of concern to the likes of Marx and Engels. But more particularly his concerns are more apt to be those of Proudhon, because in the last analysis French communists favor the latter's conception of primitive communism over Marx's concept of industrial communism.

The other head of French communism, and it is this head which confers upon French communism its label of bastard, is full of ideas of the glory that was once France, world destiny, and France's role in that destiny. Taken together the two heads of French Marxism constitute a system of thought which seeks international unity among man placed on equal economic footing, but unity overseen and enforced by France as "Super-Marx."

Such systems of belief are not confined to the rank and file of the French communist party and are certainly not lost on French social scientists who are Marxists. This supernationalism on the part of French Marxists has been one factor responsible for the fact that French Marxists are not accorded the harsh treatment accorded politically active Marxists in other European countries. In passing it is likewise worth noting that in many cases not only is harsh treatment not accorded militant social reformers who are nationalists but in more than one instance such socialists have come to occupy positions of considerable import in the French government. The current French minister of culture is the same André Malraux who authored *Man's Fate*. From 1946 to 1947 Claude Lévi-Strauss himself was Cultural Attaché to the French Embassy in the United States. One can in France be a "Marxist" as well as a member of the French establishment partially because they share the same concern for order, rather a passion for world order, and the desire that such an ordered system be headed by France. Some French Marxists have, on occasion, backed the *Force de Frappe*, and they tend to view France as a third force to both save and unite the world. Lévi-Strauss is a French Marxist, and as George Zollschan has said, "Lévi-Strauss sleeps with the medal awarded him by France." [18]

Having placed Claude Lévi-Strauss as an anthropologist, French communist, and Marxist intellectual in his social context, his work falls into place. He scrutinizes the cosmologies of the Science of the Theoretical and the Science of the Concrete, the industrial world and the primitive world, industrial communism and primitive communism and in the tradition of Durkheim and Proudhon opts, as a Frenchman, for the Science of the Concrete.

The Ohio State University

---

[18] Statement made by George Zollschan during a seminar on the sociology of knowledge at Ohio State University.

THE USE AND SYNTAX OF VALUE JUDGMENTS

JOSEPH MARGOLIS

It is a very deepseated, but altogether mistaken, practice, in generalizing about value judgments, to suppose that moral judgments or aesthetic judgments or other sorts of similar judgments have logically uniform uses within their respective domains. The practice is, familiarly, Kantian and finds its most recent expression (not entirely in accord with Kant's own preferences) in imperativism and emotivism. But we cannot, if we take a reasonably broad sample of judgments that may be construed as moral or aesthetic judgments or the like, defend a single distinctive and comprehensive model for such a set; and we cannot, if we attempt to mark off the aesthetic and the moral and other such categories from one another, provide for the satisfactory classification of any reasonably broad sample of judgments. Neither do the run of judgments of this or that sort show comfortable uniformities nor can we say with confidence what the boundaries are between this and that sort of judgment.

Let me illustrate.

It is often held, and prominently by R. M. Hare, that moral judgments are action-guiding, by which is meant that the essential use of moral judgments is to *direct* people with respect to future conduct: this is the heart of imperativism or prescriptivism. Apparent anomalies, initially of a grammatical sort, are obviated by technical enlargements of the competent scope of imperatives. So for example suitable past-tense and first-person imperatives are invented or the contexts in which relevant inquiry arises are interpreted as logically dependent on present- or future-tense and second- or third-person imperatives. The same sort of adjustment may be attempted for fictional, hypothetical, and counterfactual cases. There are, nevertheless, reasonable objections that will remain that are conclusive even at this level. For one thing, surely, moral judgments used to direct people's conduct cannot be used *merely* to direct their conduct: these cannot be merely imperatives, must be imperatives thought to be *justified* on some grounds or other. And if this is so, then the judgment of what is morally appropriate or required, *on which the imperative logically depends for justification,* cannot itself be an imperative. Either so-called moral imperatives are arbitrary, without justification, or the admission of morally justified imperatives (directing conduct) presupposes a kind of moral judgment that is not itself an imperative. From this point of view, an imperatival function assigned to moral judgments can never be more than a subsidiary function. A second objection may trade on the important differences between first-, second- and third-person discourse with respect to commands, orders, resolves, wishes, threats, advice, instruction and the like. However similar second- and third-person discourse may be alleged to be (though even this is rather dubious in important cases and depends chiefly on grammatical ambiguities), first-person discourse is quite distinctively defective in relevant ways. I cannot command myself or give orders to myself or threaten myself or advise myself or give instruction to myself; and though I can make my own resolutions, no one can make them for me. But moral judgments – in particular, "ought"-judgments of the relevant sort – appear to be indifferent, in at least some respects bearing on conduct, to the distinctions of grammatical persons. And if this is so, them imperativism must be inadequate; for it would require that the sense of "ought," used in a morally relevant way, could not be univocal for first-, second- and third-person discourse.

These arguments, however, leave the field open to alternative proposals. I wish to hold rather that, for example, moral judgments are simply not uniform, that *no* thesis like imperativism, no thesis of a universal property or use of moral judgments, will do. Concede, for the sake of the issue, that if imperativism obtains, it holds equally well for first-, second- and third-person discourse. Now, consider a difficulty of another sort, that there are moral judgments that *cannot* defensibly be construed as action-guiding in any sense in which they may be supposed to *direct* conduct. H. A. Prichard, for example, correctly insisted that, however possible it might be that behaving in this or that way (open to deliberate choice) might lead us to become *courageous* or *loving*, acting courageously or with love was *not* something one could deliberately do, on any account of human action. But, if that is the case, then the moral judgment that Peter acted with courage *cannot* be an action-guiding judgment; nor indeed can, if it is allowed, the judgment that one ought to act with courage. To hold that moral judgments are action-guiding, in the face of such counterinstances, is simply a mistake; contrariwise, to insist that such judgments are not moral judgments *because* they are not action-guiding is hardly helpful. This suggests two important themes, which we shall explore a bit further: for one thing, with reference to familiar disputes in moral philosophy, "ought" need not imply "can," some "ought"-judgments at least do not entail "can"-judgments (and are, to that extent, not action-guiding); for another, judgments of character and motivation are, as such, not action-guiding judgments, though they be moral judgments.

It is normally inappropriate, we may observe, to say of someone that he ought to be a saint or ought to act in a saintly way – which is instructive. There are, of course, very many things that a man might deliberately do that would lead to his being brave or generous or just or the like; and, therefore, we may say that a man ought to be such or to behave in such a way under appropriate circumstances, even though a man cannot deliberately be such or deliberately behave in such a way. A saintly man might deliberately do what happens to be a saintly thing; but there are no formulable practices that remotely promise to produce a saint – too much depends on natural gifts of character. We can do no more than *appreciate* that a man is a saint (or a moral monster or the like): there is no relevant sense in which we could possibly *direct* anyone's conduct to accord with saintliness. Hare, in such cases – as for instance in judging the life of St. Francis – denies that we are concerned with *moral* judgments or *moral* matters, *since* the judgments are clearly not action-guiding. But he might rather have admitted – what other sorts of cases confirm – that not all moral judgments, whether "ought"-judgments or not, are action-guiding. We may, in making moral judgments, merely appreciate a man's character, in the sense of comprehending (independent of an analysis of the logical properties of the judgments involved) that a given judgment rightly fits a given man's character and also in the sense of savoring the qualities of his character so judged.

A moral judgment might be directive (action-guiding); but, sometimes, it might be merely a matter of appreciation (and may actually not be able to be directive); and, sometimes, it might be merely informative, in the sense in which things are truly said to have a given property. There is absolutely no reason for insisting that all moral judgments, *qua* moral judgments, are, or must be, action-guiding. Some of them cannot be action-guiding; and of those that can, there is no logical constraint *to* direct anyone's life in relevantly making the judgment itself. For, as we have already seen, to direct another's conduct in a morally defensible way is tantamount to having made an antecedent moral judgment of a non-directive sort.

Any number of related considerations may be added. We say, for example, in certain circumstances, "There ought to be an end to war," "Men ought not to suffer unmerited misfortune," "All men ought to have an equal chance to be happy." Here, we attend to the presence of *evil* (surely, at least in part, morally relevant evil) that human efforts either cannot conceivably alter or cannot be expected to eliminate. We touch here on goals that relate to what men *are* able to effect; but the conditions in mind are ideal or perfect and, furthermore, no particular men are addressed or referred to in issuing a judgment of the relevant sort. These judgments are morally eligible without regard to the capacity of particular men and concern achievements that no men could conceivably effect, though the conditions in mind are conceivable and relate to human effort. The "ought" of such judgments does not imply "can" and the judgments themselves cannot be regarded as action-guiding in the required sense. Again, we advise a man, in certain circumstances, that "you ought to do what is right," "you ought to contribute to another's happiness," "you ought to be good." Here, we are not advising a man *to do* anything at all. Rather, we are pointing to the characteristic *reasons* for which morally motivated men act. Therefore, although such reasons do not apply unless men are able to act in particular ways, these reasons may be advanced and accepted without regard to any particular action whatsoever. Here, "ought" does not imply "can" and the corresponding judgments cannot be construed as action-guiding in the required sense. Again, we may say of a man, in certain circumstances, that "he ought to provide more adequately for his family," though we realize that, given his skills and opportunities, he cannot. We cannot be using the judgment in an action-guiding sense if we believe him to be incapable of the relevant action. But we may thereby draw attention to the fact that his family is entitled, has a moral right, to be taken better care of, quite independently of his incapacity.

I think it is fair to say that, among all possible moral judgments, "ought"-judgments are the ones that suggest the plausibility of the imperativist thesis. We have seen, however, that different sorts of such judgments need not, and even cannot, be construed as directive of conduct; in fact, it does not seem possible to assign to all the varieties of "ought"-judgments one would acknowledge as morally relevant a single and uniform use like the directive use. Trivially, moral judgments are sentences used to judge. But there is no reason to suppose that the logical role we assign to sentences, in being used to make judgments, could possibly serve to distinguish not only moral judgments from aesthetic judgments or from medical judgments or from legal judgments but also moral judgments (or any of the other sorts) from factual judgments. It seems impossible to deny that the only way of distinguishing one kind of judgment from another lies entirely with classifying the range of predicates that we employ. To speak of lying is to speak of a moral issue; and to speak of a breach of contract is to speak of a legal issue; and to speak of the balance of a painting, an aesthetic issue; and to speak of the malfunctioning of the kidney, a medical issue. Nevertheless, to offer paradigms is not to offer defining characteristics.

There are a number of distinctions I should like to collect at this point, that bear on the original issue of the non-uniformity of the uses and syntax of moral and aesthetic judgments and judgments of similar sorts. For one thing, the action-guiding or action-governing use of moral judgments – which is ordinarily emphasized as one of its most distinctive features – may be serviced in at least two quite different ways. In one, it may be serviced by the use of imperatives or by sentences that are used jointly to pass judgment and to direct conduct (as imperatives). And in a second, it may be serviced, in sentences used to judge (but not to direct) conduct, by a prominent sense of "ought" proper to moral judgments. The first of these two alternatives, as we have already seen, requires that "ought" not be univocal for first-, second- and third-person discourse. But the second provides the needed univocity. We may say that to judge that one *ought* to do X (in the morally relevant sense) is to judge not only that the action involved is appropriate or right or obligatory according to some admitted rule or criterion but also that anyone who would acknowledge that, in given circumstances, *he* ought to do X, would also intend to act in accord with what he recognizes he ought to do. That is, the force of "ought" lies in its bearing on the conformity of conduct and judgment. If I judge that another ought to do X, under my breath so to say, I have not directed *him* to act in any way; but I should go on to judge his *conduct* as according or not according with what I judge he ought to do. And if I judge that *I* ought to do X, or concur with another that I ought to do X, then, comme *grasping the sense of "ought,"* I cannot *consistently* not intend to do X. I should christen this sort of consistency *consistency in practice,* or moral consistency, and I should admit further that one may be morally criticized for inconsistency of the relevant sort as well as for acting contrary to what one ought to do. If the account is accepted, then it is altogether possible to admit a variety of subsidiary linguistic acts, like persuading, ordering, resolving, threatening, advising, that may service moral ends and may, in so doing, employ the same term "ought" in logically different ways. At the very least, the argument demonstrates that moral utterances may be assigned an action-guiding role without invoking imperatives. But to admit that this role may be serviced both by imperatives and by the sense of "ought" in moral utterances that are not imperatives is to admit, in an important regard, the non-uniformity of moral utterances themselves: they neither are, nor need to be, all imperatives.

A second point is this: moral utterances neither are, nor need to be, action-guiding. We have already pursued the matter in observing a variety of judgments that *cannot* be action-guiding in the required sense – judging that a man is a saint or moral monster, judging character and motivation, judging what is morally appropriate, in circumstances in which we believe the agent involved to be incapable of fulfilling his responsibility. And we have already seen that, even with respect to judgments of what one ought to do, where these are action-guiding in some sense, the action-guiding role of moral utterances may be preserved without invoking imperatives; and construing imperatives as morally relevant is, in effect, presupposing judgments that merely identify what it is one ought to do. In short, there must, on any account, be a significantly large run of moral judgments that are *not* action-guiding, that we use in merely marking out what we notice or *appreciate* regarding what is right or good or obligatory and the like.

Now, I have previously argued that value judgments are not, *qua* judgments, all of the same logical sort, that we must admit at the very least the distinction between what I have called findings and appreciative judgments.[1] I have tried to show further, in the present context, that moral judgments are not, and cannot, be all imperatives and are not, and cannot, be all action-guiding. But this means that moral judgments do not have a logically uniform use (as to direct conduct) or a logically uniform syntax (as being imperatives) or are confirmed in logically uniform ways (as being findings). There is, then, no possible way of distinguishing moral judgments from value judgments of other sorts, except perhaps by classifying exclusive sets of predicates; that is, there can be no comprehensive rule for the distinction, ranging over all value judgments, though this does not mean that particular judgments

---

[1] I have explored this in a paper, "Value Judgments and Value Predicates" *Journal of Value Inquiry*, I, No. 3 & 4 (1967). The issue has been explored also in my *Psychotherapy and Morality* (New York, 1966), Ch. 2; and *The Language of Art and Art Criticism* (Detroit, 1965), Ch. 10. The distinction here intended lies in there being a range of judgments that behave logically like factual judgments (except that we say their predicates are valuational predicates) and there being a range of judgments that logically depend on one's taste and preference (which cannot, therefore, be said to be true or false or correct or incorrect, in the manner of factual statements and judgments).

I

cannot reasonably be said to be moral *rather than* aesthetic judgments. *In context*, to judge that Peter murdered Mary may be to render a *legal* judgment. But it does not follow from deciding this that the judgment itself has *any* logically distinctive properties that could serve to mark it off as legal rather than as moral or aesthetic: the predicates alone or the use of sets of predicates in given contexts may decide the issue. To admit this, however, is to defeat a very persistent and widespread Kantian conviction.

The argument needs to be bolstered by considering non-moral contexts. For one thing, whoever would cling to the Kantian view of value judgments (as distinct from Kant's own particular version of the view) would have to decide such questions as whether moral and legal judgments are to be assigned to significantly (relevantly) distinct domains of discourse, whether moral judgments and judgments of etiquette have overlapping or coextensive domains or whether etiquette is as such a moral concern or not. Not to be able to decide such issues – and their artificiality strikes us at once – is to cast doubt on the possibility of distinguishing sharply between the different kinds of value judgments by sorting out the ranges of relevant sets of predicates.

It is not difficult, for instance, to suppose that there are runs of predicates that may be taken to be jointly moral and aesthetic. Once I give up the prejudice that moral judgments are action-guiding and grant that they may register claims (of logically distinct sorts) that accord with what I notice or appreciate, it is no longer a simple matter to propose boundaries between the moral and the aesthetic. If I judge someone's conduct to be kindly or tactful or generous or discreet or gracious or foul, have I judged in a *morally* relevant (and therefore not aesthetically relevant) way or have I judged in an *aesthetically* (and therefore not morally) relevant way? There seems to be no ready answer, short of legislating boundaries *ad hoc*. In fact, *if* the thesis that judgments of the relevantly different sorts have markedly different logical properties itself falls, there remains hardly any point in insisting on a sharp demarcation among the different sorts of judgments themselves. That is, if judging that a man's conduct is gracious is (whatever the logical properties of such a judgment) a way of marking what I appreciate or notice respecting that man's conduct, what could I possibly be preserving in insisting that the judgment is moral *and not* aesthetic?

To say that the judgment registers what it is I appreciate or notice with respect to someone's conduct is *already* to identify an ulterior use (comparable to the directive use of moral judgments) for the sake of which alone I may issue the judgment; and to identify that use – to provide for instance for what we might call *moral appreciation* – is to disorder the received (what I am calling the Kantian) view of the ulterior uses of distinctively moral and aesthetic judgments. Merely to have undermined the thesis of the directive use of moral judgments is to have seriously threatened the effort to sort out exclusive sets of predicates that may be assigned to the moral, the legal, the medical, the religious, the aesthetic, the prudential, the political, the economic domains; for, to have done so is to have eliminated the principal reason for arranging such a catalogue.

But not only may I employ predicates that are jointly moral and aesthetic (whether of the sort appropriate to findings or to appreciative judgments), I may also provide for the directive use (and other such uses) of value judgments in the aesthetic as well as in the moral domain. It is, in fact, a well-known thesis of Stuart Hampshire's, that critical judgments of the aesthetic sort are non-committal, in the sense that they do not, and cannot, make recommendations about what an artist ought to do. One may prefer, or reject, a certain work of art without, Hampshire thinks, being required to propose what ought to have been done to improve it. It is true that one may not be *required* to propose an adjustment, but the same is true in the moral domain: I may see that what was done ought not to have been done without at all being able to suggest a better way of proceeding. Nevertheless, it may be appropriate and reasonably expected that a knowledgeable critic, in judging a work to be deficient, specify what indeed *ought to have been done* to improve the work. The only point to consider is that a directive, or action-guiding, judgment may properly be made in the aesthetic domain, which will behave in the same logical way as its counterpart in the moral domain. And if this is so, then we cannot segregate moral and aesthetic judgments either in terms of the uses to which these judgments may be put or in terms of the syntax of judgments of the two sorts. What would be the point of insisting that, for example, Ezra Pound's instruction to the young T. S. Eliot, that he ought to cut the length of *The Wasteland* and begin the poem with the line, "April is the cruellest month," was a moral or quasi-moral judgment and not an aesthetic judgment precisely because it *did* direct another's action? Judgments that express our appreciation may predominate in the aesthetic domain and judgments that direct conduct may predominate in the moral domain, but there are no convincing reasons to believe that non-directive judgments cannot occur in the moral domain or that directive judgments cannot occur in the aesthetic. And if this holds for what are traditionally radically different sorts of judgments, it is unlikely that any of the less clearly articulated domains of value judgments will lend themselves to a simple demarcation of the required sort.

The discussion of issues like emotivism and imperativism tend to obscure the range of characteristic uses to which value judgments may be put and the syntactical variety such judgments (and related utterances) may exhibit. Consider remarks made to commend something. Commending is very closely related to judging yet distinct from judging. In fact, the same sentences serve both functions. I may commend a man as a good barber and may judge him to be a good barber, saying in different contexts, "He's a good barber." Sometimes, we speak loosely of sentences used to commend as being value judgments, as, typically, when P.H. Nowell-Smith speaks of the fundamental use of "good" to express a preference. The critical distinction is this: commendations may call for explanation but not for justification; and judgments, of whatever sort they may be, call for justification. Judgments are open to error and may, depending on whether they are findings or appreciative judgments, be corrected and challenged in appropriate ways. The reasons for which someone commends something may provide grounds for rejecting someone's commendation; but a commendation is not the sort of thing that can be corrected. One may commend responsibly or irresponsibly, with or without *his* own reasons, conservatively, enthusiastically, arbitrarily; but one's judgment calls for support or defense. We think of a commendation primarily as an *action* of a certain sort, as the exhibition or expression of approval, preference, liking (as in answer to an inquiry or in conversation). And we think of a judgment primarily as a formulated *claim*, as a sentence whose truth or falsity or defensibility of other sorts may be assessed. But since the action of commending is, typically, verbal, the sentence deposited is readily construed as a judgment; and since we suppose an attitude or conviction, on the part of a speaker, congruent with his claims, we construe a value judgment as a commendation (or its reverse) as well. But to allow this conflating of distinctions is to acknowledge the complexity of our use of the relevant sentences, not the force of such theories as emotivism with respect to judgment proper.

Here lies the weakness, for example, of Nowell-Smith's thesis of the primacy of the commending use of "good." "Good" used in its commending sense, as in "He's a good barber," has the sense merely of expressing approval and the like, independent of all considerations relevant to the defense of judgments, and therefore obliges us to construe the sentence uttered as a performative of the same sort. By speaking the sentence, where "good" is intended in its commending sense, I *do* commend. But "good" used in a sense proper to judgment, as also in "He's a good barber," is never simply a one-place predicate. It is always an elliptical expression for any number of more complex predicates, such as "good-in-such-and-such-a-respect," "good-as-of-such-a-kind." We understand the predicate form "good ...," where the complexity of admissible entries is not indicated, to be occupied by valuational predicates; hence, we understand *judgments* like "He's very good," even though a context be lacking in which the ellipsis may be replaced by a fully explicit predicate. Furthermore, it is easy to see how, given the initial attraction of the imperativist thesis, one might be inclined to construe value judgments as commendations (and the like); but to do so is not merely to confuse judgments with what are not judgments, it is to fail to distinguish two quite distinct uses of "good" and related expressions. In commendations, "good" does not function as a predicate at all; and in judgments, it is an elliptical form for a variety of multi-placed predicates. G. E. Moore's mistake lay in assuming "good" to designate a simple quality; Nowell-Smith's and Hare's, in confusing a non-predicative use of "good" with its predicative use.

We may give our account a firmer sense of closure if we consider a further distinction. If commendations are sub-judgments, in calling not for defense or support but only for explanation – in that our commend*ing* is explained by reference to this or that reason – verdicts are super-judgments. *Qua* verdicts, valuational sentences foreclose on defense or support. Verdicts may be preceded or succeeded by value judgments; but if they are regarded as a

kind of value judgment, once again a performative use of language willh ave
been conflated with that use we are calling the making of a value judgment.
Something is *assigned* a value by the mere issuing of a verdict. The value may
have been responsibily assigned or it may not have been. Judicious appraisal
may have preceded it, and it may, on review, be put aside on the strength of
relevant *judgments*. But however we may suppose the judge or judges to have
arrived at a verdict, a verdict does not, *qua* verdict, call for or require defense.
Sentences may, of course, be used jointly for verdicts and judgments, just as
they may, for commendations and judgments.

In beauty contests, for instance, and in many other contexts, "the opinion
of the judges," as we say, "is final." We suppose the relevant information to
have been supplied to the judges or to have been made available, and we
suppose the judges to have sorted this out in accord with appropriate criteria.
But characteristically, all we receive is a public verdict; and in many instances,
we have not the faintest hint of the grounds on which it has been determined.
If we construe the verdict *as* a judgment (as well we may), we may request
supporting reasons. But verdicts (think of judging criminals, literary contests,
dog shows) are typically rendered in contexts in which, though there may or
may not be provision for appeals from a verdict, the judgment rendered is,
qua verdict, decisive merely in having been issued appropriately. A defendant
is guilty, in the context of verdicts, if he is judged guilty; the verdict may be
appealed and a higher *verdict* may declare him innocent; or, we may supercede
the context of verdicts altogether (as in reviewing court cases over coffee) and
judge (even in the sense of a finding) that the defendant was innocent. "Innocent" and "guilty," in verdicts, are predicates properly assigned merely by
virtue of *rendering a verdict*; but "innocent" and "guilty" are also proper
predicates for value judgments, and thus construed their ascription is open
to defense and a call for defense.

Also, generally speaking, verdicts are rendered in accord with antecedently
designated distinctions: "guilty," "innocent," "not proved"; "First Prize,"
"Second Prize," "Third Prize"; "best of breed," "best of show." We do
sometimes allow, in more informal settings, certain valuational remarks to
pass for verdicts. For example, someone *whose judgment is particularly
respected* judges your first efforts at poetry to be "fine" or "very promising"
or the like. Here we see a possible convergence between commendations
(or the reverse) and verdicts. Nevertheless, the difference remains clear: in a
verdict, however formal or informal it may be, the value term is used predicatively – the difficulty being that there are no considerations bearing on the
proper ascription of the predicate other than its having been ascribed by the
assigned judge; and in a commendation, the value term is not being used
predicatively at all but only to express or indicate a liking or preference or
the like – with or without any indication that a counterpart judgment could
be defended. A commendation is no judgment at all, and a verdict is, so to
say, a degenerate judgment; correspondingly, "good" in the context of
commendations is not a predicate, and "good" in the context of verdicts is a
degenerate predicate. The confusion of these two uses and the failure to

distinguish either or both from the use of valuational predicates (proper in value judgments) is particularly márked in the accounts of Margaret Macdonald and Arnold Isenberg; and it was J. L. Austin's suspicion of both of these uses that led him to recommend a closer study of "the dumpy and the dainty."

Value judgments themselves, of course, exhibit further variety. We distinguish appraisals, gradings, rankings, assessments as well as a great many other sorts of judgment not sufficiently formalized to be distinctively labelled. Judgments of these sorts may be either findings or appreciative judgments; and they may also have verdict-like aspects. The appraisal of a jeweller, for example, may combine, in judging a diamond, considerations of weight and purity (relevant to findings), considerations of the beauty of the cutting (relevant to appreciative judgments and/or findings), and considerations of price, as in an offer of purchase (relevant to verdicts). But however interesting these varieties and complex forms may be, the principal distinction rests with contrasting value judgments proper with the related uses of valuationally significant sentences with which they may be confused; and, correspondingly, with contrasting the fully predicative use of value terms, in value judgments, and the non-predicative or degenerately predicative use of value terms in commendations and verdicts. Furthermore, returning to our opening remarks, there are no reasons for supposing that any of these distinctions regarding valuational sentences and valuational terms are linked in any logically important or exclusive way with the distinctions usually made between the various kinds of value judgments – as being moral or aesthetic or legal or prudential or the like.

The University of Western Ontaric

VALUES, VALUE DEFINITIONS, AND SYMBOLIC INTERACTION

Glenn M. Vernon

This article focuses attention upon values and value definitions from the perspective of the symbolic interactionist, with a three-fold purpose: to (1) recommend that a distinction be made between values and value definitions, (2) suggest a theoretical explanation for the development of values or for the transformation of value definitions into values, and (3) discuss some functional aspects of the use of each concept.

I. *Symbolic Interaction Perspective*

Since use is made of the symbolic interactionist perspective [1] it may be helpful to briefly state the following basic premises of this perspective, which are germane to the discussion, but for which space is not adequate for any detailed elaboration.

1. The behavior of concern is interaction (social or group behavior) not internal biological, sub-individual behavior.[2]

2. Such behavior is in response to symbols and is not *determined* biologically. Individuals respond to the labels they place upon each other and any other phenomena involved. Efforts to achieve meaning consensus are constantly underway and most likely never completely successful.

3. Symbols can be taken into account without the referent being present.

4. Man can see and experience what a label he uses calls for, even tho it may not be empirically there. In his perception, he can symbolically provide elements missing in some configuration or system and take into account the

---

[1] A more detailed presentation of the symbolic interactionist approach is found in Glenn M. Vernon, *Human Interaction* (New York: Ronald Press, 1965); Arnold M. Rose, ed., *Human Behavior and Social Processes* (Boston: Houghton Mifflin Co., 1962); Alfred R. Lindesmith and Anselm L. Strauss, *Social Psychology*, rev. ed. (New York: The Dryden Press, 1956); or Bernard N. Meltzer and Jerome G. Manis, edd., *Symbolic Interaction, A Reader in Social Psychology* (Boston: Allyn and Bacon, 1967).

[2] Analysis of human interaction would be facilitated if our language thru some linguistic device called attention to the difference between (1) a biological condition *per se* and (2) what the *individual* does about that biological condition. When, for instance, we say both that the "eyes see" and the "individual sees" we are equating the two seeing processes and attributing to the eyes "human" characteristics. Use of the eyes permits the individual to see, but eyes do not in and of themselves see, at least not in the same sense that the individual does. The use of different labels to identify the different processes would help avoid much confusion.

whole configuration. He responds to what he believes is there rather than just what is there.

5. There is no inherent relationship between symbols and their referent (that to which they refer) except the human one. The distinction between signs and symbols is the consensual connection between symbol and referent, which is absent for the sign.[3] Man decides which symbol will identify a particular referent. Such relationships then are subject to change. The same symbol may be used to identify two or more different phenomenon, and the same phenomenon can be labeled with two or more different symbols.

6. Man can take into account two types of symbols: (a) ER symbols, which have an empirical referent and which are used to identify selected aspects of the empirical world; and (b), NER symbols which have no empirical referent and which have as *one* function, in the absence of biologically derived motivators, the justification of behavior. Social behavior is in response to both types of symbols.[4]

7. Perception is always selective. The symbols used identify the aspect of the phenomenon of concern to which attention is being given, Communication problems arise when interactants perceive something differently, even tho they may use the same label to identify what they mistakenly believe to be the same thing.

8. As is emphasized in the sociology of knowledge, ignorance of certain aspects may be functional in the accomplishment of certain goals.[5]

9. The behavior of the *individual* in response to any internal biological factor is in response to the label he uses to identify it, rather than in direct response to the biological factor *per se*. Social behavior then is in response to (among other things) socially provided motives, (not biologically provided motives), which involve NER symbols used to justify the behavior.[6]

---

[3] See, for instance, Lindesmith and Strauss, *op. cit.*, pp. 53–56.

[4] Cooley distinguished (1) material knowledge and (2) social knowledge. Material knowledge as he sees it is knowledge which has an empirical referent. Social knowledge he says, is developed from contact with the minds of other men, through communication, which sets going a process of thought and sentiment similar to theirs and enables us to understand them by sharing their states of mind. His "social knowledge" appears to be at least roughly equivalent to the NER symbols as defined here. Value definitions (sentiments) are one such type of symbol. See Charles Horton Cooley, "The Roots of Social Knowledge," *The American Journal of Sociology*, XXXII (July 1926), 59–79. Leslie A. White writing in 1959 indicated "Now it turns out that there is a class of phenomena, one of enormous importance in the study of man, for which science has yet no name: this is the class of things and events consisting of or dependent upon symboling. It is one of the most remarkable facts in the recent history of science that this important class has no name, but the fact remains that it does not" – Leslie A. White, "The Concept of Culture," *American Anthropologist*, LXI (1959), 227–252. The labels used here (ER symbols and NER symbols) represent an effort on the part of the author to meet this deficiency.

[5] For further discussion see, Louis Schneider, "The Role of the Category of Ignorance in Sociological Theory: An Exploratory Statement," *American Sociological Review*, XXVI, No. 4 (August, 1962), 492–508.

[6] This emphasizes again the importance of distinguishing between (1) a biological factor *per se* and (2) what the individual does about that biological factor.

10. Decisions about behavior are emergent. They have no prior existence "out there" or "in there" – in some internal space. They can, however, achieve an existence independent of the individuals who make the decisions, in the forms of symbols (culture). Such symbolic preservation is, in fact, necessary if human societies are to persist. As Cooley suggested, symbols in effect become the "fossil mind" of man.[7]

11. There is a meaningful distinction between: (a) the decision or that which is decided; (b) the phenomenon about which the decision is made; and, (c), the deciders or those who do the deciding. With reference to values, this is the distinction between: (a) the evaluation; (b) the evaluated; and, (c), the evaluator.

II. *"Values" – One Label, Two Meanings*

The concept of "values" has frequently been used in sociological and other discussions with different and frequently conflicting meanings,[8] two of which are illustrated in over-simplified form in the following statements:

1. Cheating on an examination is bad.
2. I (we) evaluate cheating as wrong or bad.

OR

1. The Mona Lisa is beautiful
2. The Mona Lisa appears beautiful to me (or I would classify the Mona Lisa as beautiful)

Frequently both statements in each of these sets are interpreted as saying essentially the same thing. Note, however, that in statement 1, the phenomenon to which the label "wrong" (or beautiful) is attached or related is the cheating behavior (or the picture) *per se*. Presumably, then, if we accept our rules of grammar, it is a characteristic or quality of the cheating (or the picture) which is identified by the label "wrong" (or beautiful). We are talking about the evaluated. In the second statement, the label "wrong" is related not to the cheating behavior (the evaluated) but to the evaluator – to me (us, our group). There is a big difference. Use of the one label "values" to identify

---

[7] Cooley, *op. cit.*, 73.

[8] See for instance Franz Adler, "The Value Concept in Sociology," *American Journal of Sociology*, LXII (November 1956), 272–279, and "On Values and Value Theory"; William R. Catton, Jr., "Reply to Adler," *American Sociological Review*, XXV, No. 1, 85–88; William R. Catton, "A Theory of Value," *American Sociological Review*, XXIV, 310–318; and Clyde Kluckhohn, "Values and Value-Orientations in the Theory of Action," in Talcott Parsons and Edward Shils, edd., *Toward A General Theory of Action* (Cambridge: Harvard University Press, 1951), pp. 388–433. An extensive bibliography is provided in William J. Wilson and F. Ivan Nye, *Some Methodological Problems in the Empirical Study of Values* (Pullman, Washington: Washington State University (Washington Agricultural Experiment Station Bulletin 612), July 1966).

these different referents covers up this difference, which is a difference which makes a difference in sociological analysis.[9]

This dual meaning, however, may be functional or dysfunctional depending upon the goal toward which the behavior is directed. When sociology or any discipline is defined as having social-action goals, the confusion may be functional. When scientific goals are involved, however, the confusion would appear to be dysfunctional. Scientific analysis of behavior may be facilitated if we use labels which call attention to this difference and it is accordingly suggested that we use the label "value" to identify only statements of the "it is good" type, and use the label "value definition" to identify statements of the "we evaluate" type.[10] We will return to this point later.

III. *Development and Function of Values – A Theoretical Explanation*

Symbolic interaction theory provides some insights into the possible evolution of the value concept as well as the functions thereof. In an analysis of this point, attention will first be given to the developmental aspect, and then the functional aspect.

Once man became a symbol user (however this was accomplished) interacting individuals were capable of reaching a decision thru discussion or thru symbolic interaction.[11] Groups could decide thru some symbolic decision-

---

[9] One social psychologist indicates, for instance, "*Values are objects*, ideas or beliefs which are cherished. In America, such things as *money and social position are valued* highly, but we also have many values which are not economic; beauty is valued, as is art, music and philosophical speculation." (Italics provided). Thus in two sentences, he suggests that (1) values are objects and conversely objects are values, and (2) objects, such as money are valued. See Jack H. Curtis, *Social Psychology* (New York: McGraw-Hill Book Co., 1960), pp. 138–39. A team of sociologists do the same thing when they say, "... the rule that political officials should be elected is justified or 'explained' by saying that popular election is necessary if 'democracy' is to be realized. The rule itself is the norm but the *value, democracy*, is part of the normative reasoning." (Italics provided). The question here is whether democracy is the value, or whether democracy is valued. See Judith Blake and Kingsley Davis, "Norms, Values, and Sanctions" in Robert E. L. Faris, ed., *Handbook of Modern Sociology* (Chicago: Rand McNalley & Co.), p. 456. The confusion is further compounded by those who equate values and norms.

[10] Wilson and Nye (*op. cit*) following the pattern suggested by Morris, use the label "conceived values" to identify what is here called "value definitions" and the label "object values" for what is here called values. This analysis also includes a third category "operative values" (which parallels the "preferential behavior" of Morris) which they define as nonverbal behavior involved in selecting one object rather than another. There would seem to be little gained from using the label "value" for this third type. Why not just talk about the behavior *per se*. Doing so may then encourage research and theoretical explorations of the relationship between behavior and value definitions. Dewey also considers what has here been called value definitions under a "value fact" label.

[11] Lower animals coordinate their behavior and maintain their "animal social systems." They, however, do not do so through the process of symbolic interaction. It is misleading to say that animals reach decisions about their behavior, if we are going to use the same label

making process what they planned to do or what they wanted to do. Such decision making is characteristic of all human interaction. However, once such decisions are made, if they are to be taken into account in future behavior, they have to be preserved in symbolic form (verbal or written). If society is to function harmoniously and not get burdened with constantly making and remaking the same decisions, the decisions must be preserved for future attention. The initial form in which the decision is preserved might be simply, "we have decided to do such and such." However, in subsequent discussions this may appear as "to do such and such is good," or "such and such is good."

If this does happen, as has been suggested, an important change has taken place, which may escape the attention of those involved.

There are certain aspects of the symbolic interaction process which may help us understand how such a change occurs. First, the transition from "we have decided" to "it is good" may be facilitated by the fact that once the decision process has been completed, the decision can be preserved only in the form of symbols. "We" (the empirical beings involved) continue to exist and can be easily taken into account in the future. The *process of deciding*, however, is an emergent, creative phenomenon, which cannot be "rerun" for future analysis. There is no "instant replay" available. The symbols which preserve the *decision* (the "have decided" aspect) then are symbols for which there are no longer any empirically present referents. Man, however, with his ability to use time definitions, constantly takes past behavior into account. Since man is able to take into account past phenomena which are not physically present, it is an easy step when taking into account some such phenomena to use symbols such as "X is good" which refer to the present but for which there is no empirical referent. Facility in taking past decisions into account could easily lead to or facilitate use of NER symbols of the value type. This involves substituting a present-oriented NER symbol for a past-oriented symbol. The fact that man can literally label and then see that which he believes the label calls for (as hypnosis dramatically illustrates) no doubt also facilitates the development of values.

Once particular values are accepted they become a part of the culture of the group, get incorporated into the overall systematized value structure and, if of sufficient saliency, get related to the mores and become difficult to change.

This analysis so far does not answer the question why values might be developed. It only helps understand the skill which could be generalized to permit the use of values. An explanation as to why the transition might occur will now be presented. If, as has been maintained, behavior of the *individual* is in response to symbols and not directly in response to biologically given phenomena such as instincts or drives, then, when the question sooner or later arises as to why – "Why did we decide to do it this way?" or "Why

---

"reach decisions" to identify the behavior of humans, since to do so implies that the same decision-reaching process is (or may be) involved.

should I do it this way, even tho the group did decide?" – the transition from "we have decided" to "it is good" may be functional in achieving acceptance of a common set of definitions, which in turn are required if relatively harmonious interaction is to occur. The answer to the questions stated above, in over-simplified form, goes "we do it not just because we have decided, but because it is good." Since man is not restricted to the use of ER symbols, and since there is no inherent relationship between symbol and referent it is possible to translate the concepts of decision into an NER statement in which the evaluation or decision is figuratively projected or transposed into the evaluated or decided-upon behavior.

Once the transition to "the decided-upon-behavior-is-good" is made, if the statement is to mean more than just a tautological pronouncement (the decided upon behavior is decided upon) then the second half of the statement should mean something different from the first. If such a statement is viewed as non-tautological (as it frequently is) then a symbolic distinction has been introduced which leads the hearer to believe that the statement "it is good" says nothing about the evaluators, but rather identifies a characteristic of the evaluated. It may be easier to justify my behavior to you and to myself for that matter, if I am convinced and can convince you that it is some quality of the evaluated rather than some human evaluator, which I am taking into account. This aspect of values is illustrated by the following statement from the Inaugural Address of John F. Kennedy:

> To those people in the huts and villages of half the globe struggling to break the bonds of mass misery, we pledge our best efforts to help them help themselves, for whatever period is required – not because the Communists may be doing it, not because we seek their votes, but because it is right.

When I say to you "X is good" my intention is usually more than just to identify a value. I usually want you to behave toward X in a particular way. The plans of action, more frequently implicit than explicit, which accompany the "good" label are usually "seek after these things."

When the transition to values takes place, some symbol is needed to preserve the value and to take it into account in discussions. Labels such as goodness, right, beautiful, or the term currently in vogue among existentialists, "authentic," are used.

When "good" or "goodness" is used to identify the evaluated, those making such use of the term, whether deliberately or not divest themselves individually and collectively, of any responsibility for the value. To say "X is good" implies that the goodness exists in X, in the same sense that the statement "X is five pounds heavy" means that the five-poundness is a characteristic of the object, regardless of whether the viewer is aware of it. If the goodness is IN the object, then the viewer logically cannot be responsible for it. All he is doing (or so it seems) is identifying what is empirically, or may be superempirically, there.[12]

---

[12] The situation of the human neonate is quite different from that of the adult. The new-

The "it is good" statement, *if accepted*, serves to stop debate. It rests upon the unstated assumption that the decision as to goodness and badness is not a man-made decision, or as tho the beauty or the goodness (the values) are in the evaluated phenomenon. Thus, with reference to beauty and other values, Alfred North Whitehead points out: "Nature gets credit which should in truth be reserved for ourselves: the rose for its scent; the nightingale for his song; the sun for its radiance. They should address their lyrics to themselves, and should turn them into odes of self-congratulation on the excellency of the human mind. Nature is a dull affair, soundless, scentless, colorless; merely the hurrying of material, endlessly, meaninglessly." [13]

If we accept an "it is good" interpretation, we are unlikely to even consider questions such as "good for whom?" or "good under what circumstances?" or whether there are other equally "good" objects or behavioral alternatives. Once such a translation has taken place, the values may then be defended from change. Values and value definitions may both be defended. Disproving values scientifically, however, is impossible since there is nothing empirical to which one can give attention. In the absence of empirical criteria, my opinion or my conviction or the "feeling in *my* heart" is as easily accepted as a valid criterion as your opinion, conviction, or "heart." Or to paraphrase the Doukhobor statement, "If God is within me I can do no wrong," "If the proofs are within me, you cannot prove them wrong."

If two individuals differ in their conclusions about the goodness or beauty (value) of some phenomenon, these differences cannot be resolved by taking into account any empirical quality of the evaluated phenomenon *per se*. They can, however, be resolved, and consensus obtained, by producing change in one or both of the individuals (the evaluators – not the evaluated). These changes need have little if anything to do *directly* with the evaluated phenomenon. A change of reference group, for instance, may produce the change of values.

In conformity-gaining efforts, NER concepts can be compounded in an effort to increase the saliency thereof. Frequently some variation of the "goodness" – "Godness" compound is used, in which the phenomenon is interpreted as not only being good but also having some type of supernatural endorsement or as harmonizing with, or being incorporated in, "natural" law.

When I make value pronouncements about the evaluated phenomenon, I am indirectly at least also telling my audience something about me. Since there is no empirical value in the object (even tho my statement "X is good"

---

born child comes into a society which has a set of value definitions and values already established. He is initially taught just to accept both the value definitions and the values which are already there rather than to establish or create a new set of values. In this sense then he is responding to what is already there. Further, unless he is taught to do so, he most likely will see no difference between values and value definitions.

[13] Alfred North Whitehead, *Science and the Modern World* (New York: The Macmillan Co., 1925), p. 80.

implies this) I am saying that I have knowledge of non-empirical matters which the average individual does not have. Consequently, it may be that I can convince others and maybe myself that I have some magical or maybe supernatural relationships or characteristics which permits me to know about these mystical things. To the extent that I am so defined, the values which I proclaim take on increased saliency. Decisions about values rely heavily upon authority as a means of proof.

The use of values then may be functional in the attainment of consensus and the maintainance of related social systems.

The value approach may be disfunctional, however, in the sense that it may lead to disharmony. Once values are accepted, they impede change. Once we say, for instance, that birth control *per se* is wrong, especially if we use the "good" – "God" compound and link this evaluation to the supernatural, it becomes difficult to change. If, however, we say our group "has decided" (talk of value definitions) change may be easier. Whether change per se or any particular change is good or bad, however, is another question, and when stated in this manner involves a value and is incapable of scientific determination, and is not of concern to us here. Extensive use of the "value-approach" may be related to the development of "closed-mindedness," whereas extensive use of the "value-definition approach" may be related to the 1everse or "open-mindedness."

IV. *Attempted Operational Definitions of Values*

Efforts have been made by some to provide operational definitions of values, altho it is not clear just why they want to do so. One introductory sociology text,[14] for instance, indicates that "any cultural trait is socially 'good' if it operates harmoniously within its cultural setting to attain the goals which the people are seeking. This is a workable, non-ethnocentric test of the goodness or badness of a culture trait." A question which needs attention, however, is ignored. Why does one want to translate "cultural harmony" into "good," since the term good has so many other established meanings? It would, in fact, seem only to confuse the issue and the understanding thereof to introduce the second term. Since the phenomenon of concern is actually cultural (or sociocultural) harmony, why not simply talk of cultural harmony unless one is reluctant to give up discussions in value terms which may have previously provided comfort and solace or unless one falsely assumes that the scientist is able to provide scientific answers to all types of questions, including questions as to what *is* good and bad. Nothing is added to the scientific cogency of the analysis to utilize such operational definitions of goodness. A sociological analysis of social change may, in fact be hampered if the analysis starts with the premise that equilibrium and anything which contributes thereto is good.

---

[14] Paul B. Horton and Chester L. Hunt, *Sociology* (New York: McGraw-Hill Book Co., 1964), p. 87.

V. *Values, Value Definitions, and Sociology*

The hypothesis is advanced, then, that value definitions are initially developed because for continued interaction man required symbols with which to record agreed-upon plans of action. Value definitions were translated into values in an effort to establish and/or maintain harmonious interaction by providing motive language (symbols) with which to justify the decision.[15]

It is further suggested that clarity of scientific analysis can be facilitated by distinguishing between:

(A) *Value Definitions* (goodness definitions, sacred definitions) or definitions which man, the evaluator makes. The label identifies or calls attention to human decisions. Definitions are developed and applied to his world by man himself.

B. *Values* (goodness, beautifulness) which identify the evaluated, in such a way that the human evaluation is figuratively projected from the evaluator to the evaluated.

Scientific sociologists can deal with value definitions. One way to do this is to pay attention to the symbols which man uses in his evaluations. In its most simple form research about value definitions involves asking people what value definitions are involved in their behavior, and taking their answers (symbols) into account.[16] All symbols are empirical, and can accordingly be studied by the scientific method. If culture is defined as the totality of the definitions held by the group, value definitions, then, are one component thereof, and discussions of value definitions can be related to the body of literature, research, and theory dealing with culture. One can study the relationships between value definitions and other definitions such as object definitions, self definitions, norm definitions, role definitions, space definitions, time definitions, and definitions of the situation. Values which involve NER symbols cannot be handled by a method which is restricted to the

---

[15] In an on-going society, the relationship would seem to be a reciprocal one. Initially established value definitions may be translated into values and established values may be translated into value definitions.

[16] Making decisions about the meaning of particular symbols in particular situations is not necessarily an easy, simple task. See for instance, Blake and Davis, *op. cit.* Value definitions being used by others can of course be inferred. In most interaction, individuals constantly infer value definitions using some form of the role-taking process. A distinction should be made between inferred value definitions and stated value definitions. Each may serve a useful purpose. Research is needed concerning the process by which social scientists infer value definitions, as well as the relationship between inferred value definitions and respondent-stated value definitions. Note that it is value definitions, not values, which are inferred. We infer the decisions of humans as to what they will do, or as to how they evaluate. A scientist does not infer some mystical value *in* any object or behavior. Since all phenomena are multi-dimensional in nature, it is important to know to which aspect of the phenomenon of attention the behaving individual is paying attention in making his evaluations. Direct inquiry about such points may serve to identify false assumptions or inferrences about the behavior.

empirical.[17] There are empirical characteristics of various phenomena which can be identified and studied but not empirical goodness as we have viewed it. There is, as Kolb [18] has suggested, a "values *vs* science" dilemma. There is not, however, a "value definitions *vs* science" dilemma. It is important also to recognize that efforts to secure answers about values require a method different from that used to secure answers about value definitions. One method applicable to value definitions but not values, is the scientific method. It is wrong to conclude, however, since the scientific method cannot be used to secure answers about values that such answers cannot be secured. Decisions about beauty, goodness, justice, virtue and sin, are constantly being made. The method employed, however, is not the scientific method.[19] One method frequently used to secure such answers and others of a religious nature is to rely upon authority, as has already been suggested. The answers which one gets to any question are always relative to the method used to secure them. Even conflicting answers to the same question may each be right – according to its own method.

Were a distinction between values and value definitions incorporated into our discussions and text books, the likeihood of students concluding that scientific sociologists can scientifically determine what is good or bad, or that they are experts in the determination of values would be greatly reduced.

Sociologists with a social-action perspective frequently ignore this distinction. The accomplishment of their action goals may be facilitated by invoking "science," "sociology," or "scientific sociology" as the validator of their values; thereby divesting themselves of the responsibility for them.

---

[17] In the classroom in which a scientific subject matter is being taught, the teacher presumably provides information about the empirical phenomenon of concern. Since science is a method for securing answers about the empirical world which exists independent of the scientists, when the teacher makes value statements such as "X is good," his students may conclude that he is providing them with information about the empirical phenomenon of study when he is in reality providing information about himself. There would seem to be at least an element of intellectual dishonesty to permit the student to accept the first interpretation.

[18] See William L. Kolb, "Values, Positivism, and the Functional Theory of Religion: The Growth of a Moral Dilemma," *Social Forces*, XXXI, No. 4 (May 1953), 305–311. Farber and Wilson make the same point with reference to psychologists. "The psychologist is hence in a dilemma: he cannot in all good conscience make these (value) judgments himself, nor can he separate his field of research from the judgmental process which is implicit in it. What can he do? There is at present no answer to this question." The answer suggested here is to recognize that all the answers in which man may be interested cannot be secured by the same method – *i.e.* the scientific. Therefore, as a scientist one is not concerned with providing answers about values, but is very much concerned with the study of value definitions. See Seymour M. Farber and Roger H. L. Wilson, edd., *Control of the Mind* (New York: McGraw-Hill Book Co., 1961), p. viii.

[19] For further discussion of this point see Glenn M. Vernon, *op. cit.*, Chapter 7, and Glenn M. Vernon, "The Symbolic Interactionist Approach to the Sociology of Religion," *International Yearbook for the Sociology of Religion* (Cologne: Westdeutscher Verlag, 1966) pp. 135–155.

An interesting question which arises from an analysis such as this is whether it would be possible to develop and maintain a society using only value-definitions, and consequently excluding any use of values. Would it be possible to secure sufficient integration of behavior upon the basis only of "we have decided" or "we evaluate" symbols. Could a society develop a set of mores sufficient for society maintainance without convincing the members thereof (or at least a large majority) that the behavioral content of the mores IS good or moral?

The University of Maine

K

THE VALUE PROBLEM AND MARXIST SOCIAL THEORY

JOHN SOMERVILLE

Let us try to indicate at the outset what we mean, or the chief things we mean, by the value problem. In the sense in which it is being discussed, it may be broken down into questions like the following: In what sense do values exist? Out of what do they originate? Are they a necessary part of man's life? Do they play a constructive part in the life of man? Is it possible to determine scientifically, or to prove rationally what values are positive and what values are negative for man? If so, what precisely has been proved? What relation do values, and the implementation of values, have to fields like history, economics, politics, religion, physical and social science?

If these are among the chief problems which enter into the study of value, the specific question we are posing in this paper is: What account of these matters do we find in Marxism? In trying to answer this question we are first confronted with the widely discussed issue of whether Marx rejected values altogether. If one makes a detailed examination of the work of Marx and Engels, I believe it becomes clear that they did not reject values as such, but that they did reject a number of fallacies about values which we might group under the general designation, Fallacies of Misplaced Value Function. These may be broken down into two broad sub-classes: a) Fallacies of Misplaced Moralism at the Theoretical Level; and b) Fallacies of Misplaced Moralism at the Practical Level. Let us examine these in turn.

Misplaced Moralism at the Theoretical Level consists in thinking that a moral evaluation of social phenomena can by itself constitute a satisfactory social philosophy or social science, that it is not necessary to undertake detailed empirical description and analysis, and to discover general factual laws and causal relationships. An example is the tendency to think that from the standpoint of socialist theory, or humanist principles, or the theory and principles of socialist humanism or humanist socialism it is sufficient, in dealing with capitalism, to concentrate mainly or exclusively upon the identification, demonstration and condemnation of its evil aspects. In rejecting such an approach Marx was certainly not saying that capitalism has no evil aspects, or that it is unnecessary or meaningless, to make moral evaluations of social phenomena. Marx was in fact deeply interested in making moral evaluations, and in bringing them into what he considered the proper functional relationship with empirical social science. In his *Capital*, for example, he claims that socialism "creates a new economical foundation for a higher form of the

family, and of the relation between the sexes." [1] In the same work Marx
writes in a similar way about society as a whole when he expresses the conclusion that the further development of productive forces will create "those
material conditions which alone can form the real basis of a higher form of
society, a society in which the full and free development of every individual
forms the ruling principle." [2] Here we have not only a moral evaluation of
one form of society as higher than another, but a definition of the standard
of evaluation underlying the judgment, i.e., "the full and free development
of every individual" (which cannot but remind one of John Dewey's approach
to ethics), together with a statement of causal factors necessary (but not
sufficient) for the attainment of the moral goal – a statement which in its
specifics suggests Marx's differences from Dewey.

It is evident that what Marx objected to was not that the social scientist
should make value judgments, should consciously relate his work to the
attainment of moral values. What he objected to was doing this in the wrong
way, that is, attempting to make the value process perform a function it was
not capable of performing. The most frequent form of the wrong way in his
time was to imagine that moral feeling was not only an adequate substitute
for empirical analysis, but was also the main causal agent of social progress.
If Marx were alive today I believe he would say that the most frequent error
in this connection now is that there can be a value-free social science, or an
objectively neutral social scientist. The most that is possible is a social science
free from *misplaced* moralism, and a social scientist *unaware* of the values
actually served by his choice of problems and his results. The nineteenth-
century error overestimated the role of values; the twentieth-century error
underestimates it.

The remarks we have just made bring us to a consideration of the Fallacy
of Misplaced Moralism at the Practical Level, since this fallacy concerns
reasonings about how to implement values in human life, about their practice.
If ethics does not, from beginning to end, squarely face the relation of theory
to practice, it will sink into theoretical as well as practical insignificance.
This is what Aristotle understood from the start. His classic treatise on the
subject begins with the words: "Every art" [that is, practice] "and every kind
of inquiry" [that is, theory] "and likewise every act and purpose, seems to aim
at some good; and so it has been well said that the good is that at which
everything aims . . ."[3] Thus practice is brought in from the first sentence,
and in the very definition of the good as value. Aristotle proceeds immediately to note that there is a word for the overall good that everyone wants:
happiness. So ethics must be a theory of how to attain human happiness.
What human happiness is and how man can attain it naturally depend on the
kind of being man is, on how man is made, on his needs, wants and potenti-

---

[1] Karl Marx, *Capital*, ed. Kerr (Chicago, 1919), I, 536.

[2] *Ibid.*, 649.

[3] Aristotle, *Nicomachean Ethics*, trans. Peters (London: Routledge & Kegan Paul,
1906), Bk. I, Ch. I.

alities, all of which is empirically determinable. Two things stand out: man is a rational animal, and man is a political animal. So the attainment of happiness depends primarily upon two things: the full development and application of man's intelligence, and the setting up of a society whose institutions are deliberately geared to the attainment of maximum human happiness. Thus Aristotle conceived of what we think of as two works – his *Ethics* and his *Politics* – as one connected work; it is we who split them up, and deal with them separately, and as if they were separable.

What was Aristotle saying, basically? A number of interesting and important things, as fresh and challenging today as when he wrote them: that there is no impassable barrier, or unbridgeable gulf, between fact and value, that value is inconceivable apart from facts and apart from man, that value is an aspect of facts, an aspect which depends on man's necessary relationship to facts, that value arises out of the built-in needs, desires and potentialities of development of man about which he, as man in process, has no choice, that value is especially relative to man's social needs, social institutions and social problems, because man cannot be man except in and through society. Thus social science must be consciously and systematically connected with ethics; ethics must be approached as social science, or part of a social science, and social science must prove itself in application to social practice.

It seems to me quite clear that all this is perfectly compatible with Marxism, that Marx was in agreement with all the propositions in the preceding paragraph. In other words, Marx did not differ with Aristotle on the basic relation of fact to value; he differed on the nature of the facts. He did not differ with Aristotle that an adequate theory of values must also be a theory about social practice; he differed on what was involved in an adequate theory of social practice. He did not differ with Aristotle on the proposition that a correct theory about ethics and its relation to social science rests on empirically discoverable facts concerning man's nature and potentialities and is thus objectively provable; he differed with what Aristotle took these facts to be, especially those regarding slavery, classes, the possibilities of intellectual and human development of the majority, and the like. To sum it up from Marx's standpoint: though Aristotle understood correctly the relation between ethics and politics, value and science, social theory and social practice, what Aristotle lacked was a significant theory of history, a theory about the causal dynamics of large-scale socio-historical changes, and the effect of these changes upon ethics, politics, value, science, theory and practice. That is what Marxism is all about. In a sense, Marx equals Aristotle *minus* aristocracy *plus* historical social science. If one wants to make an uncharitable comparison, our average academic social scientist today might be said to equal Aristotle *minus* Aristotle *plus* empirical methodology *minus* history.

But we have digressed – perhaps fruitfully – from the Fallacy of Misplaced Moralism at the Practical Level. As the mistake at the theoretical level is to think that an empirical analysis of causal dynamics is not necessary, that moral evaluation of effects is enough, so the mistake at the practical level is

to think that a clear demonstration of the moral superiority of a certain
social arrangement or system will constitute a sufficient cause to have it
adopted in practice. This is a form, or a part, of what Engels called the
"ideological process," that is, the process of thinking that social ideas in
general, and progressive or reformist social ideas in particular, not only have
an "independent history" (independent of what is taking place or has taken
place at the economic base of society), but are the chief determinants of the
course of history.[4] It is important to emphasize that Marx and Engels consider this way of thinking fallacious ("false consciousness" as Engels puts it,
in his letter to Mehring cited above) not because social ideas and moral
judgments play no causal role whatever in relation to the course of history,
to bringing about important historical changes, but only because they do not
represent the chief causes.[5]

It is perhaps even more important, in the light (or darkness) of widespread
discussions about "ideology" at the present time, to emphasize some facts
which seem to be rather generally overlooked. One of these is that what
Marx and Engels considered false about ideology was not necessarily the
primary ideas put forward by the given thinker, but rather the assumption
that these ideas were not causally conditioned by economic factors, and (as
just mentioned) that they could themselves act as the decisive historical
causes independently of economic factors. Another important fact is that the
term 'ideology' has undergone a semantic evolution among Marxists since the
days of Marx and Engels. This evolution does not mean that contemporary
Marxists have given up the view that it is false to think that social ideas are
not conditioned by economic factors, and equally false to think that social
ideas are the main cause of historical changes. It simply means that contemporary Marxists prevailingly have given up the practice of using the term
'ideology' in a way which restricts it to those fallacious aspects of social ideas,
and use it now as a blanket term to cover all social ideas, whether or not they
include fallacious aspects. Marxists today refer to Marxism itself as ideology.
Marx and Engels would not have done that; but this does not signify that
contemporary Marxists differ with Marx and Engels as to the truth of Marxism, or its status as scientific knowledge.

As our whole contemporary discussion of ideology suffers from vagueness
– first of all in relation to the very definition of the term ideology itself – so
also does our discussion of what we specifically call value-free social science.
If we examine this matter at all closely it becomes clear that there is only one
sense in which social science can, as a matter of fact, be value-free. That is the
sense in which it can and should refrain from allowing value commitments to
distort conclusions about the subject matter being dealt with. Not refraining
from such distortion is what I have called misplaced value function, or

---

[4] *Cf.* Engels' letter to Mehring, 1893, in *The Selected Correspondence of Marx and Engels,
1846–1895* (New York: International Publishers, 1942), p. 511. *Cf.* also, Marx and Engels,
The German Ideology (International, 1939).

[5] *Cf.* Engels' letter to Bloch, 1890, in *The Selected Correspondence, Supra,* p. 477.

KK

misplaced moralism. But what is wrong is the misplacement, not the value function itself. It would be an even greater error to think that social science is uncommitted in relation to human values, or that the individual social scientist can be objectively neutral (that is, neutral in terms of actual effects and consequences in relation to the value issues and conflicts which exist in social practice, as distinguished from neutrality which merely consists in a subjective psychological unawareness of the actual effects and consequences).

It would be relevant at this point to quote, if I may, a passage from a paper on a related topic, prepared for the XIVth International Congress of Philosophy: "In this connection it is not usually noticed how profoundly partisan science is, how pervaded with value judgments, first of all in favor of man, as opposed to the rest of nature. If microbes could think, could they be expected to think that microbiology is non-partisan? Or parasites that parasitology is non-partisan? Is medicine neutral as between health and disease? Are astronomy, physics and chemistry neutral on the question whether man ought to increase his power over nature? For the scientist to imagine himself as simply neutral or non-partisan, as free from value judgments, is clearly naïve. Man is not yet in a position to say that he wants truth just for truth's sake, that he wants or loves any piece of truth whatever, just because it is true. He wants truth, of course, but he wants that particular kind of truth which has certain relationships to man, or to a God who in turn has certain relationships to man."

"There is sometimes even a question of when and where involved. Suppose in Nazi Germany there had been a proposal to publish a book entitled *The Crimes of Jews against Children*, in which every word be true, and every loathsome crime committed by a Jew against a child for centuries back would be fished up from the records and set forth in every documented detail. How many of us who were not anti-Semites would have said: 'Fine; we want and love every piece of truth. By all means publish the book in Nazi Germany'? And those who would have objected could not consistently have done so simply on the ground that this book was not 'the full truth,' for no book is ever the full truth. The fact is that the sciences abound in special studies of every kind (including studies of special crimes of special groups) to which no one objects, because there is no immediate danger of monstrous injustice being perpetrated as a result of their publication. But to allow justice to enter means that we are involving ourselves in value judgments; and to decide in favor of the oppressed means we must abandon the claim to neutrality." [6]

Considerations of this kind underlie what Soviet Marxists have called "*partijnost'*," the principle of partisanship in philosophy and science. The claim of this principle is that social partisanship is inevitable, whether through deliberate choice, tacit consent, silence, inaction, or just plain ignorance. The principle is not that it is justifiable to distort or suppress the truth, or that the

---

[6] John Somerville, "Philosophy, Ideology and Marxism Today," *Proceedings of the XIVth International Congress of Philosophy*, Vienna, 1968, (forthcomming).

Communist Party has the right to decide the final truth about everything. Of course, much has happened in the Soviet Union, and in every other sovereign state and social order, that one can readily find fault with. But one must distinguish between happenings which constitute a violation of principles held as principles, and happenings which represent the implementation of principles held as principles. This makes an important difference, if one wants to understand theory and improve practice. Otherwise, one is simply carrying on a feud.

It is not difficult to identify and summarize the basic values which Marxism accepts, defends, and proposes to use as guideliness for social development and state planning. They could be briefly formulated as follows: 1) the fullest degree of physical, intellectual, moral and emotional health and development of which each individual is capable; 2) the elimination of poverty, violence, warfare and all forms of oppression, exploitation and mistreatment of person by person, group by group, nation by nation or class by class. There is little original to Marxism in these values, as values. Most of what they contain can be found in the democratic tradition, the Christian ethic, secular humanism, and in philosophical and religious movements antedating all these. Neither is there anything original to Marxism in the conception that such values are not simply arbitrary, subjective choices, but can be proved rationally, objectively. This conception is found in the classic tradition of ancient Greece, and, later, in philosophers like Spinoza, the French Encyclopedists, Auguste Comte, John Stuart Mill, John Dewey and many others. What is distinctive to Marxism is threefold: 1) a theory of history which tries to solve the problem of the relation of economic and technological forces to the fulfillment of these values; 2) the working out, at the theoretical level, of the kind of reconstruction of social institutions which must take place if these values are to be fulfilled; 3) the organization, at the practical level, of a political movement capable of carrying through the necessary social reconstruction.

California Western University, San Diego

CLASSICAL MARXISM AND THE TOTALITARIAN ETHIC

A. James Gregor

Preoccupation with a "Marxist" ethics characterizes much of the contemporary literature devoted to the study of the writings of Karl Marx. Long neglected in the theoretical literature, Marx's ethical conceptions have become more and more the focus of attention both in the West and in the socialist countries of Eastern Europe.[1] This is particularly true since those latter countries fell heir to the moral crisis of de-Stalinization. Soviet philosophers, in particular, have been disarmingly frank in their admissions that Marxists have, in the past, neglected ethics as a discipline.[2] They conceive their current emphasis as insuring the impossibility of any further infractions of "Socialist humanism" by any future "personality cult."

In the West the analytic and interpretative works of R. T. De George and George L. Kline [3] have done much to keep philosophers abreast of contemporary developments in Soviet and East European ethical theory. Their work and the availability of adequate translations of representative Soviet and East European Marxist publications [4] provide substantial insights into the development of ethical theory in a Marxist environment. But an adequate assessment of the relationship of classical Marxist ethics and the ethics of the social order created by Marxists requires some attempt at reconstruction of the kind of ethical arguments that subtended the theoretical enterprise of the founder of Marxism himself as well as their implications for socialist

---

[1] *Cf.* R. T. De George, "A Bibliography of Soviet Ethics," *Studies in Soviet Thought*, III (1963), 83 f.; H. L. Parsons, *Ethics in the Soviet Union Today* (New York, 1965); G. L. Kline, "Leszek Kołakowski and the Revision of Marxism," in *European Philosophy Today* (Chicago, 1965), pp. 113–156.

[2] *Cf.* L. M. Archangelski, *Kategorien der marxistischen Ethik* (Berlin, 1965), Foreword (Russian names will be rendered as they appear in the translation employed); "Ethics," in Notes and Comments, *Studies in Soviet Thought*, III (1963), 203–205.

[3] R. T. De George, "The Foundations of Marxist-Leninist Ethics," *Studies in Soviet Thought*, III (1963), 121–133, "Soviet Ethics and Soviet Society," *ibid.*, IV (1964), 206–217, and "The Soviet Concept of Man," *ibid.*, 261–276; Kline, *op. cit.*, and "Soviet and East European Philosophy, and Philosophers, Today," a colloquy paper, The University of Texas, May 9, 1967 (mimeograph).

[4] A representative sample would include at least A. F. Schischkin, *Grundlagen der marxistischen Ethik* (Berlin, 1964); L. Kołakowski, *Der Mensch ohne Alternative* (Munich, 1964); A. Schaff, *A Philosophy of Man* (New York, 1963); W. Suchomlinski, *Ueber die Erziehung des kommunistischen Menschen* (Berlin, 1963); W. Eichhorn, *Von der Entwicklung des sozialistischen Menschen* (Berlin, 1964); Archangelski, *op. cit.*

society. In such an appraisal the non-Marxist philosopher is left with far less substantial treatments. There is surprisingly little literature available devoted to these vexed questions.

Few efforts have been made to explicate the relationship of Marx's own ethics to the ethics of what has come to be known in our time as totalitarian or administered society. If Stalinism was no more than an "ahistorical deviation," as is contended by Soviet philosophers, Marxist ethics should provide no rationale in its support. If the features of Stalinism reflect, on the other hand, some aspects of classical Marxism, as many non-Marxist thinkers insist, it should be possible to isolate, at least in general terms, their affinities.

The contention of this paper is that classical Marxism, Stalinism and contemporary Soviet ethics share a common logic (understood in the informal and extended sense of the term). Classical Marxism, it will be argued, provided the ultimate rationale for the Soviet totalitarian ethic. Moreover, it will be suggested that the essentials of this totalitarian ethic can be traced in paradigmatic justificatory arguments offered in support of totalitarianism of the Right as well as the Left. In effect, should the subsequent argument prove convincing, it would provide some grounds for the contention that totalitarian systems are more alike in some fundamental respects, than they are like any alternate system.

I

The publication of the early Marx manuscripts has provided contemporary scholarship with the materials that make possible a reconstruction of the ethics of classical Marxism. That Marx levelled ethical arguments is now no longer a matter of serious dispute.[5] There is, in fact, hardly a page written by Marx that is not quick with explicit or implicit moral judgment. But more than the presence of characteristically ethical predicates and normative ascriptions, Marx's work constitutes a serious effort at articulating a defensible ethic. To reconstruct that ethic is not only a compelling intellectual obligation, it also provides us with an insight into the foundations of contemporary social thought in the Soviet Union.

Marx, even in his earliest manuscripts, was concerned with formulating a *theoretical* conception of man. His original conception was a very vague "model" of man as a social being, a descriptive frame of reference simpler in obvious ways from the being it was understood to represent. As a model it

---

[5] Orthodox Marxists are the first to advance such a claim (even at the expense of historic accuracy and plausibility); *cf.* Archangelski, *op. cit.*, p. 215. Lewis' comments characterize contemporary Marxist appraisal; J. Lewis, *Marxism and the Open Mind* (New York, 1957), p. 129. For a considerable length of time it was systematically denied that Marxism was anything other than an "objective science." As an "objective science" it did not concern itself with "abstract" "values." This was Karl Kautsky's thesis in his *Ethik und materialistische Geschichtsauffassung.*

was calculated to afford a parsimonious account of, and facilitate insight into the more complex and elusive real being. In his *Economic and Philosophic Manuscripts* of 1844 this model was reduced to stenographic formulations, and the relationship between the individual and "social-being" was regularly reduced to one of identity. "The individual *is* the *social-being*. His life ... *is* ... an expression and confirmation of social life. Man's individual and species life (*Gattungsleben*) are not different ...." [6]

Framed in such a manner the model becomes a definition and is recognizable as an Hegelian inheritance. It was the common heritage of almost all the Left-Wing Hegelians of the period. Moses Hess, himself such an Hegelian, and a mentor of both Marx and Engels, identified this model as that of "modern German Philosophy." "The individual ... according to contemporary German philosophy," Hess indicated, "*is* the 'species, the totality, humanity ....'" [7] This vague and ambiguous conception remained central to Marx's theoretical accounts. "Man," Marx contended, "*is* the human world, the state, society" and the human essence was understood to be no more than "the *ensemble* of social relations." [8]

Such a conceptual bias produced in Marx a conviction that a "real science" of society could only be established by making "the social relationship of 'man to man' the basic principle of ... theory," [9] and that relationship was construed to be, in some sense, an identity. The theory which sought to explicate this relationship drew inferences from a set of descriptive sentences which could be taken as premises. The premises which thus served as postulates for the theoretical system were understood to be broad empirical generalizations capable of generating theorems of increasing specificity which themselves were subject to empirical confirmation and disconfirmation. The theory was expressed in terms of very broad (and consequently vague) sequential laws which conceived determinate changes in the productive forces generating changes in the division of labor in society which in turn entailed alterations in productive relations. The ordering of the constituent propositions indicated the implications of the conceptual model by providing an inventory of determinants, directing the strategy of research and explanation by isolating the prime variables. Variables were identified as belonging to the productive forces, the relations of production, the superstructure or class interests (to specify only the most prominent categories). Changes in variables belonging to one or another category are related in a law-like manner, indicating the direction in which variables influenced each other. The theory established the cognitive implications of the initial definition.

---

[6] K. Marx, *Economic and Philosophic Manuscripts* (Moscow, n.d.), pp. 104 f. Hereafter referred to as *EPM*.

[7] M. Hess, "Die letzten Philosophen," in *Philosophische und sozialistische Schriften: 1837–1850* (Berlin, 1961), p. 381.

[8] Marx, "Contribution to the Critique of Hegel's Philosophy of Right," in *Early Writings*, trans. and ed. T. B. Bottomore (New York, 1964), p. 43; and "Theses on Feuerbach," in Marx and Engels, *The German Ideology* (New York, 1947), p. 198.

[9] *EPM*, p. 145.

Marx defended his use of his theoretical scheme and the initial definition of man with which he had begun with standard arguments. The notion of man he advanced was (1) intuitively more tenable than the mechanistic and atomistic conception of "bourgeois" social theory; (2) it had specific empirical referents and consequently could generate a variety of verification studies; and (3) it provided a more parsimonious account of the range of phenomena under scrutiny.[10] All of which can be said in the language of contemporary theory construction in the social sciences. But social science is ideally concerned with the formulation and issuance of "if-then" or "theoretical" propositions, descriptive or explanatory accounts systematically relating recurrent phenomena for purposes of prediction and control. It does not conceive the issuance of imperatives, or the identification of ideals towards which men should aspire, to be among its legitimate concerns. Marx's analysis, on the other hand, characteristically delivered itself of conclusions unmistakably normative – couched in the language of advocacy rather than empirical assessment. His analysis led to "the doctrine that man is the supreme being for man ..." and ended "with the categorical imperative to overthrow all those conditions in which man is an abased, enslaved, abandoned, contemptible being ...." [11] Marx's prose, particularly of this early period is charged with imperative force. "Man is the highest being for man," [12] an evident value, is conjoined with the injunction, "One must rekindle in the hearts of ... men their human self-consciousness, freedom. Only this sentiment ... can make out of a society a community of men devoted to their supreme ends ...." [13]

Thus Marx's model of man supported normative conclusions as well as discharging scientific or purely descriptive functions. What is of interest in the present context is how one and the same theoretical model can serve in such diverse capacities. What this account will suggest is that the initial conception employed is "normic" in the sense that as a theoretical model having a *prima facie* descriptive character it reveals itself, in fact, possessed of normative force capable of providing support for imperatives. How this is possible is, if this account is not thoroughly mistaken, instructive.

Marx's theoretical account of man identifies him, as an individual, with his society, with the human macrosphere or with the *ensemble* of social relations which constitute society and/or the macrosphere. The individual man, Marx argued, was neither a particular thing nor possessed of an abstract essence. Man, Marx seemed to argue in some critical contexts, is an existence which *is* social activity, a variable in an interactive context.

The cognitive meaning of such formulations is obscure enough – but such

---

[10] *Cf.* Marx's discussion in Marx, Engels, *The Holy Family* (Moscow, 1956), p. 142; and *The German Ideology*, particularly Part I.

[11] Marx, "Contribution ...," p. 52.

[12] *Ibid.*, p. 59.

[13] Marx, "Briefe aus den 'Deutsch-Franzoesischen Jahrbuechern,'" in *Werke* (Berlin, 1961), I, 338 f.

formulations have the species traits of definitional, empirical or theoretical propositions. How can they be understood to support normative conclusions? They support normative conclusions because implicit in such an account is at least one proposition rich with normative force. The emotive features which even elementary analysis reveals makes manifest how it is possible for Marx to negotiate the transition from presumably descriptive propositions to normative results.

The procedure reveals its traces in a variety of places, not only in Marx's earlier writings, but in his mature work as well. Thus in the notes Marx wrote for his *Contribution to the Critique of Political Economy* he contended that "Man is in the most literal sense a *zoon politikon*, not merely a social animal, *but an animal which can develop into an individual only in society.*" [14]

Cognitively this appears to be little more than an implication of the vague putative identity relationship conceived to subsist between the individual and his society. But such an implication has what Stevenson [15] has baptized "vectoral force" – it not only describes or defines but it tacitly *recommends*. The implication has persuasive force. To identify the conditions necessary for the realization of individuality entails, *psychologically*, their recommendation. One *ought* to defend and foster the conditions requisite to such fulfillment.

Marx's recommended definition of man, defended by appeals to its theoretical fruitfulness (when expanded), confirmation and parsimoniousness (when applied in the empirical domain), has emotive implications that permit the transition from cognitive premises to normative conclusions. Marx's definition has the dual characteristics of a condensed theoretical proposition which can function in an articulated social science theory and can serve as a normative ideal as well. Men *should* fulfill themselves and if man, in some unspecified sense, *is* society, *is* the ensemble of social relations – if society is the necessary ground of individuation – society and macrosocial relations have at least an instrumental, and by virtue of the identity relation, intrinsic value. Fulfillment *means* the unalienated identity of the individual and his productive community. This seems to be one of the implications of saying that man's essence *is* an *ensemble* of social relations, of saying that man *is* the human world, the state and society. "What is to be avoided above all," Marx argued, "is the re-establishing of 'Society' as an abstraction *vis-a-vis* the individual .... Man, much as he may ... be a *particular* individual ... is just as much the *totality* ...." [16] Such a conceived relationship is taken to support the normative conclusions – and Marx's ethics takes on an empirical or naturalistic character.

This conception of man was central to the "humanism" of the Left-Wing

---

[14] Marx, *Grundrisse der Kritik der Politischen Oekonomie (Rohentwurf)* (Berlin, 1953), p. 6, emphasis supplied; *cf.* N. Rotenstreich, *Basic Problems of Marx's Philosophy* (New York, 1965), Chapter IV.

[15] C. Stevenson, *Facts and Values* (New Haven, 1963), p. 102.

[16] *EPM*, pp. 104 f.

Hegelians. For Moses Hess it meant that "Only as a *social being* is the human being *truly* and *really alive*" [17] and Marx could maintain: "... my *own* existence *is* social activity .... My *general* consciousness is only the *theoretical* shape of that of which the *living* shape is the real community, the social fabric, although at the present day *general* consciousness (*Gattungsbewusstsein*) is an abstraction from real life and as such antagonistically confronts it." [18]

By identifying the individual with a "totality" (whether it be society or the state) one can, by a series of not too complicated substitutions, *demonstrate* that without society the individual is not *truly* an individual, not *truly* human and further, that the interests of the "totality" and the individual must ultimately coincide. Thus the justificatory arguments for normative judgments succeed in taking on a quasi-demonstrative character and have implications for social and political conduct.

As a consequence, Marx's purpose: the resolution of the social contradictions which compromised what he called the "unity of human essence ... *the practical identity of man with man*," [19] could muster formal as well as empirical or theoretical warrant in its support as well as provide the rationale for political conduct. In this sense Marx's arguments are curiously Hegelian in character and implication, and the "individuality," "fulfillment" and "freedom," promised is an Hegelian "individuality," "fulfillment" and "freedom," the unity of the particular with the universal. It is harmonizing of the ego with its otherness.[20] The "human emancipation" which constitutes Marx's explicit moral ideal during his early revolutionary activity is understood to be a "genuine and harmonious species life ..." [21] which, in the *Communist Manifesto*, was to be formulated as "an association in which the free development of each is the condition for the free development of all." [22]

Marx negotiates the is/ought hiatus by harnessing the implicit recommendation contained in the seemingly descriptive and definitional propositions which identify (in some unspecified sense) the individual with his social macrosphere. If man *is* his society, a disharmonious, contradictory and debased society can only engender a disharmonious, contradictory and debased individual. Marx's conception of alienation is, in fact, predicated on this putative identity relationship. To become a fully human being, harmonizing existence and essence, the harmonious identity of the particular with the universal must be restored. This harmony of ultimate interests is the condition of the "development of human powers as such" which Marx, in his maturity, made the "end in itself." [23]

---

[17] Hess, "Ueber die sozialistische Bewegung in Deutschland," *op. cit.*, p. 284.

[18] *EPM*, p. 104.

[19] Marx and Engels, *The Holy Family*, p. 56.

[20] G. W. F. Hegel, *Reason in History* (New York, 1953), p. 33.

[21] Marx, "On the Jewish Question," in *Early Writings*, p. 16.

[22] Marx and Engels, "The Communist Manifesto," in *Selected Works* (Moscow, 1955), I, 54.

[23] Marx, *Grundrisse* ..., p. 387.

II

Contemporary Marxists seem at least intuitively aware of the nature of the argument advanced by Marx. While the "normic" model of man advanced by Marx is defended by appeals to theoretical fruitfulness, empirical confirmation and descriptive economy, it is recognized that the model serves more than theoretical and descriptive purposes. Once it identified the locus of *fulfillment* and *freedom* moral judgments have gained a foothold. Fulfillment and freedom recommend themselves as self-evident values. Marx's normic conception is recognized as providing the foundation for Marxist ethics and Marxist political activity.

Thus Adam Schaff can argue that "the propositions of socialist humanism and its precepts ... flow from the theory of historical materialism, and in particular [from] the specific understanding of the individual as a social product – as a product of 'the totality of social relations'. ..."[24] Schaff is sufficiently well informed to know that no conjunction of descriptive propositions can ever provide the ultimate basis for ethical conclusions. Among the set of propositions from which a normative judgment derives there must be some element of value. Schaff therefore does not pretend to offer a demonstration but makes recourse to metaphor and speaks of socialist ethics "*flowing*" from the Marxist theory of history.

This transition from descriptive to normative domains is possible only because individuality, freedom and fulfillment are *defined*, by Marx, in terms of social relations. Apart from social relations there is, strictly speaking, no individuality, no personality, no humanity. If one accepts such a definition (actually a redefinition, for it was formulated to counter the prevailing "bouregeois" atomistic model of man) a reasonably specific set of values (psychologically) follow. What would one oppose to Marx's account? Depersonalization, inhumanity, slavery or debasement as values? Marx's initial definition, advanced in descriptive guise, identifying the individual and society, mobilizes sufficient commendatory force to deliver the ethical conclusions which remained central to the Marxian enterprise throughout the life of its founder and now provide the legitimizing rationale for Soviet political conduct.

Ethical arguments emanating from the Marxist countries regularly traffic on such a "logic." A seemingly descriptive account of man's "essence" is identified with the totality of social relations and what results is the prescriptive ideal of a "human society" or a "social humanity."[25] Thus what Marx referred to as the "supreme end" for man, his fulfillment and freedom, the full development of his personality,[26] is only possible within the harmonious

---

[24] Schaff, *op. cit.*, p. 60.

[25] D. Bergner, "Dialektischer Materialismus, Psychologie und Ethik," in *Wissenschaft contra Spekulation*, ed. G. Heyden (Berlin, 1964), pp. 208 f.

[26] *Cf.* the "Collective Work," *Die Grundlagen der kommunistischen Erziehung* (Berlin, 1964), p. 46; and F. V. Konstantinov, *Grundlagen der marxistischen Philosophie* (Berlin, 1964), p. 650.

and intricate network of socialist social relations realized in harmoniously integrated social collectives of varying form, function and extent. The perfection of man, the fulfillment of the self, requires the perfection of the relations and institutions of the society in which he lives. Society is man's essence; the more perfect society, the more perfect man. Thus Marxist ethics conceives a substantive identity between collective and individual interests. Marxist philosophers therefore characterize the distinguishing trait of Marxist ethics to be the resolution of what "bourgeois" ethics held to be the inevitable antagonism between the individual and society.[27] Thus the central achievement of Marxist ethics is understood to reside in "harmonizing the private interest of the individual with collective or social interest." [28] As a matter of fact, this putative harmony is the analytic consequence of defining man's essence as the totality of social relations.

<h1 style="text-align:center">III</h1>

The identification of the individual with any aggregate of men (the society or the state) accomplishes a variety of tasks. The most important for our purposes here is to effectively empty the concept "freedom" of any descriptive content. Freedom has been traditionally defined in terms of the absence of social and legal obstruction to the individual's freedom of action. For Locke perfect freedom meant a state in which men could "order their actions and dispose of their possessions and persons as *they* think fit . . . ." Once, however, the individual is, in some fundamental sense, identified with his collectivity, restraint and absence of restraint lose their descriptive significance and freedom cannot be non-vacuously characterized. Once such an identification is accomplished, the individual who is constrained by his collectivity is only *seemingly* constrained. Since the collectivity is his greater self, in submitting to its demands he answers a law he has, in some sense, laid upon himself. He remains, according to this rationale (the empirical constraint notwithstanding), the autonomous moral agent who freely acts to obey his truer self. Freedom and constraint conflate and the instances of the one are no longer distinguishable from instances of the other. There remains only seeming freedom (acts undertaken which conflict with the interests of the collectivity) and real freedom (acts undertaken which harmonize with the interests of the collectivity).

Thus Soviet moral philosophers have argued, "A correctly understood personal interest is an interest that is always compatible with collective goals," [29] which is a reformulation of the judgment made by Engels in 1845: "In communist society . . . the interests of individuals do not conflict, but are identical . . . . Public interests no longer differ from the interests of each

---

[27] K. Mácha, *Individuum und Gesellschaft* (Berlin, 1964), pp. 9, 14 f., and 297 ff.
[28] Shishkin, *op. cit.*, pp. 32 and 238.
[29] *Ibid.*, p. 264.

individual." [30] Such judgments rest on a putative identity relationship between the individual and his community and provide the charter myth for
the rule of the single party.

Only as long as freedom is negatively construed as the absence of collective
restraint imposed on the individual's freedom to act in his own interest is a
real distinction between freedom and constraint, between private and public
interest, possible. As long as freedom is so understood a free act is one undertaken by the individual as a self-directed activity, motivated by whatever
self-regarding interests and personal motives. Any conflict of interest between
the individual and his collectivity can then be squarely faced and mediated
by an appeal to the respective merits of the individual versus the collective
interest in each particular confrontation. The most generous interpretation
of Mill's first principle, "All restraint, *qua* restraint, is an evil," is that which
interprets it as a formal or procedural maxim which requires that any
restraint imposed by public power upon the individual's freely chosen activity
be justified by public, neutral and relevant reasons.[31] It does not necessarily
imply that freedom of individual action is valuable in and of itself, but it does
advance an initial presumption in favor of the individual's freedom to act
which must be overcome. In view of the individual's vulnerability to society,
his intrinsic powerlessness against any organized collective or unorganized
aggregate, such an initial presumption has much to recommend it. It merely
means that the burden of justifying restraint imposed upon the individual
rests upon the stronger public power. It means that the individual's defenses
against collective demands, at best never very imposing, are not further undermined by requiring that *he* justify to the community every act he undertakes.
He cannot be required to show that his every act is compatible with collective
interests without a recognition that what will result, in all probability, will
be a community with a high conformity index. This stultifying eventuality
seems to be anticipated by Soviet philosophers with satisfaction. "[P]eople
are cultivating the habit of framing their actions," we are told, "in accordance with the demands and opinion of the collective." [32] Elsewhere it is
insisted, "The community of interests, the social, political and ideological
unity of men in socialist society provides the foundation for complete
personal happiness." [33]

Marx effectively exposed the shortcomings of the arguments advanced by
"bourgeois" philosophers in support of the "atomic conception of man." He
correctly recognized that the case for psychological individualism was un-
convincing. There was no empirical warrant for the characterization of man
as an atom and of society as an aggregate of atoms. Marx's alternate con-

---

[30] F. Engels, "Zwei Reden in Elberfeld: I," in K. Marx and F. Engels, *Werke* (Berlin, 1957), II, 539, 542.

[31] S. I. Benn and R. S. Peters, *The Principles of Political Thought* (New York, 1964), pp. 259 f.

[32] G. Shakhnazarov, *et al.*, *Man, Science and Society* (Moscow, 1965), p. 251.

[33] Archangelski, *op. cit.*, p. 302.

ception of man enjoyed a more compelling empirical warrant; it could, with suitable semantic and syntactical specification support instructive verification studies. And yet Marx's conception of man led to an interpretation of individual rights and freedoms as *derivative* and consequently advanced a *prima facie* presumption in favor of the interests of the collectivity as exemplifying the true or more profound freedom of the individual. Contemporary Soviet Marxists draw out the implications of this procedural presumption in a variety of contentions:

> To learn to live in a collective means to regard oneself an integral part of it and always to remain true to the guiding principle of collectivism: one for all and all for one. When people take their stand by this rule, they harmoniously blend their personal interests with those of the community . . . . Building a new society, therefore, implies that personal interests coincide with those of the community . . . . [C]reative endeavor adorns the collective and its members and is no longer an expression of the subordination of personal to communal interests, but their *confluence* . . . . Whoever violates the collective's rules, lets down or even shames his comrades, is in for heavy criticism . . . . Private life is the sphere in which a person lives when he is not engaged in productive or public activities, that is to say, the part of his life that he sets apart for himself. Is this the purely personal affair of everyone? No, a person's private life is inextricably bound up with public affairs . . . .[34]

and further:

> When the social interest is lifted to the level of the principal interest of the personality then there can be no renunciation of personal interests as the enemies of Marxism contend, rather personal interest thereby finds its highest fulfillment . . . . The new communist ethics declares: Think above all of social interests, conceive them as your own most important interest and you enhance thereby the collective as well as your own personal well-being.[35]

All of these contentions could be made compatible with arguments that construed the collective and the individual interests *substantially compatible* while recognizing the distinction between them. And it is true that Marxists frequently argue in such fashion.[36] But the more ominous contention is that there obtains, in some obscure sense, an *identity* of interests between the personal and the social interests. And it is this contention that gives moral priority and control privilege to the collective as against the individual. Lenin, in the tradition of classical Marxism and under the direct influence of Hegel, argued such an identification with the claim that "the individual *is* the *universal* . . . . Consequently the opposites (the individual is opposed to the universal) are identical . . . . Every individual is (in one way or another) a universal." [37]

---

[34] Shakhnazarov, *op. cit.*, pp. 254, 255, and 258.

[35] Shishkin, *op. cit.*, p. 261.

[36] This is particularly true of non-Soviet Marxists. *Cf.* J. Lewis, *Socialism and the Individual* (New York, 1961).

[37] V. I. Lenin, *Philosophical Notebooks*, in Lenin, *Collected Works* (Moscow, 1961), XXXVIII, 361.

It is this sort of persuasive definition that permits Soviet Marxists to speak of a unitary collective will that expresses the interests of all classes, strata and individuals in the population.[38] If "the individual is an ensemble of determinate social relations," it is possible to argue that he is but a "part of a greater, encompassing social whole," which because of a single pattern of social relations governing the activities of all, evinces a single and coherent will.[39] Such a unitary will represents the will of all and finds expression in the will of the single party.

This kind of argument provides the rationale for the logic of substitutions which make the will of the party the will of the proletariat and which makes the will of the proletariat the will of the Soviet people and which makes the will of the Soviet people the ultimate will of humanity. All that is necessary to complete the legitimation of totalitarian dictatorship is the recognition that the will of a single man is in some manner identical with the will of the party. Under the rigors of such a system of identifications any activity which is incompatible with the collective will as it finds expression in the periodic programmatic statements of the Party and the laws of the state is *prima facie* the product of ignorance or perversity. When faced by deviation of whatever sort one must either educate (the increasing emphasis in the Soviet Union even today on the tutelary and pedagogical responsibilities of the ideological agencies of the Party) or punish (the "Builders of Communism" are admonished to be unrelenting in their opposition to the "enemies of the people").

While it is perhaps an exaggeration to say "In the ideal totalitarian state 'everything that is not compulsory is forbidden,'" [40] there is an evident tendency in a totalitarian system to move in just such a direction. Soviet legal development is characterized by a conscious extension of law to cover the most intimate and personal relations.[41] It is the logic of identities, a heritage of classical Marxism, which subtends such developments in the total or administered state. It is the logic of identities which permits one man or a select group of men to speak in the name of the interests of all. It is the unified and harmonious will, the exemplification of the identity of all with all, that institutionalizes anxiety, for under such circumstances the individual who deviates from collective norms (as they find varied and changing expression in the determinations of the unitary party) can only expect to be accounted a fool or a criminal. Thanks to the identification of public and individual interests, the individual who pursues his own concerns can expect to be apprised either as one who cannot assess his true interests, a fool, or one who chooses to be anti-social, a criminal. It is interesting to note that the identity relationship between the individual and his community permits transit only in one direction. The collective interests are the individual's true interests.

---

[38] *Cf.* F. Burlatsky, *The State and Communism* (Moscow, n.d.), p. 85.

[39] Mácha, *op. cit.*, p. 289.

[40] R. T. Holt, *Radio Free Europe* (Minneapolis, 1964), p. 26.

[41] H. J. Berman, *Justice in the U.S.S.R.* (New York, 1963), p. 365.

But should the individual attempt to argue that because there obtains an identity of interests between the individual and his collectivity everything the individual does must be in the collective interest, he is immediately characterized as "petty-bourgeois," a defender of "outworn and moribund views which are incompatible with the essence of [the] socialist order." [42]

One of the critical arguments in the armory of arguments used to defend totalitarianism is this system of identifications between the individual and his collectivity, between private and public interests. Critics of totalitarianism, even when they are of Marxist provenience, see the perniciousness of "hairsplitting about harmonizing the particular and the general ... the individual and the social ...." [43] But the apologists of totalitarianism are loathe to surrender such arguments as a vindication of their political policies. For while such arguments have but little cognitive substance, they have high emotive salience and impressive persuasive force. Their use is manifest in the standard arguments in support of totalitarianism. How ubiquitous they are can be indicated by documenting their presence in the arguments advanced to support "non-Marxist totalitarianism," paradigmatic Fascism.

IV

Giovanni Gentile was not only the principal intellectual apologist of Mussolini's Fascism, but he was the unacknowledged author of its official ideology, the "*Idee fondamentali*," the philosophic portion of *La dottrina del fascismo*.[44] Central to that ideology was a conception of man most succinctly described by Gentile himself in his posthumously published *Genesi e struttura della società*:

> The human individual is not an atom. Immanent in the concept of an individual is the concept of society .... Only this identity can account for the necessary and intrinsic relation between the two terms of the synthesis which requires that the concept of one term must involve the concept of the other .... I hope that the importance of this concept will escape no one, for in my judgment it is the keystone of the great edifice of human society.[45]

---

[42] Archangelski, *op. cit.*, pp. 303 f. In its entirety this reads: "Some men argue in the following fashion: Since the personal and the collective are not to be distinguished, one must in the first instance pursue his own interests and thereby serve the collective well-being. But this argument is fundamentally erroneous. In it petty-bourgeois aspirations find expression, and whoever takes this position defends outworn and moribund views which are incompatible with the essence of our socialist order."

[43] M. Djilas, *Anatomy of a Moral* (New York, 1959), p. 90.

[44] The English text is to be found in J. Somerville and R. Santoni, edd., *Social and Political Philosophy* (Garden City, N.Y., 1963), pp. 424–428. Gentile is now recognized as the author of the first part of the *Dottrina*. *Cf.* N. Tripodi, *Vita e ideali di Giovanni Gentile* (Rome, 1954), p. 16.

[45] G. Gentile, *Genesi e struttura della Società* (Florence, 1946), pp. 32, 34, and 39.

The central thesis was that between the two terms "individual and the state" there was "a speculative identity." [46] Thus Gentile could argue that "the state is the very personality of the individual" and at the same time is the unitary will of the nation.[47] The conclusion to which the argument leads is express: "In the way of conclusion, then, it may be said that I, as a citizen, have indeed a will of my own; but that upon further investigation my will is found to coincide exactly with the will of the state, and I want anything only in so far as the state wants me to want it .... Since the nation, as the state, is of the essence and nature of our very being, it is evident that the universal will of the state is identical [tutt'uno] with our concrete and actual ethical personality." [48]

Gentile's affinities with classical Marxism in this respect have not gone unnoticed. Gentile himself, republishing his early essays on Marx in 1937, indicated that the germs of his philosophical position were developed in his reflections on Marx.[49] Ugo Spirito, one of Gentile's foremost students and a prominent intellectual during the Fascist period, confirmed that Gentile's rationale was "inspired by the Marxist dialectic" which took "its point of departure from the identification of the individual and the state ...." [50]

Gentile's rationale follows essentially the same logic and provides the same occasion for the convenient substitution of leader, party, state, nation, class and individual interests as does classical Marxism. All interests are conceived as harmonized, the analytic consequence of conceiving a "speculative" identity to obtain between the individual and his collective.

In 1932, in a Fascist apologetic approved by Gentile, Spirito argued, "The individual must finally become aware that in the process of conquering his true liberty, he cannot stop at intermediate and hybrid forms .... He must seek and find an absolute identity between his own goal and that of the state ... because private and public are the same thing ...." [51]

How convenient all this is to totalitarian rule is self-evident. The principal Fascist theoreticians were quick to indicate that the totalitarian conception of man was unalterably opposed to the "liberal idolatry" that conceived the "empiric individual" as possessed of inalienable rights which he could oppose to the sovereign rights of the state.[52] The rights and freedoms the individual enjoys are the rights and freedoms of the state with which he is indentified.[53] This central identity of the individual and his collectivity was intoned in the official *Dottrina*:

[46] G. Gentile, "Individuo e stato," an appendix to U. Spirito, *Scienza e filosofia* (Florence, 1950), p. 291.

[47] G. Gentile, *Che cosa è il fascismo* (Florence, 1925), p. 36.

[48] G. Gentile, *La riforma dell'educazione*, 5th rev. ed. (Florence, 1955), pp. 25, 14.

[49] G. Gentile, *I fondamenti della filosofia del diritto*, 3rd rev. and enl. ed. (Florence, 1955), p. vii.

[50] U. Spirito, *La filosofia del comunismo* (Florence, 1948), p. 13.

[51] U. Spirito, *Capitalismo e corporativismo* (Florence, 1933), p. 33.

[52] *Cf.* R. Farinacci, *Storia della rivoluzione fascista* (Cremona, 1937), III, 238, 265.

[53] Gentile, *Genesi* ..., pp. 58 f., and *Che cosa è il fascismo*, pp. 109 f.

Man as Fascism conceives him is an individual who is at once nation and fatherland
.... Fascism is an historical conception in which man is not what he is except as a
function of the spiritual process in which he participates .... Liberalism negated the
state in the interests of the particular individual: Fascism reaffirms the state as the
true reality of the individual ....[54]

V

The collectivity with which the Fascists identified the individual was the
"true state." In its name they mobilized a revolution against the *de facto*
state. Once ensconced in power the logic of substitutions that provided Fascists their ethical rationale rendered the dominance of their state absolute
and all encompassing. The Bolsheviks, in their struggle against the Czarist
state, on the other hand, originally held that the state was an oppressive force
that must "wither away" in the course of their victorious revolution. The
individual was to be identified with his *class*. The state was only a product of
the contradictions which arose in a class riven society. When classes no
longer existed the state could no longer exist, for the state is a machine for the
repression of class enemies. Lenin had made it clear that Marxism conceived
the state as nothing more than "an organ for class rule, an organ for the
oppression of one class by another" and consequently "so long as the state
exists there is no freedom." [55]

At the Twenty-Second Congress of the Communist Party of the Soviet
Union in 1961, however, it was discovered that "the substance of the state"
had "changed radically under the impact of the socialist revolution." [56] The
state is now conceived by Soviet Marxists as the "state of the whole people,"
a state which represents their unitary will,[57] a political conception unknown to
Marx or Lenin. All classes, strata, collectives and individuals in the Soviet
Union are now conceived as united by a single harmonious identity in the
"all people's state," in which private and public interests lose their distinctions, in which freedom and constraint, and democracy and dictatorship
lose their respective meanings.

The logic of identities, now employed by Soviet thinkers to render the
state and the individual one, provides for political conservatism and pervasive social confirmity. The institutional and social forms assumed by totali-
tarianisms of the Right and the Left approach each other and find their
rationale in charter myths that display a surprising similarity. In the case
of Soviet Marxism and Fascism the similarity has a common intellectual and
philosophic source, the neo-Hegelianism of Karl Marx. But the convenient

---

[54] B. Mussolini, "Dottrina del fascismo," in *Opera Omnia* (Florence, 1961), XXXIV,
117 and 118.

[55] V. I. Lenin, "The State and Revolution," in *Selected Works in Two Volumes* (Moscow, 1951), II, Part 1, 204 and 299.

[56] Burlatsky, *op. cit.*, p. 5.

[57] *Cf.* N. Khrushchev, *Report on the Program of the Communist Party of the Soviet
Union* (New York, 1961), pp. 106–109.

logic provided by the argument of the ultimate identity of private and public interest affords so many organizational and control advantages to the revolutionary leaders of our time that it appears and reappears in the writings of the apologists for a variety of totalitarian and quasi-totalitarian systems that do not share that source.[58] If Marx had not formulated it, its very political convenience would have brought it into the world without him.

University of California at Berkeley

---

[58] *Cf.* A. James Gregor, *Contemporary Radical Ideologies* (New York, 1968).